STILL INNOCENT ABROAD

David M. Addison

Other Books by
David M. Addison

An Italian Journey

A Meander in Menorca

Sometime in Sorrento

Bananas about La Palma

Misadventures in Tuscany

An Innocent Abroad

Confessions of a Banffshire Loon

The Cuban Missus Crisis

STILL INNOCENT ABROAD

Further Misadventures of an Exchange Teacher in Montana

Being Part Two of
An Innocent Abroad

David M. Addison

eXTREMIS
publishing

Still Innocent Abroad: Further Misadventures of an Exchange Teacher in Montana
by David M. Addison

First edition published in Great Britain in 2016 by Extremis Publishing Ltd.,
Suite 218, Castle House, 1 Baker Street, Stirling, FK8 1AL, United Kingdom.
www.extremispublishing.com

Extremis Publishing is a Private Limited Company registered in Scotland
(SC509983) whose Registered Office is 51 Horsemarket, Kelso, Roxburghshire, TD5
7AA, United Kingdom.

A CIP catalogue record for this book is available from the British Library.

ISBN: 978-0-9934932-2-5

Typeset in Goudy Bookletter 1911, designed by The League of Moveable Type.
Printed and bound in Great Britain by IngramSpark, Chapter House, Pitfield, Kiln
Farm, Milton Keynes, MK11 3LW, United Kingdom.

Cover artwork and stock images are Copyright © Shutterstock Inc.
Cover design and book design is Copyright © Thomas A. Christie.
Author image and internal images are Copyright © David M. Addison and Fiona J.
Addison.
Internal map designs are Copyright © Richard Addison.

The State of Montana and the United States of America

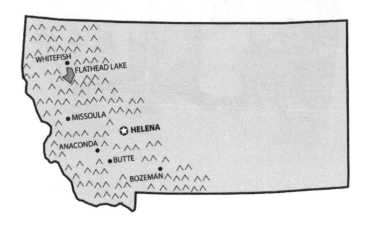

Prologue

It is October 1978. As this narrative opens, my wife and young family and I have been in the United States for two months to the day. From the moment we arrived, we were bombarded by a succession of culture shocks and soon came to realise that just because we share a common language (more or less), that does not necessarily mean we do things the same way as our transatlantic cousins. This I found especially true of Montana which, I was delighted to see, still had something of the "Wild West" about it so familiar from my boyhood, raised as I was on a diet of TV Westerns, in monochrome of course, as it was a long, long time ago.

It was all very bewildering at the start as we struggled to become accustomed to our new surroundings: our house (the house from *Psycho*); buying a car (the Big Blue Mean Machine); meeting a host of new people; and not least of course, as far as I was concerned, getting to grips with the American educational system, to say nothing of parents on the warpath. And along the way we had some hair-raising adventures as we began to explore our environment. That is the subject of *An Innocent Abroad.*

Now, as this book opens, I am coming more to terms with the culture shock, coming to appreciate that I was very fortunate indeed to have been placed where I was, in Emerson Grade School in western Montana in the foothills of the

Rocky Mountains. I have friendly colleagues who have shown me every consideration, have met many other interesting people besides, and seen some spectacular scenery.

But I have only been in Montana a matter of weeks. The adventures have barely begun. I am still an Innocent and there were to be more misadventures and shocks galore in store...

Chapter One

In which I meet an admirer, learn something about hunting elk and go backpacking in the wilderness.

It was a more-or-less spur of the moment sort of thing yet I had agonised over it for a long time. I had a dilemma: to go backpacking with my colleagues, Steve and Blake, or attend a meeting of Reading teachers. As an exchange teacher, as a guest of Uncle Sam, I felt it behoved me to attend the meeting. After all, was that not what I was here for - to learn more about, and experience, the American educational system? On the other hand, am I not on a cultural exchange also - and what could be more of a cultural experience than to go backpacking in the wilds of western Montana?

"It's up to you, Dave. But it's an experience you'll never forget," Blake had said, not that he was trying to influence me in any way of course.

And so recreation won the day over education.

I want to take some photos to remind me of this unforgettable experience, just in case the memory, sometime in the future, is not what it is now; a time perhaps, when I may be living in a mansion with lots of servants (though who all these other residents are or what they are doing here, in my house, I just don't know, but I wish they would go away. To tell you the truth, some of them are completely gaga). Unfortunately I am out of film, so in order not to keep my friends waiting, that is why on this fine October morning I am up early, not quite before the sun exactly, but so betimes that when I arrive at K-Mart ("K-Mart, fall apart" according to my students, but my favourite store, because of its outstanding bargains) - it is not even open yet.

Rushing back, armed with rolls of film, just slightly after the arranged pick-up time, it is to discover that Steve had phoned to say they are running late. Time to have a shower and breakfast and time to spare too before Steve's red-and-white truck pulls up outside. As usual, even at this early time in the morning, he is bouncing with energy.

"Here, try these on, young man," he says, thrusting a pair of walking boots at me. They belong to his wife, Jackie. Last night, at a soirée we had held for Steve and Blake and spouses, Steve had said he thought they might fit me. I hoped so, for if not, I would have to buy a pair and what worried me most was that Steve wouldn't let me buy them from K-Mart.

"Well, hello, Miss Hélène, you little cutie, have you got a sweetie for me?" he bends down to address her as she joins us in the family room. There's no denying she is my daughter: she looks just like me and there is no denying either she is cute. Everyone tells us so. And so did she once. "I'm cute," she had said, but she was only parroting what people had said to her as if it were an incontrovertible truth. Which it is.

Steve had been tickled pink when she had offered him a "sweetie" when he had called in one day and she had invited him into her "house" in the garden, actually a child's climbing frame. Then she had overcome her shyness, but now she is coy and embarrassed and doesn't know what to say.

Thankfully Jackie's boots are a perfect fit and we take our leave of Iona and the children and set off on the great expedition - only not quite. We have to go back to Steve's house as he had forgotten, or had had second thoughts about taking some sort of fly.

4

Next to Blake's house to pick him up. And not just him. I am dismayed to find that accompanying us is his bow ⁃ an intriguing arrangement of pulleys and a wire that seems to go on forever. The whole thing is as tall as me but what attracts my attention more, with a horrific sort of fascination, are the arrows, the most vicious-looking instruments of death it has ever been my misfortune to come across. I repress a shudder as I try not to think of what that tip, consisting of four razor blades, does to the hapless animal at the receiving end. It had been disingenuous of me to imagine that this would be a mere backpacking trip. I had already actually eaten or helped to eat, two of his victims ⁃ an elk and a black bear. I was especially sorry about the bear. But he did taste very nice indeed I have to say. Very sweet. Because he had been eating berries, Blake had said.

Next to the supermarket for some supplies. There's some comfort in that. It means that it's not going to be a matter of having to catch our supper or go hungry. In fact, I'm staggered by the size of steaks that Steve and Blake buy and my stomach rebels somewhat at the sight of this enormous hunk of raw meat. They look as if they might have come from a mammoth. But Montana, of course, is a cattle-rearing state, east of the Rockies especially. It's a state of two halves, except thirds would be a more accurate division and description. In the east, the vast and sprawling, as-far-as-the-eye can see, conservative, cattle-rearing, Big Sky Country (the state's nickname which you see everywhere, most notably on the car number plates) and the mountainous, more cosmopolitan, liberal west, though having said that, you see many cowboys in town ⁃ and I am not just referring to the builders and plumbers.

After that, it's back to Blake's house again, for a fishing rod for me, despite my protestations that it really doesn't matter ‑ I'd be quite happy to watch. It doesn't look as if my friends are the most organised people in the world and yet here I am putting my trust in them, letting them take me to the back of beyond, a place so secret that they have not even told their wives where it is precisely.

I have had some experience of the wilderness in Montana already, seen forests like a green sea stretching from horizon to horizon with not a landmark in sight. I know that if somehow I ever got separated from my guides I'd never find my way out. What's more, they are practical jokers *par excellence* and I am half prepared for them to pretend to abandon me at some stage in the expedition. Although I wouldn't be able to see them, I know they'd be watching me just to see how I would react, for a laugh. For my part, I was determined to be masterful and not give them the satisfaction. I thought I might just lie down and pretend to go to sleep. They'd soon get tired of that!

The next and final stop is to Bob Wards.

"He needs a fishin' permit," says Steve to the assistant before he has time to ask what it could be his great pleasure to do for us today. Everyone who works in the service industries here is a graduate of Uriah Heep Academy, majoring in servility and obsequiousness, the purpose of which is to make the consumer feel a really valued and special customer, but which in my case at least, provokes a strong desire to vomit.

It's just as well Steve is doing the talking as I am so overwhelmed by the arsenal of guns and rifles on display that my mandible is somewhere in the region of my navel and my vocal cords been reduced to a state of temporary paralysis. There are more rifles here than bottles of wine at my local supermarket. But even more incredible is the thought that on the production of one's ID and the funds of course, anyone could just walk in off the street and buy one - or a dozen or two, if they are planning a revolution or merely a bank raid.

"Sure." Then turning to address me, adds, "That'll be three dollars, suh. Where y'all from?"

I know, despite the plural form of address, he means me, and me alone. I'm not dressed like an outdoors man or a Montanan for that matter.

"Scotland!" he says. "Well, what d'ya know! I ain't never talked to a Scotsman afore. Would y'min' talkin' to me a little? Jus' say anythin' you like. I just wanna hear your axcent."

I am not unaccustomed to this phenomenon. Since I arrived in Missoula I have frequently been astonished by the reaction people have when they find out I come from Scotland, conferring upon me what it must feel like to be a minor celebrity. What's more, even back home, I have been told what an attractive accent I have. Iona often tells me that I like the sound of my own voice and could talk for Scotland. Now it seems as if I am just about to, for real.

I go into some detail, telling him what I am doing here, halfway around the globe, in a place I had never heard of before, though what I really want to say is that though the fishing permit sounds like the bargain of the week, a bargain is only a bargain if it is saving you money you would have spent anyway. For me it is $3 wasted. I have no desire to do any fishing: I am unlikely to catch anything (I hope) and since we are going to be in the wilderness with no-one around for miles, who's going to ask to see it anyway? Not at all in keeping with Montana's Wild West image. I can't imagine my cowboy heroes of the small screen gunning down baddies one minute and in the next breath applying for a poncy hunting or fishing permit.

"Gee, I sure wish I had a axcent," opines my new admirer.

"Where are *you* from?" I ask, to return the compliment, though I have a pretty shrewd idea from the drawling sing-song, elongated vowels.

"Alabama."

I thought so. And I'm not surprised he'd like to talk like me either.

We stop at a hamburger joint in Lolo, a few miles out of town, for by now it is getting on to lunchtime already and we have miles to tramp before we sleep. It is only right I treat my companions - after all they are taking me on this treat, not to mention stumping up for the mammoth steaks.

After a few miles we turn off onto a forest track. Steve has the wheel to hold on to but Blake and I are joggled about so much that the phrase "bumping into someone" was never truer. Still managing somehow to keep our hamburgers in our stomachs, the track eventually peters out and we come to a halt in a small clearing. Retrieving his bow from the back of the truck, to my astonishment, Blake and Steve also bring forth guns, complete with holsters, which they proceed to buckle and strap on. Now I know for sure the Wild West still exists.

Thus armed and wearing our backpacks (mine being lighter than the others, befitting a wimp and a novice), Blake and Steve's towering over their heads, we set off, in single file, down a track, through the trees. Eventually that track too peters out and we emerge from the forest into a sort of moorland strewn with boulders and brush already attired in its autumn motley.

Mountain ranges ripple into the distance like a rucked-up carpet. I pause to catch my breath and drink in the scene that had suddenly appeared before my eyes, as well I might, for the scenery certainly is breathtaking. The reason for this unexpected and sudden vista Steve explains, is because there was a fire in 1910 which raged from August until November, sweeping through three states - Washington, Idaho and Montana until eventually, the rain and snow put it out. Nature began it with a lightning strike; Nature put an end to it. "And so it goes," as Billy Pilgrim was so fond of saying in *Slaughterhouse-Five*.

And it isn't long before the going, which had been easy up till now, also takes my breath away as we begin to climb steadily uphill. I become aware of the weight of my backpack, and Jackie's boots, which had felt perfectly comfortable at the start, begin to pinch my toes.

But then we get a few moments' respite, as reaching the top of a ridge, Blake disencumbers himself of his backpack, plants his bow upright in the brush and from his pocket, like the Pied Piper, produces an instrument rather like a sawn-off recorder and settling himself down on a rock, proceeds to blow into it.

"He's buglin' for an elk," Steve informs me as we sit down beside him.

A rather plaintive sound fills the air and the valley below. It's meant to reproduce the mating sound of a bull elk though it sounds more to me as if the poor beast is suffering from terminal gastroenteritis rather than from a burning desire for a bit of alfresco passionate sex. It surprises me that Blake is bugling like this in the open as there is no way that even the most myopic of female elks could mistake him or us for one of her own kind.

But that's not the idea. Despite the alleged charm of my accent aforesaid, it has to be said my dulcet tones never did me much good in the mating game, but of course I was usually being seen at the same time as being heard. But in elk world, it seems if she likes the sound of his voice, and if she is in the mood, she'll send an answering message along the lines of: "I'm down here. If you want it, you'll have to come and get it."

So that's where we would have had to have gone, back down the mountain into the trees, Blake bugling from time to time to tell her to be patient, he'd soon be with her. Only as we got nearer, would we need to be more cautious as the stalking began. I suppose that's what those who enjoy such pursuits call the "joy of the hunt".

Fortunately, if any lady elk was listening, she had obviously not read *The Joy of Sex* or maybe she had figured out that once he had had his wicked way with her, he'd bugger off and leave her to bring up the kids on her own. In any event, answer came there none ⁃ to my immense relief. What I feared most of all was that the arrow was unlikely to be instantly fatal. I dreaded the sight and the sound of the stricken animal's suffering and not least the merciless (or merciful) bullet or knife-cut which would put an end to it. Then there would be the guts and the gore as the poor beast was disembowelled. It's not my idea of fun.

I was never intended to be a hunter. I attribute this soft centre to my mother especially, as she was very fond of animals. She also told me my father did not want to follow his grandfather, father and three elder brothers into farming because he couldn't bear to rear animals only to send them off to slaughter. What chance then had I of not fearing this death? Had I been aware that this had been on the agenda, I would have gone to the meeting of Reading teachers, no question about it.

And, it suddenly hit me, another reason that made my unspoken prayers that Blake would be unsuccessful even more fervent - how would we get the elk out? There was only one way and my backpack was already making me feel like the Hunchback of Notre Dame. But that was a hundred times better than a hunk of freshly-butchered meat dripping with blood to add to my load.

And so we resume our trek over hill and dale, stopping every so often for Blake to have a bugle with the same happy result as before, until at last, there below us, lay our destination, Lake X. I don't know if I'm in Idaho at the moment, but when we get there, I know I will be as that is where the mysterious lake is situated and whose name is not revealed to me in case I blab and the world beats a path to it. I also know I will be heartily glad to get the pack off my back, the boots off my feet and let the poor cramped toes expand to their normal size or quite possibly larger.

First job is to set up camp. I let Blake and Steve put up the tent. Like the cooks in the adage I reckon too many hands are more of a hindrance than a help though it wouldn't surprise me if I hadn't put up more tents than Blake had shot elk as that was our accustomed summer holiday, camping on the continent, usually in France.

While they are doing that, I make myself useful by gathering some brushwood for our campfire and in the failing light (for we had trekked for hours to get here, the bugling breaks notwithstanding) Blake begins to cook our evening meal. The steaks seem to flow into the pan like Salvador Dali's melting clocks.

Meanwhile, with the aid of some tinfoil, potatoes and corn on the cob are buried amidst the glowing charcoal. Ever since our arrival in Missoula, friends, neighbours and colleagues, all have been desperate to foist this yellow delicacy upon us, as if to save us from starvation like the way the indigenous Native Americans saved the first white settlers during their first winter. And a fat lot of thanks they got for that, history was later to show.

Perhaps it is the fresh air, perhaps the exercise, perhaps the smoky flavour, but a steak never tasted so good. Unfortunately, there was only tea with which to wash it down. It had never occurred to me to bring some wine or beer. Blake and Steve are not great drinkers, unlike my neighbour and friend, Al the cop, who would no more think about embarking on an expedition like this without some sort of alcoholic sustenance than an astronaut would take a walk in space without his life-support system. A robust red would have been a fitting accompaniment and well worth the weight, and of course, much lighter on the return journey (because naturally, we will be carting out all our trash with us) but alas, I had not thought ahead. I am an Innocent, as I said, even if I can speak enough American now to write "trash" instead of "rubbish".

Later, after our meal, when the velvety dark sky is pricked with a myriad of stars, the glowing embers are restored to flames that leap and dance at least a foot or two high, depending on their mood. By that flickering light I observe Blake and Steve in their quilted jackets and their woolly hats, while I, hatless and in my thin waterproof jacket, extend my hands to the fire.

What, if I hadn't applied for this exchange, would I be doing now I wonder? Well, still tucked up in bed, given the seven hours time difference, but that apart, I'd be looking at another routine and boring Scottish Sunday. I never dreamt I'd ever be in a place like this. Out there in the inky darkness beyond the radius of the fire, if we didn't know any better, we three could be the only people on the planet, the stars the closest visible source of life and perhaps none there either.

Yes, I know this will be an expedition I will never forget, just like Blake had promised. What I didn't know was the real reason why it was going to be so memorable was just about to happen...

Chapter Two

*In which I hear some queer stories and have an
encounter of a very strange kind.*

What else do men do when sitting round the
campfire, but chew the fat. What else *is* there to
do when you have no beer and it is as dark as
Hades but not half as hot?

Steve regales us about his student days at Western
Montana College in Dillon, little more than a two-horse town
about sixty miles from Butte, the so-called "Butt of the
Nation" which I imagine does not impress the residents one
bit. We have been there and I'm not making any comment
except to point out it is a truth universally acknowledged that
a mining town never won a beauty contest yet. Dillon, on the
other hand, is just a sleepy little dormitory town.

And it was in the dormitories that some of the
escapades took place as Steve and his mates went on knicker-
raiding parties. That was nothing: they once bricked up a
door to one of the dorms, had water fights with the fire hoses
in the halls (corridors) and even rode motorbikes along them.

"There was this shy, innocent guy," Steve says, getting
into his stride. "He'd never been out with a girl afore so we
fixed him up with a hooker from the cathouse in Butte along
with a pal. We didn't tell him that of course. We told him it
was just a blind date. The pal took them to the town dump
(how romantic, I thought) an' when they got there, we were
waitin' for them. We started flashin' our lights an' honkin'
our horns."

He pauses, chuckling at the memory.

"One of us pretended to be the girl's father and yelled, 'I'll teach you to fool around with my daughter!' an' started blastin' off a shotgun. The pal pretended to be hit. 'Make a run for it,' he managed to get out before collapsing, apparently mortally wounded.

"Our guy didn't wait to be told twice! He was outta that car faster'n a jack rabbit. It took him four hours to get back. His clothes were all ripped an' torn an' he was bleedin'. He said he'd crawled through a barbed wire fence. But that wasn't the end ⸱ we had one more surprise for him. The guy that had pretended to be shot was lyin' on the bed, laid out like a corpse. Boy, you shouldha' seen his face!"

Steve is unable to continue for the moment, laughing at the recollection. "But you shouldha' seen him a moment later when the 'body' sat up and said, 'How ya doin'?' Boy, his legs just buckled clean under him an' he hit the deck just like that!"

Even in this light, I can see Steve's eyes shining and his moustache bristling with the excitement of it all. Thank God that poor guy's heart was strong I couldn't help but think. But that, I'm afraid, is as much sympathy as this poor individual gets. His torment is our vicarious pleasure. It puts me in mind of Tam O' Shanter listening to Souter Johnny as he told his "queerest stories". Pity, like them, we are not quaffing the beer, but our laugher, especially mine, is ready chorus to Steve's stories and thus encouraged, he regales us with more tales from the cathouse.

"I was there a few times," he admits candidly, "but I only ever got round to doin' anythin' once. I don't remember the other times," he goes on, not so candidly. Perhaps he is being economical with the truth; perhaps he was there so often he couldn't remember the details. Perhaps he sees the disappointment or disbelief in my face for ‑ "There was one time I do remember," he says hesitantly, seeming to dredge it up from the depths of memory.

"Yes?"

"Well first of all they wash your ding-a-ling for you then they give you a kinda menu of the tricks on offer. I took 'Around the World' for $20."

"What's 'Around the World'?" I ask as casually as I know how.

"I dunno either," he grins. "I passed out."

"Passed out?"

"Yeah. Well you see, we used to drink a lotta beer afore we went. To get the courage, see? An' one of my pals," he adds as if he has just remembered it, "he used to jack off afore he went in so he would last longer."

If that sounds like a good idea, to get more value for money (such a thing as an Aberdonian might have thought of), Steve would have done well to have brushed up on Shakespeare's Scottish play where the porter says of drink: "it provokes the desire, but it takes away the performance".

And so to bed. But not in my case, after completing my journal, like Mr Pepys. I will have to do that when we get back to civilisation. And a fat chance of getting to sleep either. I have never been any good at sleeping in strange beds and unfamiliar surroundings so I knew right from the start that in a sleeping bag on hard ground, in the confines of the small tent, sleep would always be elusive. And it always irritates me beyond words when people like Blake just drop straight off to sleep as soon as their head hits the pillow. I could put up with that, but what I really can't stand is the snoring. Once that starts I know it will drive any possibility of sleep further and further away. I lie awake, becoming more and more frustrated. How dare they enjoy a good sleep when I can't? Will I ever manage to fall asleep? And the more you worry about it, the further and further it recedes.

Steve appears to be asleep too and so I am the only one who is aware of the wind getting up, tugging and pulling at the flysheet as if hell-bent on uprooting the whole tent. Although it does drown out Blake's snoring, what with the racket and expecting at any moment to see the stars, sleep becomes even more of an impossibility. Incredible, I think, how my companions can sleep like babes through all this.

But not for much longer. Suddenly we are swaddled in nylon. It was that, rather than my involuntary cry of surprise and pain when the pole landed on my unprotected nut that awoke my companions. No point in all of us going out in that gale. Besides, they are far better equipped with warm clothing, so I just lie where I am while Steve and Blake do what is necessary. When they return, it is my chance to sleep before Blake starts snoring again. But you can't call sleep to order, or at least I can't. It just will not come. Perhaps the sound of the wind tugging at the tent will lull me to sleep but it is not in the least a soothing sound and I lie awake, half expecting to be crowned again.

We are all awake when something strange happens. Suddenly, the interior of the tent is suffused with a curious light. It seems to pulse and is bright enough to let me see the look of alarm on my friends' faces. They are now sitting bolt upright in their sleeping bags. Had I been able to see my own face, I'm sure it would have registered puzzlement, wonderment and the beginning of fear. I can feel my heart beating faster. Out here in the wilderness, so far from any human habitation, what on earth could be causing this mysterious light? Naturally I thought of the fire straight away, but Steve and Blake are only too well aware of the havoc that fire can wreak in these parts and had been meticulous in extinguishing it hours ago.

"What is it?" I breathe.

Silence. Then Blake clears his throat before saying in a low voice, "Static electricity."

We mull that over in our heads. Even he did not sound convinced and neither were we.

"A UFO," Steve whispers.

Strangely enough, I find this more convincing than Blake's explanation. I know of several cases where people allege they have seen flying saucers and other unexplained lights in the sky which can move at amazing speeds and in ways that defy the laws of physics as we know them, which is not very much in my case. There have even been cases of people reporting they have been teleported into such vehicles where aliens with blank, elongated faces and dark, almond eyes have done experiments on them before returning them safely to earth to tell the tale. And, what's more, these people have all been captured in remote places, in just the sort of place where we are now.

"Maybe it's the fire," I suggest though why I am whispering I just couldn't explain, though it seems to me that that still has to be the most likely explanation.

"Naw, we put that out for sure, hours ago, Dave," Blake assures me. Then with a certain bold resolution as if the curiosity has got too much for him, he announces, "I'm goin' outside." And with that, he begins to scramble out from the cocoon of his sleeping bag.

To me, his speech has something of Titus Oates about it. And we all know, too, what killed the cat. But better him than me, I think logically, if he is going to be abducted by aliens. If they have conquering the planet in mind, better they conduct their examination on a specimen like Blake and not a weakling like me. If they took me to be a representative sample of humanity they may as well start the invasion tomorrow.

"Here, take my gun," says Steve, offering him the aforesaid.

"It's OK," Blake says, reaching for his own.

When I had been at his house once he had confessed to sleeping with a gun under his pillow. He lives in the very last house in Missoula, if you go in a certain direction, up in the hills. He needs a four-wheel drive to get out in the winter and in particularly snowy years, he needs a snow plough, though he spells it "plow". His orthography apart, this presents no problem to him whatsoever as he possesses, not only a tractor (for his fencing business) but the plough as well. When you know you are going to get snow, it is something worth investing in. Meanwhile, back home, the trains stay in the stations and the motorways grind to a halt because of an inch of snow. The funny thing is we get at least that much every year.

Being at the end of the trail, so to speak, in the middle of the night, when car headlights rake his bedroom window, the first thing Blake thinks is that no-one should be up there at that time of night without good reason and his hand automatically grabs his gun. He knows if it were people up to no good it would be too late to phone the cops because by the time they got there, they could be already riddled with bullets, because of course, the intruder had just been down to Bob Wards (or any of a score of other similar establishments you would care to mention) and bought himself enough weapons to equip an army. Or just one would be enough.

My car, the Big Blue Mean Machine, my six-year old Plymouth station wagon has a sticker on the windscreen that shows that the previous owner was a member of the National Rifle Association: a bald eagle bearing crossed rifles upon a shield bearing the stars and stripes. It's not their motto, but it may as well be, the Second Amendment: the right of the individual to "bear and carry arms" and which the NRA robustly defends.

Ratified in 1791 just eight years after the jittery nascent republic was born, it might have made sense then, but makes none at all now. But try getting an amendment through the Constitution, never mind an amendment to an amendment. Maybe Montana and the other western states are different from the rest of the country but I wouldn't go knocking at someone's door in the middle of the night, lost, and asking for directions, not if I didn't want to end up looking like a colander.

I had asked Blake how many guns he possessed.

"Thirteen," he had replied without even having to think about it.

My God! I thought, but why I was so surprised I couldn't say. He wasn't the first person I had met with so many weapons. I had seen a display case of them in Matt, my principal's, house. He might well have had others under his mattress for all I knew. I hadn't asked anybody else. It felt a bit like asking how much money you had in the bank.

Pausing only to put on his quilted jacket, Blake goes out to see what he can see, while Steve covers him from inside the tent. Surely if it was someone intent on murdering us in this remote spot, he wouldn't announce it by flashing a light like this? Maybe it *is* aliens after all. As Sherlock Holmes remarked, when you have eliminated all other possibilities, however unlikely it may be, what's left has to be the explanation.

It doesn't take him long. It was the most likely explanation after all - the fire. Like the wolf in *The Three Little Pigs,* the wind had huffed and puffed and blown new life into the apparently dead fire after all.

Just as I had said. Politeness prevents me from pointing this out to my seasoned backpacking friends.

They had me going for a moment and they weren't even trying to wind me up this time.

Chapter Three

*In which I have more shocking experiences in the
wilderness and come home to another.*

When I awaken, it is light, the wind has dropped
and there is no-one in the tent. I fumble for my
watch. Inexplicably, it has stopped. If it had been
a UFO last night I would have known what caused it. How
long have my companions been up I wonder. I bet I am in for
a ribbing when I make my appearance. If so, the sooner it's
done the better.

"Good afternoon, Mr A!" says Steve.

"So you finally got up, huh!" says Blake.

I expected no less, so I have my speech ready.

"What time is it? My watch has stopped."

"Time you got up," says Blake with his usual sang-froid
tone and expression.

"It's 7.45," says Steve, more mercifully.

That *is* early for me and considering how I hadn't slept
all night, later, much later, would have been excusable.

"You should have told me," I say, withdrawing my
head like a tortoise into the tent, where, given its confines, I
get dressed as slowly as one of those species would if they
wore clothes. I'll wash my wrinkly face and paws in the lake
afterwards. It's incredible that Blake and Steve hadn't
disturbed me when they got dressed. Shows how tired I must
have been after that eventful night.

Breakfast, I am pleased to learn, is baked beans and
sausages, just like cowboys on the range, after which it is fly-

fishin' time. Steve initiates me into the art and leaves me to it. The etiquette apparently, is that you don't fish in another man's waters, so he leaves me to my own devices. That suits me. I need not officially strive to catch anything and my lack of success could easily be put down to being a novice.

Presently, at the other side of the lake, my eye catches sight of Blake hauling a big fish out of the water. Maybe I looked away at the vital moment, maybe I was too far away to see clearly, but it seemed to me that as I watched, he unseamed it from head to tail without bothering to kill it first. I had witnessed such a thing once before when, as a boy, I was taken on a sea-fishing expedition. The fish, which I had thought long since dead as it lay on the bottom of the boat, writhed in agony and shed pints of blood as its head was sawn off. It put me off fishing for life.

Some time later, when Blake asks me if I'd like to accompany him hunting, I agree. If this surprises you, dear reader, then you should realise just how mind-numbingly boring I find fly-fishing, especially when the tedium is unrelieved by successfully not catching anything. Besides, I trust that Blake's bad luck will hold out and he will be unsuccessful again. But most of all, what makes my mind up for me is when Blake points out where we are going, to the top of the ridge behind the lake, he says that the last time he was there, as well as elk, he saw a mountain goat and a couple of black bears. Now that really *would* be something to tell the folks back home, and I don't just mean in the house from *Psycho* either.

Armed with the dreadful arrows, we scramble up the steep, scree slope and coming to the top, look down on a sight I never expected to see. Was this how the Children of Israel felt when they first saw the Promised Land, I wonder? I had expected something similar to our side of the mountain, but down there, too green and lush for Canaan, it has to be Arcadia. And if there are no houses to be seen, then neither are there any bears. Perhaps they are picnicking in the woods. And if I am disappointed in that, despite Blake bugling fit enough to crack his cheeks, I am pleased to see that the elk remain as elusive as before. Clever elk.

I think I am pretty smart too when we get back to the lake and I find a place where there appear to be no fish. This means I can cast and cast to my heart's content and be confident that I'll catch a big cold before I ever catch as much as a minnow. But I hadn't reckoned on Blake's helpfulness.

"You havin' any luck over there, Dave?" he calls from across the lake.

"Not much," I reply in what I intend to be interpreted as a tone of regret.

"C'mon over here, they're jumpin' like crazy! Here, let me change your fly," he says when I join him. "Try that."

And what do you know, a moment later, I feel a tug at my line. I have just caught my first fish! It's a tiny little fellow, so small that to my relief, Blake deems it too small to die and puts it back, perhaps to die another day when it is bigger and plumper. I even catch two more.

And talking of eating, it is time for lunch. What could be better than cutthroat trout straight out of the lake? Blake is the designated camp cook apparently. Whilst he conjures up appetising smells from the pan, Steve fishes on and on, getting the most of his fishing permit, like a good Scotsman would. A normal Scotsman. When Blake goes back to the lake, Steve comes for lunch. Poor fish. Don't they ever get a break? It's only polite to engage Steve in conversation while he eats so at least the fish are spared my efforts, feeble though they may be.

It was a bit silly I suppose, in retrospect, but I have seen pictures of men fishing in fast-flowing rivers up to their oxters. I mean, it's not as if I am half as dedicated as they seem to be, so what possessed me to walk out to the lake on the fallen trunk of a tree like a pirate's victim walking the plank, I just don't know. At least I should have known that a plank is a darned sight easier to walk than a tree trunk. And if only I had used my fishing rod as a balancing pole, the best use I could have put it to, but I didn't.

It wasn't far above the water, so the cry and the splash were practically simultaneous. It wasn't deep but the shallowest water is as just as wet as the deepest. It wasn't funny but my "friends" seem to find it hilarious, the sight of me struggling to stand up, gasping for breath with the shock, not to mention the freezing water.

Feeling a complete idiot and as much removed from Mr Walton's "compleat angler" as it's possible to be, I wade back to shore. This was meant to be an expedition that *I* would never forget. Seems to me my friends will never forget it either, dine out on it even, telling tales of the Scotsman who only caught minnows and who, in his desperation to catch a bigger fish, tried to cast farther into the lake by walking along a log.

Naturally, I never anticipated such an outcome and have brought no change of clothing. Fortunately the sun is beaming its benevolent rays from a cloudless sky, as warm as, warmer even, than a summer's day in Scotland. Even more remarkable when I remember we are at an elevation of at least a thousand feet higher than our highest peak, Ben Nevis - and this is in October!

There is nothing else for it but to strip to the skin, wring out as much water as I can from my clothes and spread them out on boulders to let the sun do its work. And then, when I'm sure, absolutely sure, that Blake and Steve are fully engrossed in their fishing, I slip out of my underpants and do the same with them. My altruism knows no bounds, or you might say, my Calvinistic background dictates that too much enjoyment is not good for a person. I don't want them killing themselves laughing at my wee willie winkle, still shrivelled up like a maggot at its recent immersion in the ice-cold water. God knows how fish manage to swim about in it all day without catching their deaths, though of course many of them do.

By the time Steve and Blake have had their fill of fishing, my clothes have dried out considerably but not completely. I decide not to wear my underpants, profiting from a mistake I once made at Lourdes. Suffering from nothing other than a severe case of curiosity, I decided to have a holy bath. Two muscular men, taking an arm each, tipped me backwards, stuck me right under, bobbed me up again and stuck a plastic Mary in my face (which a Protestant non-believer like me dared not, not kiss). No towels were provided and I, who had not expected to get even slightly damp on that broiling hot day, never mind get soaked from head to toe, had no such thing with me. I had therefore, to put on my clothes over my wet body and walk about, steaming like a train before catching one of its diesel descendants for the two-hour train journey back to our campsite. I ended up with the worst cold I have ever had, and the worst nappy rash I had had since I was a baby.

Once the tent is down and we have all the gear packed into our backpacks, I notice Blake and Steve appear to be having a conference. It looks serious. What could it be? Is this them deciding at what point they'll scarper and leave me, just to see what I'll do? Well they are not being very subtle about it if that is the case and little do they know I have my strategy already prepared. But I was wrong.

"Say, Dave, would you like to fire a gun?" Blake says.

You can't go to Las Vegas and not, at least, put a coin in one of those infernal machines and you can't come to the Wild West and never fire a shot, even if it is not in anger. Even better, they strap their gunbelts on me and take a photograph of The Compleat Westerner, a gun at each hip. But not quite. I only have a baseball hat and that just won't do at all. I must get a proper cowboy hat before I leave.

They set an empty gas canister into a tree some twenty yards away and stand at least that distance behind me. They trust me, but not that much. For the moment, I am the master ⸗ could be the joker. I could, for a laugh, ignore the canister and turning on them say, "Reach for the sky!" like they did in my cowboy films.

Methinks that was what the conference was about: would I be likely to pull that sort of trick, and if I did, which of them would shoot me first? To this day I do not know the answer because, of course, I was not so foolish to play such a stupid prank. I know you never, ever, point a loaded gun at anybody, even in jest. Besides, mathematically challenged though I am, I can at least count up to two and I realise that after the photograph, they have entrusted me with only *one* of the guns.

I draw it out of the holster and align the sights on the gas canister. This is not about being quick on the draw. I have seen it in the movies: I grip my wrist tight with my left hand and rather than firing directly at the target, I begin *above* it and slowly bringing the sights down and holding my breath ⸗

I squeeze the trigger. Really, you would think I had been letting off firearms all my life.

The blue canister flies out of the tree and lands feet away. I'm not sure if it is the feeling of the kick from the revolver or the sight of the target spinning away that gives me the greater shock.

"Good shot, Mr A!" says Steve, retrieving the canister for my inspection, There's where the bullet hit, plumb in the middle and if he sounds surprised, then he is the lesser surprised of the two of us. Well three, if you count Blake, who is speechless. It seems not only can I shoot my mouth off, but I could shoot for Scotland too, at least based on the evidence of this solitary experiment.

And so we say goodbye to Camp David (not to be confused with another of the same name) and since I shot the canister, I have the duty (and honour) of carrying it out. But far from being a burden, it buoys me up somewhat, the living testament of my prowess with the gun. Dead-eye Dave. I may keep it for the year, put it on the mantelpiece as a conversation piece.

I know it is never going to be the most comfortable of treks home and my heart is as heavy as my backpack as I heft it onto my shoulders. The boots too, seem tighter than before, my feet sorer, the hills steeper and the stops for bugling fewer, which is a good and a bad thing. Once, far below, we see a herd of elk but Blake deems them too far away to shoot one. That, at least, is a blessing, but it is the only one I can count.

Steve has gone on ahead and is out of sight, leaving Blake to keep me company. I am conscious that I am slowing us down but I am going as fast as I can hirple. Then all of a sudden, a loud bang rents the air and reverberates for what seems a long time before the air becomes still again. Blake and

I have stopped dead in our tracks, looking at each other, wondering what it could mean, when round the bend comes the answer. Steve, grinning from ear to ear, has something big and feathery dangling from his hand.

"This little sucker just popped its head roun' a tree and winked at me," he explains. "Next minute, pow!"

Speaking as a sure-shot myself, I have to say I am impressed with Steve's reactions, the speed of his draw and his aim. I call Steve "The Bird Man of Emerson" because birds are to him as elk are to Blake. Not knowing that feathers are my phobia, he had kindly brought me three of his victims last week, in all their glorious plumage, for me to pluck and disembowel for our culinary delight later.

Despite my squeamishness, but strangely fascinated, I hear myself asking, "What is it?"

"A blue grouse," Steve replies, holding it up so I can see it better. I wish he hadn't done that. There was no head where a head should be, just blood dripping.

After what seemed a great deal of time later, we are back at the truck. The last mile seemed endless. Nearly four hours it took in all to reach the truck and I was never so thankful to see a vehicle in my life.

Steve and Blake are loading their weapons and rods into the back, followed by their backpacks, when - "Hand me up the bird, Dave," I hear Steve ask as if it were the smallest request in the world.

I should have put some distance between me and the feathery one that had literally lost its head, but if my intention had been to show my bravery by standing next to it, then it had badly backfired. When Steve came round with his tribute, it seems I had managed to conceal my phobia from him or he would never have asked this of me. He'll never know therefore (till he reads this), just how much guts it took for me to pick up that big, bleeding bird and hand it over to him - as quickly as possible. I must not let my huntin', shootin', frontiersmen friends see just what a complete and utter wimp I am.

"An' you know somethin' else - he's even scared to pick up a dead bird!" I can just hear them telling their wives, and to anyone else who would listen, like this was the climax of our weekend. Another reason why I might need to keep the canister. Just to remind them that they'd better not get too cheeky. *Nemo me impune lacessit* as the motto of our emblem, the thistle, has it.

We are behind schedule, so we stop in Lolo to get a burger (again) and make a phone call to let one wife know, so she can phone the others to say we have not been eaten by bears or been attacked by a moose and it would be premature to cash in the insurance policies. We would be returning to the bosoms of our families just as soon as possible. It's good for them to know this so they can have them at the ready. Being in the wilderness for a day and a night, sleeping cheek by jowl with two men in a tent, can do strange things to a man.

"Care to come in for a brew?"

To my surprise they accept. It is already 9.30. I know they are early bedders and tomorrow is a school day, unfortunately. Perhaps they want to see the look on Iona's face when they tell her of my exploits. But somehow, when they get to the bit about me falling in the water, I feel she does not respond with the correct degree of shock, horror and amusement, that she seems vaguely distracted in some way, as if there is something on her mind, something worrying her.

Finishing their beers, Blake and Steve announce they had better be going.

"Just a minute," Iona says hastily, standing up. "There's something I'd like to show you."

Leaving us looking at each other somewhat mystified, she leaves the room and reappears a moment later with a full-length leather coat.

Naturally, Blake and Steve, those connoisseurs *extraordinaire* of women's wear, admire it profusely, while initially I am rather lost to find any words at all, let alone ones of effusive praise.

"Diane and Jackie took me shopping," Iona explains. "I got this in a sale. It was $99 reduced from $149!"

She knows if there is one thing I approve of it's a bargain, as long as of course, it is something you need (as opposed to want) in the first place, as I said earlier. I have confessed that I "need" a cowboy hat to take back as a souvenir and if Iona "needs" a full-length leather coat, so be it. However, just in case her husband turns out not to be the reasonable, kind, accommodating and generous person she fell in love with and married, when you have news to tell him which you suspect might give him a cardiac arrest, it is advisable to have his friends around him at such a time, is it not?

Chapter Four

In which I have some transport problems, a cyclist blows a fuse and another fuse has miraculous properties.

I am in the habit of cycling to school so Iona has the use of the Big Blue Mean Machine but today after school I discover I have a flat tyre and so it is literally what we on our side of the Atlantic at least, call a "push bike". It is a lot slower and harder than mere walking, I can assure you. Since it was all right this morning, could it possibly be sabotage and it's not a puncture ⁄ some joker has let the tyre down? And I'm not necessarily suspecting one of the students either.

Misfortune is compounded when the darned back wheel, for no reason at all, decides to jump out of its forks so the wall of the tyre is hard up against one of them. It's like the brake is hard on all the time. The gods are certainly having a good laugh at me now, for pushing it in this state is even worse than cycling up those infernal hills which, in my youth, lay between me and my school, though I never dismounted, preferring to stand on the pedals in the lowest gear and which had very painful consequences indeed when it slipped out of gear, as it sometimes did, and I just about split myself in two when I made a sudden excruciating contact with the bar. It makes my eyes water even now, after all these years, to think of it.

As readers of the first volume already know, Marnie, my exchange partner, fancies herself as a bit of an antique collector and down in the basement, amongst all the junk, the boxes and the books, the cobwebs and not least what Scots call "oose" (fluff), down there where I'm sure Norman Bates keeps his mother (only I haven't probed too deeply for fear of what I may find) - one day when I was feeling exceptionally brave, I found treasure: the bicycle aforesaid and such an antique that Mrs Bloomer herself might have been seen displaying her knickers on it.

After checking with Perry, Marnie's ex (whom she had divorced within the space of two weeks after she had discovered his dalliance with a younger woman), that it would be all right to use it, I set about making the bike serviceable. That it was a lady's bike didn't bother me one whit. Back home I also cycle to school and that too is on a lady's bike. I found it in a skip, what Americans would call a "dumpster".

When you are as poor as me, you have to take what you can find. Beggars can't be choosers. Not the family motto, but it might just as well have been, for I would have you know that teachers are the poor relations when it comes to the professions, at least back home, and one of the reasons for my discontent - for after I had paid the bills there was precious little left for anything else. Life was just an endless routine of work and fed up to the back teeth, that was why I had applied for the exchange. Marnie's reason, as you have probably guessed, was to get over her divorce, especially after the happy new couple moved into a house just a couple of blocks away. A courageous thing for Marnie to do, not just on her own, but accompanied by three children ranging in age from eleven to six. But desperate times call for desperate measures.

Pushing the bike back was actually the most strenuous thing I did all day by far and a rummage in Mrs Bates' basement flat reveals an inner tube that looks completely new.

How odd in a house that has nothing less than fifty years old in it! How Marnie is going to revel being in Scotland! There, she will get a fine appreciation of just how old everything is, though of course, we take old things for granted and I'm not just referring to the way we treat our pensioners.

If that was a happy circumstance, the last thing I need to hear is there is yet another problem with the Big Blue Mean Machine - by which I am using "mean" in its American sense, which is to say not being very nice to someone, a term very popular with the young and which they don't hesitate to let you know when you tell them to do something they don't want to do - which is quite a lot of the time.

I had bought the Plymouth for a song, or I thought I had. Since then I have spent a fortune on repairs. There's always something going wrong with it. Now it's the lights. Fortunately, I have a ready supply of willing helpers who have helped me with such things as the brakes and as for the bigger jobs, such as regrinding the valves and the cracked cylinder head, Steve has put me in touch with Dennis, his tame mechanic and now mine. Probably his best customer. But lights that don't work sounds like something I can fix for myself, such as a loose wire or something.

"Oh, and the indicators don't seem to be working either," Iona calls after me.

Damned car. Should never have bought it. The plan is to tour the country after school gets out in the summer, south to Mexico, north to Canada, south east to Florida and north again to Washington DC where I will be debriefed and where I will sell the car, hopefully. And what am I putting my trust in to cover all those miles, more miles than I can even begin to calculate - this wreck! The only good thing is if it continues to break down at this rate, I'll practically have a new car before we set off on that epic adventure.

Hopefully the fault with the lights and the indicators has a common cause. But some time later (and after not a few curses) when I have unscrewed every screw in the dashboard fascia and still not been able to trace the fault, Perry happens to come along. It's been a while since I saw him, since that time when he did my brakes and introduced me to the lovely lady whom, I suppose you could say, was responsible for me being here.

Seeing me wrestling with the car, he has kindly stopped to see if he can help. He has been visiting a member of the family, the one that was left behind, his dog, a "German Shepherd" as the Americans call it, "Alsatian" as we call it and "Fritz" as he calls this particular member of the canine race. I had no idea he was so attached to the brute. I call it "brute" because I have not had a happy relationship with Alsatians in the past. It stems from the time when, as a mere toddler, the policeman's dog (they were to policemen in those days as handbags are to women) not only bit me but seemed to have a desire to devour me whole, beginning with my head ~ an incident which had the tragic consequence of making my mother miscarry.

When Marnie asked me, therefore, if we would mind adopting Fritz for the duration, as the father of two toddlers, I had absolutely no hesitation in rejecting her request out of hand. Fritz, I was assured, was not like that at all, more likely he'd lick me to death than eat me. But I stuck to my guns. What if he thought I was really, really tasty and couldn't stop at that?

Fritz was therefore sent on his holidays just along the street to live with Al and Terri. Terri is Marnie's friend and our mentor. Now realising that Perry was so fond of Fritz, it begs the question: why did *he* did not take him? But I probably don't need to exercise my brain too hard on this. I bet it was because the new wife, Karen, didn't want Fritz either. Poor Fritz! No-one wants him and that might well include Terri but there she is, stuck with him.

Maybe a plan was hatched out between Marnie and Terri: when we saw what a friendly beast Fritz was, perhaps they thought we would fall in love with him and he could come home again. "Friendly beast" is an oxymoron and therefore suspect and if indeed that was their thinking, there was one serious flaw in their logic. I'm here to see the country, explore the local area and the last thing I want is the encumbrance of a dog, thank you very much. Mind you, it would be comforting to have him in the bathroom every time I take a shower in that house from *Psycho*...

It takes Perry only a moment to diagnose the problem. A mechanical genius as well as a hotshot lawyer. His surname should have been Mason, one of my black and white TV boyhood heroes.

"It's the switch," he announces definitively.

Too bad he hadn't happened to come along earlier. And would he have called in to see us, I wonder, after seeing Fritz? And that might have presented us with a certain embarrassing problem, for to be perfectly frank, unable to live with some of Marnie's "antiques" any longer, we, or rather Iona, had banished them to the basement. I am talking about the jawbone of a rat, phalanxes of Coca-Cola bottles with their rusty helmets, rusty baking implements tastefully displayed on weathered wooden boards riddled with woodworm and the yoke with the broken ends strung up with some red wool against the red, flock wallpaper. We left that where it was, as well as, because we couldn't do anything about it, what we had dubbed the "hairy Viking chair", the back and seat apparently fashioned from the pelt of a mammoth.

A long time ago, I had banished the dust-collecting rag rugs, placed as they were, on top of the polished wooden floors. Several times I skid on them like an ice skater and once they had damned nearly killed me. That had been the last straw. It would be hard to explain to Perry all these absences without causing the greatest offence, for if there is one thing Perry and Marnie have in common, and I know this for a fact, it is their love of "antiques" - maybe the very thing that initially attracted them to each other. Ironic then, that he should have traded her in for a younger model. You might have thought that Marnie would have become even more attractive to him the older she got, like Agatha Christie memorably said when she pointed out the advantage of being married to an archaeologist.

Anyway, expert though he may be in I don't know how many things, no matter how hard both of us try, I with my slim fingers and Perry with his stubby ones, we just can't get at the switch. And even if we did, what would be the point as I don't have a replacement? The answer is staring me in the face. There is nothing else for it but to go round and see Dennis and the quicker the better, before it gets any darker.

Damned cyclists! I always give them wide berth. But how can you do that when they just suddenly loom at you out of the gloom? This one for instance, cuts a corner off the pavement and damn near rides straight into me. Typical! The rules of the road don't apply to them apparently, boldly going where they please. I don't know who gets the bigger shock, him or me. I saw him all right, saw him approaching the junction, but never expected him to suddenly cut across my path like that.

"Where are your lights, buddy?" I can't hear him but in my rearview mirror he appears to be shouting very loudly indeed and although I can't lip read either, I have a fairly good idea that that is what he is saying, except maybe not the "buddy" part.

You see! Typical! It's always the motorist's fault. "What about *your* lights?" I could have retorted had I been so stupid to stop and point out his hypocritical sin of omission, for he didn't have any lights at all. The Plymouth does; it's just that they aren't working at the moment, which is why I am on my way to do something about it - as I would have told him, though to be fair to him, he could not possibly have known that.

It's bad enough driving without lights but if I am caught by the cops driving without indicators as well, they will throw the book at me - unless of course, one of the cops should happen to be Al. I know one or two of his mates slightly but not well enough, I feel, for them to let me off with a wigging rather than a fine. In some ways a fine would be preferable (if it were not for the fact that I've got to find $99 for a leather coat) as these cops are pretty tough-looking hombres, let me tell you, and I wouldn't like to get on the wrong side of them.

Happily, Dennis is in his workshop, as I thought he would be. If he can't fix the lights it will be a long walk home. I'm not trying that trick again. Fortunately, he can. It *is* the switch, and it gives him some trouble too, *and* he has a spare. What a wonderful man! But if he could do the indicators as well, he would be twice as much.

But Dennis looks doubtful.

"Dunno, Dave. That would be in the steerin' column. Probably a faulty switch too. A new one gonna set you back about $20. Can't do it tonight anyhow."

"No, no! I quite understand." It was good enough of him to stop what he was doing and fix the light switch. "The main thing's the lights. Thanks for that. Would it be OK to bring it round tomorrow night?"

"Sure."

I'm just leaving when suddenly I remember something.

"Oh, you wouldn't have a spare fuse for the radio would you? I took it out to use in the heater."

Dennis has a fuse for every occasion, but I wasn't expecting what happened next, and I bet neither did he. When he put the fuse in the radio, incredibly, the indicators started working again! What a relief to have the blinking things working again! If this story indicates anything (pardon the puns), it is, to paraphrase William Cowper's immortal words: like God, mechanical devices move in mysterious ways their wonders to perform ⁓ especially as far as a technophobe like me is concerned.

Dennis took $15 for the switch but wouldn't take anything for the fuse, and as long as those fuses that work the lights and indicators don't blow, any careless cyclists I should happen to encounter on the way back should not have any reason to blow one either.

Chapter Five

In which I reflect on being culture-shocked and Iona has a far more shocking experience of her own.

Blake is off today and his place is being taken by a substitute.

"What do you find is the biggest difference between here and Scotland?" she asks. I take it she is referring to the educational systems.

That's easy. The informality. Informality in dress, both on the part of students and staff, the informality of the students' behaviour and last and certainly not least, the informality of the staff towards the students ⁃ if Blake and Steve are anything to go by. But are they? Just this morning for example, to give just one example out of many, Steve and I had been in the hall as the classes filed in for the start of lessons.

"Hey, Rhonda! Rhonda the Honda," Steve greeted one tall, gangly girl cheerily, "c'mon over here!" Taking her hands, he held them out in front of her and bent the wrists up and down. "Now you are all revved up you can go!" he laughed. Eaten up with embarrassment, the girl turned and fled. "Mouth moves at a mile a minute," Steve said, apparently to me, but really intended for her ears which I am sure would have been a deep shade of red if you could see them under her long hair. Just before she disappeared into my room, he raised his voice yet again, "Hey Honda, show us your tyres!"

He gets a real kick out of being with the students. This informality I found rather shocking at first. Now I am getting more used to it, I'm more bemused than anything else. Another thing Steve does, which shocked me at first, is he mimes eyeing up the more attractive girls as if looking through a telescope. And as for Carly, the most attractive of them all, who, without too much stretch of the imagination, could make it as a model - he makes no bones about admiring, frequently giving her a wolf whistle and telling her how easy on the eye she is. For her part, Carly is covered in confusion, though she must have heard it many, many times before.

That's why I'm here, to observe different methods and the methods here are the complete opposite of all I had ever been taught. The golden rule, dinned into me again and again by lecturers at training college, headmasters, heads of department and fellow teachers was: *Don't get too friendly with the kids or you're lost.* The precise opposite of what I was seeing here - and yet it seems to work very well.

Nat, the Math teacher, the fourth teacher in the upper school, is not like them at all. But then he has been compulsorily transferred from another school this session and has not had time to get to know the kids yet. But I doubt if that would make any difference; he is altogether a much more serious sort of a person. So just how typical are Blake and Steve and Emerson school? A substitute teacher should know.

"The kids in the other schools are less well behaved than they are here, at least the ones that I've been in," she tells me. "I can't see that they'd get off with that sort of stuff in those."

If that is true, I am certainly glad I am in Emerson. It would be too much like home. I've already had my problems with some students' behaviour and which I'd told Bill Kennedy about. Bill is an English teacher at Hellgate High and who had been on exchange to England last year. He had listened to my tale of the troublesome parents sympathetically.

"I had a similar experience last year," he confided. "At parents' night, it was school policy to have the meetings in the assembly hall, supposedly for our protection." He gave a sardonic little laugh. "Well this parent had a go at me, really shouting at the top of her voice and everything. It was terrible!"

My turn to be sympathetic. Stroppy and over-protective parents are the bane of teachers everywhere. You don't have to go on an exchange to know that.

To my surprise, Bill gives another little chuckle. "She later apologised and you know what, Dave, she invited me and Sharee round for dinner!"

"Maybe you were on the menu," I suggested. "My mother used to say to me 'I'll have your guts for garters'. Maybe that's what it was all about."

* * *

It is Wednesday morning and Judy, the comely school secretary, makes a brief appearance in my room in order to deliver a message.

"Phone call from your wife," she tells me. "You have to phone home at lunchtime. And you've not to worry," she adds before I have time to ask if she has any more details, which she probably doesn't.

And so, for the next hour or so, that's exactly what I do ⸱ worry. If it *is* bad news, it can't be that bad or I would have been sent for or told to phone right away, so it can't be an emergency either. Having said that, the fact that I have received this instruction at all must bode ill of some sort.

Good news could always wait until I got home. It's not even a Friday when I am in the habit of going to the football game after school with Art and then to the Happy Hour (or longer) in some bar or other for half-price beer and free food and where we are later joined by Sam and some others. Art and Sam are 6th grade teachers. Art is Marnie's "special friend", or so she had described him to me when we had met in Washington DC.

"I've just had the most awful morning." The distress in Iona's voice is plain to hear when I call her from the phone at the end of the corridor.

"Why, what's happened?" I ask, alarmed now, despite having eventually persuaded myself there was probably nothing to worry about too much.

"It's George..." I hear her say and can imagine the tears in her eyes, just about to brim over. I want to hop on my bike right away and rush round but the journey time would leave hardly any time there at all, certainly not enough to deal with the crisis this appears to be.

"What? Why? What's happened?" I demand in increasing alarm.

"He fell in the bathroom and hit his head," Iona resumes a few seconds later (though it seemed like minutes to me), her voice under control again. "He was really, really angry, really red in the face. His mouth was just open, screaming in rage. It was like he had forgotten how to breathe out. I just didn't know what to do..."

Thank God I wasn't there. I wouldn't have had a clue either. I would have been panicking, flapping about like a headless chicken, more of a hindrance than a help. Even now I don't know what to say as I picture the scene and how terrifying it must have been for Iona.

"Are you still there?"

"Yes."

"Well say something!"

A hug would have better than a hundred words. "God, that must have been ghastly for you! What happened next? I take it he is OK now?"

"Yes. He passed out. But when he came round he was having convulsions, his eyes were glazed and his eyelids were twitching."

"God!"

"I didn't know what to do, whether just to leave him or pick him up while I phoned Dr Romero."

Oh my God, neither would I! Poor Iona having to cope with this all alone.

Thank God we had finally got around to buying some medical insurance for Iona and the kids, and not so long ago either. As the exchange teacher, I was given $2000 of free medical insurance but they had none ‑ a bit of a sore point actually as that was one thing that Marnie and her children didn't have to worry about ‑ they had inherited our medical practice and dentist and anything from a filling to a major operation would all be taken care of free, gratis and for nothing thanks to me, the taxpayer (and a few million others).

By contrast, on our side of the Atlantic, where we are now, the American system seems to me to be a return to the bad old days of the 1920s, to the days of A. J. Cronin's Dr Finlay, where you had to think twice before calling out the doctor and hoped you never had to. Likewise we hope and pray that we will all enjoy good health and avoid accidents. We have gambled on $6000 being enough insurance and in another development which had come as rather a surprise to us, we had discovered that rather than being general practitioners, doctors here tend to specialise. Confronted with a bewildering array of choice from paediatricians to geriatricians and everything in between, we had settled on a paediatrician, Dr Romero, reckoning that on the balance of probability, the kids would be the ones most likely to need medical attention - and he could attend to us too, if need be.

As for a tooth doctor, we don't intend to do anything about that until we need to, but Iona's friend, Carolyn, whom she had met at a newcomers' welcome meeting, happens to be married to a dentist. He is setting up a practice in the town, so we know where we will be going if we need dental treatment, literally, since John's practice is just round the corner from us in Lincoln. That is probably where we would have gone anyway.

"So what happened?"

"He said to bring him straight round. He'd be waiting for us. But then - " her voice chokes and it is some time before she can go on. "When I went back to the bathroom…he wasn't moving, wasn't twitching or anything…I couldn't see him breathing….He was as white as a sheet. I thought he was…de -" and then she does finally break down, leaving me at the other end of the line feeling incredibly helpless and inadequate and once again groping for the right words of sympathy and empathy, and not finding them, remaining silent. I think I'm in shock myself.

"Go on," I manage to say finally.

"I phoned Carolyn. I wasn't even dressed. And there was Hélène to get ready too. I couldn't possibly have driven…"

"So what did the doctor say?" I cut in.

"Well he gave him a really thorough examination. Said he wasn't epileptic or suffering from meningitis… It never crossed my mind ⸍ "

"Good God! Nor mine! How is he now?"

"Dr Romero said to keep a close eye on him and so far he has been as right as rain. As if it had never happened."

"Well, thank God for that!"

"It was really, really scary!"

"I bet it was! Poor you!"

"I hope to God he doesn't put us through that again. I nearly died of fright. It's a wonder I didn't have a heart attack."

But of course he did ⸍ and not before very much longer either.

Chapter Six

In which we attend the Homecoming Parade and learn some astonishing things about American culture.

Thank God it's Friday. But it's not a typical Friday. Art is not going to the game as it is Homecoming Day tomorrow and he is too busy preparing one of the floats for the parade. Apparently it is going to be one of the largest ever with over 120 floats. I had no idea what all the fuss was about, but now I know that "Homecoming" refers to the start of the university year. I had heard of a "Homecoming Queen" thanks to the Monkees' hit single *Daydream Believer* but hadn't been curious enough to find out what it meant. It still seems an odd term to me to use however, since surely "home" is what they have just left, from all four corners of the state (the fourth largest and more than one-and-a-half times the size of the UK), not to mention many other states from all four corners of the country, or so I presume.

And so I am back in the house from *Psycho* unprecedentedly early for a Friday evening and after the kids are tucked up in bed I am sitting in front of a log fire, well bits of wood really that I have been in the habit of picking up in the forest until such time as I go logging again with Al. I am reading *The Amityville Horror* and I have a Bacardi and Coke by my elbow.

I had used the "free" time after school to visit the liquor store, the first time I had actually bought anything from there. Incredible, considering that I have been here two months now. Beer and wine, you can get from the supermarkets. Hard liquor you have to get from the liquor store. And what an Aladdin's cave it turned out to be! As well as the gallon of Bacardi, I bought a gallon of Californian Riesling for $7 and the whole lot cost less than an ordinary-sized bottle of Bacardi back home! Of course the American gallon is not quite as large as ours, but still! No wonder I am congratulating myself on my decision to apply for the exchange and toasting my luck in being sent here. The book, I suppose, I could have read back home, but reading it in Mrs Bates' house gives it such an additional spookiness that when I was finally able to put the ripping yarn down, I hardly dared go to bed…

Nat had asked if we'd like to go to the parade with him tomorrow and so with that prospect in store, my cup of happiness is complete. What a difference to my weekends back home with no money to spend on entertainment, or even alcohol, and two days of inactivity in which the best thing that could be said for them was that I was not at school, but before I knew it, it was back to Monday morning again. That was the treadmill I was stepping off when I took the big step of applying for the exchange.

* * *

It's another beautiful autumnal day, the sky a cloudless deep blue when Nat and his family come to pick us up. His wife, Mae, works for a realtor, an estate agent, as we would call it. Their two girls, Laura and Sara, aged nine and ten, are both wearing fetching caps that remind me of the ones boys used to wear in the Twenties only theirs are in gingham of green and blue respectively.

Somehow Nat manages to find a place to park and we take up our position about halfway down North Higgins, not too far from the start. It seems as if all Missoula has turned out for the spectacle, but thanks to Nat we are in good time and get a position at the front of a crowd that imperceptibly grows to two or three deep on both sides of the street. But for the lift, we would not have had such an advantageous position, as arriving early for anything has never been part of my philosophy. In fact, left to our own devices, there is no telling when we may have arrived as Iona had reported yesterday that when she was down at the university with George (who is deaf) having his hearing tested, on her return, she found the car wouldn't start. Not knowing what else to do, she just left it for a while and when she tried it again, it started first time. I diagnosed a loose battery connection and tried to wiggle the cables about but they seemed tight enough. It would be typical if this morning, with all of us relying on it, the Big Blue Mean Machine took it into its head not to start again.

With so many floats, not to mention all the other participants in the parade, I can imagine the organisers must be working flat out to get everyone marshalled in the right order. No wonder, therefore, we must hang about for what seems a lifetime in the deceptively crisp sunshine before we hear the banging of a big bass drum which signals that the parade has got underway at last.

It's a piece of pure Americana. Marching bands from each of the high schools and the university; cheerleaders likewise, in their assorted liveries with short skirts and fluffy pompoms on their wrists, stopping every so often to give us a demonstration of their razzmatazz and fuelled, it seems, by chewing gum.

And here come the Girl Scouts in their yellow and green, like our Boy Scouts. To my ears it sounds strange - "Girl Guides" sounds better and not just because of the alliteration. I expect this change of nomenclature is something to do with making girls seem more equal, something to do with the Women's Lib movement which I find much more to the forefront here than in Scotland. Perhaps that explains why I have not seen a woman in a dress or skirt till now and you could hardly call the cheerleaders' costumes typical women's wear. They all wear what they call "pants" (and I should hope they do).

It was one of the first things I noticed when I got to Missoula. Just another of those little culture shocks that reminded me I was in a foreign land, that although many things are recognisable and familiar, I have the sort of feeling Eccles did in Ray Bradbury's short story *A Sound of Thunder*. When he returned from his time-travelling trip to the time of the dinosaurs during which he accidentally stood on the butterfly, Eccles found things the same, but subtly different.

Every club and society in Missoula seems be using the opportunity to showcase their organisation. As they pass, they scatter sweets (candy) like confetti on both sides of the street for the kids to pick up. And in the scramble if you don't succeed, not to worry - another one is coming right behind, such as this for instance, The Big Brothers and Sisters of Missoula.

"Who are they?" I ask my guides.

They tell me it's a volunteer organisation designed to support and mentor kids mainly from single-parent families. Sounds like a good idea. I wonder how many single-parent families there are in my classes and how many are on the program (as they spell it here) as many of my kids, or so I've been told, come from poor and dysfunctional backgrounds. If we have such an organisation in Scotland, I've never heard of it, but it seems to me an eminently good idea. The problems in the classroom stem not so much from the kids themselves but the parents who have next to no parenting skills, having been shown none themselves. Not that I am thinking of starting up a branch when I get back, mind you.

Here comes the float Art must have been working on but there is no sign of him, only one person who looks rather embarrassed to be stuck up there with only Snoopy and his kennel for company. There is some writing on the roof: *School's OK, You're OK in the USA* and underneath a banner: *Missoula District No 7 Schools*. You might have thought Snoopy's companion would have put in a bit of an effort, tried to look at least a bit like Charlie Brown or one of the gang. In fact, it is hard to see why he is there is at all. Maybe the only teacher in the entire district not to renege on riding the float. Snoopy, a kid in a costume, looks much more relaxed, waving to the crowd. Despite the superfluous teacher (I presume) I consider this a rather appropriate tableau as when I saw my classroom for the first time, the desks looked just like the ones in a *Peanuts* cartoon.

As well as Snoopy, there are some other cartoon characters, like refugees from Disneyland, free to roam at will. I'm afraid I don't recognise this character however, if indeed he is meant to be one specifically. About seven feet tall and with black-and-white fur, his bulbous bear belly wobbling as he comes down the street, he waves to the crowd and stops every so often to shake paws with the kids. He stops in front of us, maybe because Hélène stands out in her orange dress.

And if he is taken with her, as he appears to be, the feeling is mutual as she is gazing at him in wonderment.

And the bear is not the only one attracted to Hélène, for the next character to stop is a clown who is already a fan of hers, not that we recognised him at first, not until he spoke.

"Well, hello, miss Hélène!" says the clown, giving her an orange balloon to match her dress but that was maybe a coincidence as the ones he gives Laura and Sara do not match their hats. Checked balloons he does not have. It is none other than Steve representing the Lions Clubs International.

In what seems rather out of place for a parade of this type, there is bit of politicking. Several cars decorated with balloons and banners are urging us to vote for so-and-so for the senate, for sheriff, for district attorney, even a judge and other public offices. The senate I can understand, but I am somewhat surprised, if not shocked, to learn that these others are not a matter of coming first in an interview, admittedly not always a totally reliable method of choosing the best candidate, but a whole lot better I would have thought, than leaving it to Joe Public in the polls. I can just see all the crooks and shady characters voting for the one they reckon they might be able to hoodwink or would be the most lenient, or open to bribery, while the law-abiding folk, apart from the liberal left, would be inclined to vote for the one promising to be "toughest on crime". It seems a strange way of working but you can't deny it's certainly democratic.

And here's the Democrat in "Democracy", a cowboy leading a fine roan over whose back is draped the Stars and Stripes and a banner bearing the legend: *Go Democrat, Go Griz.* You might have thought borrowing a donkey from somewhere would have been more fitting since that is their somewhat surprising choice of animal symbol. The

Republicans you can make some allowances for, elephants not being as plentiful here as buffalo once were on the plains of Montana. The nearest I have seen to one is Mt Sentinel which does bear some resemblance to a recumbent pachyderm, but not nearly as much as Arthur's Seat in Edinburgh.

The Griz, I could scarcely not know, is the university football team, their symbol a grizzly bear. Despite being mere students and their opponents, like them, other students in other universities, they arouse great passion and fervour amongst the faithful (which seems to be practically everyone). But why they should get so worked up about amateurs playing such a tedious stop-start game with more stops than starts is a mystery to me and one I suspect, I will never be able to fathom. Nor will I ever understand why our fast and furious, end-to-end national game of what they call "soccer" has almost uniquely, never caught on in the United States like it has throughout the rest of the planet.

I've kept the best till last, though they were not the last by any means (and apologies to the star of the show, the homecoming queen herself). The bands, the balloons, the cheerleaders and the floats, all that I had been expecting, but I was not at all prepared for the sight that greets my eyes now - a formation of bright-red little vehicles like Noddy cars, each being driven by big men dressed in red with a fez on their heads.

"Who are they?" I ask Mae, desperate to know. It's as if a brigade of Lilliputians had been specially drafted in for the occasion.

"The Ancient Arabic Order of the Nobles of the Mystic Shrine." I look at Mae as if to say: "Are you winding me up?" It sounds as mysterious a mouthful of words as I have ever heard. And if that is the answer it sounds as enlightening as the question. I am amazed Mae can remember it, let alone trot it out pat like that.

"They're Shriners," Mae laughs. "Sort of Freemasons. They're a charity organisation, raise money for hospitals."

"But why the little cars?" I bet George would love one and so would I have once - but then I grew up.

Mae shrugs. "Search me," she says. "It sure is a bit whacky, but the fez comes from its origins in the east."

Well, to me that is just another mystery, as I associate the fez with Turks, not Arabs and I don't associate Turkey with the real east either. But mine not to reason why. It takes all kinds and if the Shriners get their kicks by driving what look like pedal cars like overgrown infants, why not? They are not doing anyone any harm after all. Indeed, quite the reverse. I have taken quite a shine to the Shriners. But I'm not going to start a branch of them either when I get back. I'd never live my little red pedal car down amongst my pupils who would mock me mercilessly.

After more than an hour, the parade is over, and as it heads for the university, we head in the opposite direction for a coffee shop and cinnamon rolls. That's another thing that astonished me when we first arrived in the United States. If we Brits are supposed to have chips with everything, as Arnold Wesker would say, then the Americans have cinnamon. I was not unfamiliar with the spice before coming here, but here you can't avoid it. I'm not exactly sure what the spice of life is but I know what the answer would be if you asked an American.

Over the coffees, I tell Nat and Mae we have a similar parade in Aberdeen, but it happens in what is known as "charities week" and that out of all the universities, Aberdeen consistently raises the most money for charity on a per capita basis in the entire UK. Which is ironic really as if the Scots as a nation are renowned for their parsimony, the buck is said to stop at Aberdeen. There used to be a postcard of Union Street, the main thoroughfare in the Granite City, where the top half was teeming with people while the bottom half was completely empty, not a soul to be seen. The card was entitled "Aberdeen on a flag day". They can laugh at themselves too.

I happen to mention the latest malfunction of the BBMM and after taking us back, Nat has a look under the bonnet. He pronounces the battery terminals very dirty, cleans them up a bit and says that should cure my problem.

Whilst he is doing that, I have a moan about another of the Plymouth's failings. Whether you want it or not, the heater insists on blasting hot air out on your feet. It will not be much longer before I will be heartily glad of it if a Montana winter is anything like I've been told to expect, but in this wonderful Indian summer we have been enjoying where the temperatures have been reaching the eighties, it was certainly something I could do without.

Nat can't stop it working but he shows me where the heater is in the engine compartment and how I can manoeuvre the thing that looks like a hairdryer so that it will only blast out mildly hot air for the moment. At least it avoids another bill of which there have been far too many already. But I know it will only be a stay of execution. What will be next?

It seems set on ruining me. I will say one thing for it though. Gas-guzzler it may be but petrol is so cheap here it actually costs less to run than my medium-sized car back home - twice the car for half the cost. And I can hardly complain about that.

Chapter Seven

*In which I make a new friend and some incredible
coincidences come to light.*

Some time ago I met a man in a pub, or bar, as you do.
When you have an accent like mine, people are always
very interested to engage you in conversation, as I said
earlier. His name was Steve Smith and he was a reporter for
the *Missoulian*. Though I read it every day, I did not
recognise him from the little photo in his column.

"You must get in touch with the Scottish Heritage
Society," Steve had said. "Let me have your telephone
number. I'll get them to call you."

Time passed and I had heard no more which did not
upset me unduly. I'm here to immerse myself in American
culture; I can get all the Scottish culture I want back home.
Truth to tell, I am petrified that they'll invite me to Scottish
country dancing which I just can't stand. My father was the
headmaster of a small rural school and his assistant was a
Scottish Country Dance zealot who took classes after school
once a week. Apart from having no sense of rhythm, which
made me hopeless at it anyway, what I resented most was the
warm summer days when my friends were out roaming the
woods while I had to endure this enforced incarceration,
listening to diddly-diddly-diddly-dee-dee and having to dance
with *girls* in front of my father who teased me about my
choices after.

"Hello. Is that David Addison I am speaking to? This is
Gloria Andrew from the Scottish Heritage Society."

So the call has come. The voice is warm and friendly but of course this could just be the sharks circling before the bite.

"So tell me, David," says Gloria, after the preliminaries have been made, "what part of Scotland do you come from?"

"Oh, you won't have heard of it. A wee place called Banff in the North East, round the corner from Aberdeen. I usually like to tell people that I am just round the bend."

"Oh, my Lord! That's where Dave, my husband's ancestors come from! His great-grandfather was provost of Banff! In fact we were there this summer and we just had a *wonderful* time!"

In her excitement, Gloria seems not to have noticed my joke. I notice, however, she puts so much stress on the first three letters of "provost" it's as if the illustrious ancestor were very much in favour of "vost", whatever that may be. And in case you don't know, in Scottish local government, the provost is the head of the town council, the equivalent of a "mayor" in England, or the USA for that matter.

It's unbelievable, it really is! Gloria is the second person I've met since I came here (well I am sure I will meet her now) who has heard of Banff. This is astonishing: I wouldn't mind betting a lot of people in Scotland have never heard of it. Its transatlantic cousin in Canada is far more famous and (illustrious), I have to admit. With her next utterance, Gloria astounds me even further.

"Do you know Aberchirder?"

That's proof she has been there all right. Not a lot of people have heard of that either, let alone know how to pronounce it correctly.

"Yes indeed! I have cousins from near there, though we normally call it 'Foggieloan' or just 'Foggie' though why they call it that I haven't the foggiest," I add wittily, not really laughing at my own joke, more as a hint to Gloria that I was making one, another one. But once again it falls on stony ground.

"Isn't it something to do with the Gaelic? Doesn't it mean 'boggy meadow' or something like that?"

"Yes, it probably does!" I agree, impressed with her knowledge even if she hasn't quite got the pronunciation of "Gaelic" right. I'm chastened to realise that it takes someone five thousand miles away from Foggie to tell me something it had never occurred me to question before. And what else, I wonder, do the people in the Scottish Heritage Society know about Scotland that I don't? And when they find out I can't do the dancing, a pretty poor ambassador they're going to think me.

"Are you familiar with Portsoy?" Gloria continues in the same effervescent tone as before.

Am I familiar with Portsoy! As if my father-in-law had not committed the crime of his life there when he was at a Boy Scout camp by ringing the church bells and arousing the good burgers peacefully sleeping the sleep of the just in the middle of the night! And did I did not pass through it every day on my way to school in the school bus? And have I not cousins who have farms near there? And have I not got relations sleeping the Big Sleep in the cemetery? And did the love of my life (until I met Iona) not come from there also?

"So you will know George Clark?"

Is there anything else this amazing woman can say to astonish me?

"Well, yes I do! He was at school with me at Banff Academy." He was one of the ones who got on the school bus at Portsoy.

"We met George on our trip and he's been over here to visit with us. He's just left as a matter of fact."

Good grief!

Gloria says we must come to her house soon and see the slides of their trip. I'll look forward to that. I might even find out more about my dear own home town.

Chapter Eight

In which we make an excursion and attend a party.

It is Sunday afternoon. In Scotland, one of the worst times of the entire week when time hung heavy and the thought of school in the morning just would not go away, like the toothache. But not here and not this Sunday. I have a plan.

It's another glorious day, the Plymouth starts first time, glides silently onto Higgins then takes the I-90 for a short distance as far as the 200 and then on to the 83 at Clearwater junction. Had we carried straight on we would have ended up in Butte, but today we are going to what I call "The Lake District". I don't know what they call it here, if anything, but if they don't, that's what they should call it. Blanchard Lake, Harper's Lake, Elbow Lake, Salmon Lake, Placid Lake, Seeley Lake, Lake Inez, Lake Alva, Rainy Lake and Summit Lake. And if you don't find a lake out of that lot to suit you (and why ever should you not?) there are plenty more of them further off the "highway" as they say here, whose names I have not mentioned, not to mention a host of other little ones which quite possibly have not yet been "named for" (as they say here) something or somebody.

That would be a grand thing, to have a lake named after you. It was up this way, a few weeks ago that Al and his dad and I went fishing at Lake Placid, not named for the stillness of the waters as you might expect, but after one of Al's ancestors, Placid Albert. But somewhere between Al's dad and Al, the gentle genes were kicked into the long grass, for if there is one thing Al certainly is not, it is placid. If it were to be named after, I should say "for" Al, it would have to be Megaphone Lake or Whiskey Lake. And if it were the latter, he would surely drink it dry.

But before we embark on this scenic drive where we will have a picnic somewhere, we stop at Clearwater Junction because there is an attraction of another type ‐ a massive Hereford bull with the bluest eyes I've seen since I last saw Blake. He has piercingly blue eyes that bore through you like gimlets. When he tells you a story with a dead‐pan expression, you, or at least I, who have only known him for a matter of weeks, can't be sure if he is joking or not, no hint of a twinkle out of the blue to give you a clue.

We pose by the twenty‐foot high Hereford to have our photographs taken. Actually it is nothing more than an advertising hoarding and I am not going to tell you what is written on it as the cheque seems to have got lost in the post. However, what I can tell you is that the writing is in white and at the bottom it says: CLEARWATER JCT MT. And that is all ye need to know.

It is a splendid run, sometimes the road running close to the lakes, sometimes not, the only indication that one is near, a sign pointing to it through rank upon rank of conifers standing as straight and stiff as soldiers. We pass through only one settlement ‐ Seeley Lake, a ribbon development along the shores of the lake of the same name. If we were to follow the 83 to its end, we would end up in Bigfork, but time does not permit us to go that far today so we stop at Summit Lake to have our picnic. The previous lake was Lake Alva, a name which has resonances for me of home, for Alvah, near Banff, is the home of my ancestors.

There is food for the eyes too as we eat our picnic by the lake. In the distance, the magnificent Mission Mountains are looking even better with their new coating of fresh, gleaming white snow. They could be a toothpaste advert, if only the teeth were not so jagged and splintered. And in another harbinger of winter, the needles on the tamarack trees have donned their autumnal yellow livery. While conifers cannot hope to compete for autumnal splendour with their deciduous cousins, especially the maple (three of which we are lucky enough to have growing opposite us in Lincoln) the bright yellow of the tamarack, either on its own or set against the dark green of the firs and spruces, is nevertheless a splendid sight.

Admiring the scenery, however, has not been the sole purpose of our trip. In the *Missoulian* I had spotted a company, Rustic Inc. in Seeley Lake, were giving away unwanted off-cuts to anyone who could be bothered to pick them up. With the back seat folded down, a space is created in the back of the Plymouth roomy enough to carry a coffin but in the summer intended to provide sleeping accommodation of a less permanent sort. Today we intend to pile it high with wood till we can pile it no higher, the faithless station wagon at last earning its keep. But now it is sitting so low on its springs I'd better take care not to cause any sparks from the exhaust pipe hitting the ground.

This should last us for quite some time I think, well pleased with my afternoon's work, though hardly enough to see us through the winter. But I know I am going to go logging with Al again before then.

Last time, after what had seemed a massive haul to me, enough to keep the home fires burning for ever and a day, Al declared that was not nearly enough yet and we would need to make two further trips at least. It was not something I was looking forward to, as it was, without exaggeration, the hardest work I had ever done in my life - and dirty too, as the trees had been charred black by a lightning fire and felled by the forestry people. That was why they were free to take away.

I was sustained in my labours that day by the knowledge I would be getting a cut, and the pleasing prospect of sitting in front of a roaring log fire while outside it was snowing a blizzard were sufficient antidotes to the back-breaking work to keep me going. But the only wood I had seen since that day were the splinters in my fingers. Hence the trip to Rustic Inc.

* * *

"Hey, Dave, where y'bin for Chris' sake! Y'gotta come over here an' have a drink. It's Rob's birthday."

It's Al's voice booming down the line. I've just finished unloading the wood and stacking it by the back door. The timing makes me suspect that Al has had his spies out waiting for this moment. Rob is at Hellgate High. He is also our most regular babysitter. Iona is not keen on me joining the party: she thinks Al is a bad influence on me. But you can't just ignore your babysitter's birthday can you, even if he is about fifteen years younger than you and under federal law, several years short of legal drinking age?

"See you got some wood," Al says, pouring me two fingers of whiskey into a glass. (So he had been on the lookout!) I should point out that two of his fingers are the equivalent of four of mine and I once saw him use them to tighten the nuts on a wheel of his truck whose "number plate" happens to be "BIG AL". For a small fee, instead of a number, you can have a nameplate on your vehicle and Al had wanted me to call the Big Blue Mean Machine "SCOTCH". But not being half as addicted to my national drink as he is, and to his great disappointment, I opted to have what Americans call the "regular" version ⁓ a 4 to signify Missoula and after a dash, the other digits which are framed by the outline of the state. The plates belong to me, not the vehicle, and when I sell it at the end of the year, they will make an unusual souvenir.

I don't know why, but each time I see Al, I can't stop thinking about the Mafia, unless it is his swarthy skin and his tinted glasses which always seem to be on the darker side of clear. This means you rarely see his eyes but you can get a hint, all the same, of what he's really thinking for he has a moustache too, the most expressive I've ever seen, that quivers and bristles animatedly as if it had a life of its own.

It has been nearly two weeks since I saw him, just before he and Terri had invited Little Al's girlfriend's parents round to dinner. As well as prospective in-laws, they are also Little Al's employers. They have a sewerage business which they run as a sideline to their main jobs and where Little Al is the sole employee. Indeed, I had had to get him to sort out a blocked drain in Mrs Bates' basement bedroom. Little Al has been offered a partnership in the business but that seems dependent on his marrying their daughter (who happens to be pregnant). Is that an offer he can refuse? Anyway, they are here now at the birthday celebrations so presumably the meeting must have gone all right, whatever Little Al's decision was.

It's not everyone who has a Scotsman as a neighbour and Al is keen to show me off to his prospective new friends and/or relatives-to-be.

"Dave's from Scotland," he tells them. "What Dave don't know about Scotch ain't worth knowin'." He wraps his arm around me affectionately whilst I modestly look at the carpet as well I might, for Al's misconception stems from a time when he asked my opinion on a bottle he had got from the liquor store and I appeared to give a very knowledgeable and detailed analysis.

"Hiya, hon," says Terri, appearing from somewhere and embracing me from the other side, "what you bin doin'? Ain't seen you in ages."

It's true and I feel guilty about that. They were our first points of contact and very helpful and hospitable they have been too. I could not have been luckier. Terri had even loaned me her VW Bug until I had bought the Plymouth. The fact that it was so unroadworthy I was terrified to drive it, was neither here nor there. It was the thought that counted.

"Oh well, you know... teaching."

To my surprise, this elicits an outburst of basso profundo mirth in my right ear from Al and a piercing contralto in the other from Terri, making the empty space between them dirl like a bell. From this I conclude the party must been under way for some time. Further confirmation comes when before detaching herself, Terri gives my bum a hearty squeeze. If my cheek had been one of those horns that cars had in the olden days I would have pooped.

That was the last I remember seeing her that evening, but as ever, Al is the amiable, generous host. Your glass is never allowed to be empty, even if Al chooses what you should drink. Hélène is playing with Amy, Sandi's daughter. Al describes Sandi as his "Italian" daughter and I suspect the favourite of all his children, for his Italian heritage is the one of which Al is most proud. The funny thing is his surname is Hertz.

Iona is talking to Sandi and of course has to look after George as well, while Sandi has Daniel, only a few months old. Grandpa, Al's gentle, kind father is there too, sitting at the table in an upright chair, glass in hand, his head nodding as if half asleep. He looks ineffably sad and when he is not looking sad, there is a vague air of bewilderment on his wrinkled countenance as if he were halfway between this world and the next. Like George, he is deaf, only his is not congenital. No-one is talking to him. I am all too aware, as the father of a deaf child, how ostracising deafness can be and I would dearly love to speak to him now but I have been buttonholed by Little Al's potential mother-in-law who seems to have an insatiable desire to know all and everything about Scotland, on which subject, fortunately, I am more knowledgeable than on my national drink.

Naturally we have no babysitter, it being the birthday boy's day off. We have stricter rules than those in the Hertz household where it is not an uncommon sight to see small children still up when the little hand of the clock is pointing to double figures, whereas we believe in getting them tucked up in bed two hours before that at least.

"Aw, shit, you can't go yet, man!" Al booms.

I tell him that we must, that the kids have to be put to bed, that there is school the next day.

I wouldn't mind betting that Al thinks that is women's work, fit only for cissies. The moustache quivers in consternation, if not contempt, before the mouth below opens.

"Once you get the kids to bed, c'mon over an' have a drink. Eeeona can do the babysittin'. She don't drink worth a squit anyhow."

"Sure," I hear myself saying. You don't argue the toss with a cop who doesn't need a spanner to undo the nuts on his wheels, especially after he has had a drink or two.

Actually, it *is* a bit of a wrench to leave this convivial gathering. Apart from that, I wouldn't mind coming back because I have a special reason for doing so. When I went on the logging expedition, it was such hard work that it had taken my mind completely off the fact that the other sort of work, the one that I had come to do, was starting the very next day and I didn't have a minute to think about it, not a second to feel nervous. And after it was over, I was too tired to think of anything apart from a shower and bed.

Likewise tomorrow. After school, we have a parents' evening and I am not looking forward to it one little bit. I have already fallen foul of a couple of parents and am not relishing the re-acquaintance. Just how many others have been waiting for this opportunity to have a go at me I have no idea, but worrying about it is not the best soporific in the world.

Al and his alcohol would certainly take my mind off it.

Chapter Nine

In which I meet the parents of my students, reflect on what might have been and on American education.

It's the end of another uneventful school day. The kids have gone home and will be replaced by their parents in half an hour. I am as prepared as I can be and would rather get on with it right away. The waiting's the worst. I hope. Even back home with a lot more information about the pupils to hand than I have here, I find meeting some parents a bit of a challenge. It's easy with the kids who are bright and hardworking, but just how do you tell parents, diplomatically, that their offspring have not got "the write stuff" and never will?

Matt, my principal, materialises in my room. The door is open in readiness to welcome my visitors but because of the carpet, I had not heard him coming. That was another thing that had struck me when I first arrived ⸱ that the school was fully carpeted whereas Marnie's house was not. If only it had been the other way about.

Matt clears his throat and gives a little cough. "Ahrrum... How's it going, Dave?"

I know from his nervousness this is just a preliminary, that he's come to tell me something he thinks I'm not going to like. I've probably done something else wrong, though my conscience is clear. I have been a bit of a thorn in Matt's side, not deliberately, but my methods were not going down well with a number of parents. I was too strict for a start, gave out too much homework for another (although I thought it negligible compared to what I give my pupils in Scotland) and had been accused by one of moral corruption and incitement to murder even! More embarrassingly, Matt's lack of support for me in that matter had provoked a meeting of my colleagues who felt he did not support the staff in general.

But now I've agreed to cut down on the (miniscule) amount of homework, withdrawn the offensive material (to write a murder mystery story or a horror story) and not had any rows with any students recently. I've even relaxed the strictness, tolerating behaviour I never would have in Scotland, having come more to terms with my students' informal attitude to me as well as their lackadaisical attitude to their work which shook me to the core when I first arrived. I felt, after six weeks of school, that I was beginning to fit in, not rocking the boat any more. So what could it be that I'd done wrong this time?

"Fine," I lie with faux cheeriness.

"Good. That's good, Dave..." There's an awkward pause as Matt gulps for air and his Adam's apple bobs up and down like a yo-yo and his face reddens slightly. I wish he'd just spit it out. As I said, the waiting is the worst thing.

"Dave... well, it's just you see... the way you got your chairs set out..."

There now. He's said it. I look past him to where the students' desks are arranged in serried rows just like in *Peanuts*. What could be wrong with that?

Catching my eye, Matt says, "No, no, Dave. It's these chairs here," indicating with a nod of his head the two innocuous specimens in front of my desk.

"Yes?"

Matt shuffles his feet. "Well, you see, the thing is, Dave... it looks too formal, too unfriendly. It would be better if you came out from behind the desk and sat *with* the parents."

This is bad news indeed. It wasn't much of a barricade against hostile parents but it was at least something and when you are trying to explain to fond parents why their child is consistently getting D or E grades, to do so from behind a desk I felt would give me some air of authority, might just be enough to persuade them to take my assessment at face value, not to question it, might just be enough to get me out of the hole of having to explain to them that the real reason for the bad grades was not lack of effort on the part of the student or lack of skills on mine but when the writing skills were being handed out, they were "in the line" as they say here, for some other skill.

"Oh, oh, I see," I say, springing up with alacrity to remedy the situation. (Is that all it was?)

"That's just grand, Dave," Matt says, grinning. "I know our parents are just goin' to have a grand time talkin' to you." He puts his arm round my shoulders and gives an encouraging squeeze. "I want to tell you again how lucky we are to have you with us, Dave."

I don't let this show of affection go to my head as I am accustomed to Matt's blandishments. In fact, they seem even harder to swallow in the light of the succession of troubles I've been bringing to his door practically from the moment I arrived, but it's nice of him not to hold them against me.

So there I am feeling somewhat naked and defenceless with this cosy arrangement of three chairs, awaiting my first customer. Now, it may not be a truth yet universally acknowledged, but in my philosophy, the more you worry about something, the less bad the event turns out in practice. Thus it was with the parents. In fact, I quite enjoyed it in the end as the conversation invariably turned away from the kids to questions about Scotland and my impressions of Missoula and Montana.

As for the troublesome parents aforesaid, they did not turn up, as they tend not to do in Scotland either. It would have been nice, however, if they had let me know this in advance so I need not have worried at all. But unlike Bill Kennedy, if no-one raised their voice to me, no-one asked me to dinner either. Which was a bit disappointing.

* * *

School is over for the day. No kids tomorrow, nor the next day, then the weekend. A kid-free zone for four whole days! It's what they call the MEA days (Montana Education Association) where a city is selected to host a series of meetings which you can either attend or, if you prefer, attend meetings in your district, or just stay in your school doing your own thing, which is meant to be of an educational nature, naturally.

Steve and Blake regard them as the most mind-numbingly boring events on the planet and consider them as ME days, by which I mean they get someone to sign them in somewhere and do something *they* want to do, which is to go hunting instead. "You don't want to be bothered with all that bullshit, Dave," they had told me.

Taking them at their word, I began hatching a plan of my own which was to visit my relations in Abbotsford, near Vancouver. Most Scots have relations in the former colonies but mine are my English mother's cousin, his wife and family whom I had never met before. It is the sort of trip that would be considered absolute madness at home and I'm not sure that it is not madness here either ⁃ a round trip of 1,200 miles with the slight matter of the Rockies to be negotiated also ⁃ just for a long weekend. But when you live 5000 miles apart, it seems a mere skip and a jump in comparison, especially on roads as straight, wide and empty as they are here. And what with school being closed for the kids from Thursday to Monday, it seemed a perfect opportunity to meet up before the passes became choked with snow.

I had been in touch by letter and by phone (blow the expense) and it was all arranged. Steve and Blake had assured me that Matt would certainly give me his blessing. But I hadn't reckoned on his innate caution and fear of doing the wrong thing in case it rebounded on him, and he wouldn't let me go. The funny thing is that I would have thought that Steve and Blake might have anticipated that. In fact, knowing them to be the jokers they are, I'm not so sure they didn't know that all along and when they saw me disappear down the stairs to his office, they chuckled with glee at the thought of Matt gulping like a toad when I outlined my modest proposal. Which is exactly what happened.

And it is intensely frustrating because there was absolutely nothing I could usefully do in school, nothing to prepare, no correction to undertake. I can honestly say I have never worked less hard in my life: classes half the size producing half the amount of written work I am accustomed to.

Now, if I had been asked to *address* a meeting of the Language Arts teachers, that would have been a different kettle of fish ⁃ I would have rather relished it in fact. I was a little disappointed, not to say a tad insulted that I hadn't been, as the Bureau had told us that in all likelihood we would be asked to give talks and to come prepared for such an eventuality. I hope my decision to go backpacking with Steve and Blake rather than attend a meeting of Reading teachers that Saturday had not sent out the wrong signals. I am a bit worried about that, lest people thought I was here on false pretences, not at all interested in the educational side of the exchange.

But probably these meetings were organised months in advance, long before my arrival. And what these mysterious meetings were about and who organised them I don't know, but no-one had thought to tell me or recommend one. As the sole Language Arts specialist in the school there was no-one to consult. I could have asked Matt to find out more for me I suppose. In fact I was rather surprised that he hadn't already come along and "suggested" which one I should attend.

I sincerely doubt there is anything I would have usefully gained from any of these meetings anyway, unless it was to confirm how far ahead of the game we were in Scotland. As we had discovered, in the matter of deaf education, Missoula was light years ahead of us but when it came to the teaching of English to "normal" children, they had much to learn, as a speaker from Washington University, DC had tried to tell a meeting of Reading teachers I *had* attended shortly after my arrival, and that had gone down like the proverbial lead balloon. Like the slogan on the roof of Snoopy's kennel, they thought that School's OK. If it ain't broke, don't fix it.

The trouble is from what I have seen, it's very badly broken indeed.

Chapter Ten

In which the honeymoon comes to an end.

It is a happy bunch of us chattering like excited school kids, who are off to the Depot to celebrate having no classes for the next two days, followed by the weekend. But like moths drawn to a flame, some of us must stop and admire the goods on display in an "antique" shop.

So this must be the sort of place that Marnie got her rusty knives and other rusty kitchen implements from, together with the yoke without ends and the mammoth-pelt chair, all of which she is inordinately proud of. Amongst the non-desirable items here, as well as guns and rifles, there is a chainsaw and even a pair of mouldy old boots. There really is! But just as incredible in my eyes is the ugliest coffee table I think I have ever seen, a rustic, monstrous, knobbly thing that does look old enough for Methuselah's mother to have mixed his baby food on it, but even more incredible than that is how Art and Sam and Kathy Kuhn, George's teacher, go into raptures over it. There is no accounting for taste I suppose, but it seems to me that Americans regard something old as synonymous with desirable, regardless of its appearance.

If you are a mite surprised to learn that George, who is twenty months old, has a teacher, you would be right to be so. In fact, he must be the youngest student in the whole of Missoula, if not Montana, maybe the whole of the United States. Iona goes along too to learn the signs that Kathy is teaching him but also to change his diapers, which naturally Kathy is extremely happy about.

As it happens, I am her student too since I attend her evening classes at the university where we learn to sign so that we can involve George in family life. It's called "Total Communication" where the spoken word is reinforced by signs and George already knows his animals and his colours, even if his chubby fingers are too small to make the sign for "yellow", so he takes his mum's hand and manipulates her fingers until it makes the word. And if I am disgruntled about Matt's decision not to let me go to Canada, I have to thank him for pulling the strings that allowed George to be enrolled in the preschool Hearing Impaired Unit despite his lack of years (not to mention my lucky stars for being sent to a school that had such a thing in the first place).

At the Depot we put $2 in the kitty for drinks. Because it is Happy Hour, the food is free and the beer half price and when it's all over, despite the countless bottles of beer we have quaffed, and being amongst the last to leave, I even get a dollar back. What an amazing country! It is a lively gathering and gives me the opportunity to speak to colleagues further down the school with whom I don't normally come into contact.

It's amazing just how little people seem to know about Scotland. When I first arrived, one person had even asked me if we had Coca-Cola in Scotland. God knows what sort of backward place she thought I came from. I was so shocked I merely said we did. Too late I thought of asking her if she realised that those two indispensables of 20th century life, the telephone and television, were invented by Scots.

I feel privileged and happy to be an ambassador and enlighten anyone who will listen. Maybe it was the beer talking but Mo Momoko tells me that what I said was "fascinating" and she could listen to me for hours. As a matter of fact I *have* been there for hours and like Tam O'Shanter, the hour has approached when I "maun ride". Unlike the unhappy Tam, however, I do not have a "sulky, sullen dame" at home who is "nursing her wrath to keep it warm", or at least I hope not, but I may have overdone it on this occasion, for I have been enjoying myself so long amongst the "nappy" that it is quite dark. So dark in fact, that since Marnie's old bike does not have the luxury of lights, I decide to cycle on the pavement, or sidewalk, lest some idiot of a motorist driving without lights knocks me down.

* * *

So here I am, where instead of kicking my heels in school I could have been shaking the dust off them - Canada bound. And all because Matt does everything by the book. And what a boring book that is!

It's very quiet at school. There is no sign of Matt. He's probably at a meeting of principals, but might be duck hunting as Steve cynically suggested. But no escape for us as he has left a spy in the camp. She's a 4th Grade teacher by the name of Sally Monk who was not at the Depot yesterday. She must be forty-something, unmarried, and comes originally from Oklahoma. That's OK for short, but it is definitely not OK with Art and Sam and Steve and Blake. Matt has deputed her to patrol the corridors, not to see what we are doing, but simply to check that we are present.

If she *had* come into my room to see what I was doing, she would have found me catching up on my journal, writing a letter to my mother and reading a book. The rest of the time I spent twiddling my thumbs and trying not to think of the wide, open highway and the road to Canada.

Lunchtime is a potluck served in the staffroom. I have contributed some cheese dips. It looks pretty meagre compared to what others have brought. My first experience of this admirable institution where everyone brings a contribution, either a savoury or a sweet and everyone mucks in, was at Matt's house before school started and where our contribution had been some shortbread which Iona had made. Matt and his wife didn't know what to do with it, putting it on the savoury table, where it looked a very humble contribution next to the massive casseroles and salads and quiches. No-one else knew what it was either and left it untouched, thus missing out on this Scottish delicacy. I should therefore have known better by now but this solecism is compounded when Steve and Nat persuade me to phone Iona and invite her and the kids to come along.

I am embarrassed by my offering and apologise to Mary Mason, one of the 3rd Grade teachers (the one who had asked me about Coca-Cola), hoping she would just shrug it off and she would say something like, "Don't worry about it!" or "You're welcome!" But what she actually says is, "You oughta have asked what a potluck was."

It was an innocent mistake but if my colleagues thought I was still an Innocent about the way things were done here, so much the better. But the next day, when I go into the staffroom and cheerily greet a couple of colleagues chatting in the corner, they just carry on with their conversation as if they hadn't heard me.

Is it a result of my perceived parsimony of yesterday, fuelling the myth that the Scots are the meanest nation on earth? Or is it merely that I have been here so long now that I am becoming part of the furniture, just as I am in Scotland where no-one lifts their head out of the newspaper when I walk in the room? Just think ' less than twenty-fours hours ago I was an ambassador, a raconteur with "fascinating" facts and stories and now I am reduced to this.

I have been enjoying something of a celebrity status up till now but I think the honeymoon may now be over.

Chapter Eleven

*In which we set out on an expedition and have
encounters of an unpleasant kind.*

After school Iona takes the car to Brownies to get Big
Buns for our tea. Then I go to my signing class,
where amongst other things, Kathy signs to the
Carpenters' *Close to You*. It strikes me as very graceful and
beautiful but what makes me feel ineffably sad is the thought
that George will never hear any music from birdsong to
Beethoven. I suppose there is some comfort in the notion that
never having heard it at all, he will never know what he is
missing, unlike Beethoven for instance. But he could always
hear it in his head, so maybe I shouldn't feel so desperately
sorry for him either. Though I do.

After that it is on to John and Carolyn's who are
lending us sleeping bags. Once I finally get out of school on
Friday, we are going to head for Glacier Park which shares a
border with Canada, so you never know, we might set foot in
that country this weekend after all. The idea of the sleeping
bags is we are going to try out the Plymouth as a dormitory
for the first time and also intend to call in on Lindy, Marnie's
friend in Whitefish with whom we have a standing invitation
to stay. With a bit of luck, she might make good her promise
and put us up for the night.

She's a bit of a sore point actually which is why I had
not picked up the phone and formally reminded her of her
offer. When we left Scotland I had been particular to have all
the meters read, everything paid up so Marnie would start off

from scratch, as directed by the Bureau. Had Marnie done the same thing? Had she heck! In fact, Lindy's whole family had been staying in her house for two months after Marnie had left while Lindy took some credits at the university and, for all I know, burning the midnight oil all night and the kids never turning a light off in their bedrooms, not even during the day. Which is not unlikely as it is a very dark house. The bill has yet to hit the doormat "an' forward tho' I canna see, I guess an' fear" - as our national bard put it.

She may have left without settling the electricity bill but had left a note to say she had paid the papers (gee, Lindy, that was really nice of you). Letters had been exchanged between me and Marnie whose response had been for *me* to approach Lindy for the money, an abrogation of responsibility, if ever there was one.

In fact, Marnie's approach to the whole exchange had been laid-back in the extreme. She's just not one of the most organised people on the planet. And another thing she fails to realise is the differential in our salaries. She is earning as much as my headmaster (to say nothing of the alimony I presume she is in receipt of) whilst I, promoted teacher though I may be, all I am in receipt of is free milk for the kids because we are so poor - and very grateful indeed I am for it too. No doubt about it, compared to me, Marnie is rolling in it.

So how embarrassing would it be to pick up the phone and ask Lindy for her (greater) part of the utility bill (when it comes) considering she had not made the offer, and to have to explain the reason I was asking was because I am broke and not because I am the stereotypical mean Scot. For the honour of my nation at least, I felt I really couldn't do that, even if we lived on bread and water for the next month whilst the kids lived on milk which I now have to buy.

Still, it might be a sort of quid pro quo if she put us up for the night. Not that we have an address, mind you, but we do have a telephone number. Too short notice in any case, to phone and invite ourselves and no small imposition with two small kids, but it wouldn't do any harm just to call in on her and see what happens. Besides, Whitefish is such a tiny wee place that everybody must know everybody else, especially if you happen to be a teacher, like Lindy.

* * *

Friday. No sign of Steve or Blake or Art today. The first two gone hunting presumably rather than honing their teaching methods which is what Art *may* be doing, as to the best of my knowledge, he is not the rootin', tootin', shootin' sort. No sign of Matt again either for that matter. Out for a duck, Matt's preferred species to hunt? No, I'm sure he's playing it by the book and he's where he is supposed to be. Once again, the top floor is like a morgue with only me and Nat and Millie, the librarian - apart from Sally Monk making an unwanted guest appearance from time to time, taking in the rarefied air of the third floor from her habitual denizen on the ground floor, just to see if we are still here.

So Steve and Blake's absence will be noted, but as experienced hunters, I am sure they will know how to cover their tracks. And if they haven't, I bet Matt would be too embarrassed to ask where they had been, seeming to question their integrity and professionalism. Which is when I have an epiphany - maybe this is not about them at all, but me. Matt knows where I'd far rather be; maybe it's all about spying on *me*. The more I think about it, the more I think that is what Sally's sallies are all about. I hadn't been thinking about skiving off anyway but even if I had been, I would know it is out of the question now. I'm an ambassador, a teacher on an educational exchange and I really must not dirty the nest.

Bored out of my skull, I go down to see Sam. He has both his kids with him, Tom and Amy.

"Just go, David," he says. "The highway is your oyster," and he makes a broad sweeping gesture with his arms and gives vent to another of his gurgling laughs. There's a touch of Kerouac in that and I just love the way Sam speaks in that slow lugubrious drawl of his, almost as if it were too much effort, an apparent reflection on his laidback philosophy of life.

I do go, but not until noon, which is getting on for lunchtime, and then allowing an hour for that, give or take, and then making some allowance for the creeping Monk not beginning her rounds straight after that, my absence might not be spotted till nearly going-home time - if I am lucky. Despite my best intentions, the utter futility of wasting any more time in school got to me and I succumbed to temptation.

* * *

Just before Arlee, about fifteen miles into our journey, Iona discovers that George is not wearing his hearing aid. The mould is there but not the aid itself. He's forever doing that, taking it out and hiding it somewhere. We reckon it's not worth going back for. We might be lucky and find it straight away, but on the other hand, it could take us ages and if he hid it again, somewhere on our trip, it's unlikely we would ever get it back.

Soaring over the crest of a rise in the Big Blue Mean Machine, the magnificent Missions suddenly pop into view, serrating the clear blue sky. We are in the Flathead valley and some thirty miles out of Missoula we come to St Ignatius, a little settlement in the Flathead Indian Reservation. We had been here before when we visited the nearby National Bison Range.

St Ignatius is just a two-horse town, founded in the 1890s when the Catholics came to the valley and founded the Mission. We stop at The Trading Post for a few moments. It looks like a set from a cowboy movie with shops made of logs and high, square frontages that hide the pitch of the roof and wooden sidewalks and rails to hitch your horse, or if you are nearly three like Hélène, a very convenient thing to swing on. It also has a totem pole. It is a tourist trap I suppose - if there ever are any tourists in this neck of the woods, apart from us. No danger of our wallets being fleeced by the natives today anyway since everything is closed.

At Polson, at the bottom of Flathead Lake, we elect to take the more minor road up the eastern side, through Woods Bay and Bigfork. We will probably come down the western side on our way back. Flathead Lake, nearly thirty miles long and half as broad as that in some places, is the biggest natural freshwater lake west of the Mississippi. The scenery is very pleasant and in some places reminiscent of a Scottish loch, hemmed in by the trees and the hills which do not look very high in these parts, though their actual height might be deceptive since we are already probably as high above sea level as Ben Nevis, our highest peak.

This idyll is suddenly shattered by a terrible smell that fills the car. I glance in the rearview mirror to where Iona is looking after the kids in the back.

"Phew! What a guff! Has he...?"

I can see from Iona's screwed-up face that she has been pole-axed by the same smell.

"No, it's not him!" she says indignantly on his behalf. "God, that's truly awful! What the hell could it be?"

"Pooh, farm!" chips in Hélène, but it's not like any farm I've ever smelt before and being brought up in the countryside, I am not unaccustomed to some vile smells as the fields are spread with manure. Pig manure, cow manure and hen manure, all these I have smelled and hated and the latter is the foulest by far but this goes far beyond this. This is so pungently poisonous you don't want to take another breath in case you pass out.

Then ahead I see a little, black, furry mound lying motionless on the road and as we get nearer, the stench gets noticeably stronger, though I wouldn't have thought that possible. I think I know what is causing it now and when I see the band of white I know I have just seen my first skunk and I smelt him long before that. We all did.

It took miles before the fumes left the car and we were able to inhale clean, fresh air again. It was a revelation. I was very familiar, of course, with the expressions "You dirty skunk!" and "You smell like a skunk!" from those TV Westerns I consumed as a boy and therefore knew they were rather unsanitary animals, but I had never imagined they would smell anything as bad as this.

That's another North American experience notched up. I could die happy now, having smelled a skunk. And if I never smell another one, I'll not be sorry. But I am sorry I ever suspected George. On our future travels, if we have the misfortune to encounter this again, I'll know not to blame the innocent.

Kalispell, the Gateway to Glacier Park, is the biggest town in these parts, even boasting traffic lights, but we do not stop and carry on to Whitefish. It's a quaint little town with very much a Wild West sort of feel to it. Although the buildings on the main street are made of brick, they have the same sort of frontages as we had seen at The Trading Post and many have canopies overhanging the sidewalk so you very much get the feeling that you could be walking down a street in frontier times. As well as the usual cafés and restaurants and bars, there are, of course, gun shops and fishing tackle shops by the score ⁄ and taxidermists. Matt doesn't need one of those. He stuffs his own trophies, birds and fish alike, to which Sam would be the first to add ⁄ the staff.

What strikes me most however, and adds considerably to this frontier feeling, is that the cars and trucks are not parked parallel with the street, but face inwards, at a $45°$ angle. How many times had I seen the cowboys ride into town and casually hitch their horse to the rail, if they even bothered to do that, and left to their own devices, the horses always stood facing inwards, just like the cars are now. Such an arrangement would be impossible in Scotland, but here, with plenty of space, you can do that on both sides of the street and still have a street twice as wide as the average street in Scotland. That's another thing that Marnie will have to get used to ⁄ how much narrower our roads are, and how much busier.

Instead of stopping a kid to ask the way to Lindy's house, we ask a policeman in the police station. Policemen are approachable back home. They are our servants after all, here to help us. Thanks to Al, I have met a few cops in Missoula and they all have a sinister look about them with their dark uniforms, dark glasses and bulging biceps. I suppose it's good to have guys like that on the side of the righteous. I don't know what they do to the ungodly, but they certainly terrify me, as Wellington said of his own troops.

"Em… er, excuse me, but do you happen to know where Lindy Collins lives? She's a teacher," I add helpfully.

There is something about the cop's attitude that is making me nervous and I feel not a little bit stupid. Already I am wishing I had asked a kid and I've only just walked in through the door.

He looks at me closely as he might a possible suspect in a murder enquiry. Either that or someone who is a bit unhinged. Why doesn't he say something? The silence is so unnerving I feel I must break it before he slaps the cuffs on me and throws me in the cells for wasting police time.

"I'm an exchange teacher from Scotland you see and she said if ever I was in this area to look her up. Only I don't have her address you see." Still no answer. "All I've got is her phone number. Look," and I fish the crumpled piece of paper from my pocket and hand it to him. He smoothes it out and looks at it. It seems to take him forever to read the numbers. That's all it is - numbers, not a secret code. As if I'd present that to him anyway.

"Well, I dunno," the law at last delivers the words I have been hanging on for. "I dunno if I oughta do that. Her husband's a judge, see."

Is he indeed! I never knew that. But I don't really see what difference that makes. I hardly look or sound like a Mafia hitman, accompanied as I am by Iona and the kids. But I suppose it could be a cunning disguise and he can't be too careful. After all, with all these guns floating about, anybody could be a potential assassin.

"Oh, right. Oh yes, I see! In that case would you mind phoning and asking her if it's all right for us to call in on her?"

Hesitantly, still keeping his eye on me as if I might metamorphose into a gangster if he doesn't, he dials the number. There is silence while the phone is ringing at the other end and then he speaks.

"Your mom there, son?" He listens for a moment followed by, "All right, son," then he puts down the receiver. "No-one in at the moment. Best call back later."

"Yes. Yes. Right."

This is a bit of a blow, but gathering my composure, I manage to mutter, "Thanks for your help."

Taking back the proffered scrap of paper with the phone number on it, we flee.

Chapter Twelve

A fright in the night.

There was a wooded area we had noticed just before we had come into town and it looked as if it might be a suitable place to camp. As forest tracks go, it's not bad at all, certainly nothing like the one we had gone through in the Skalkaho Forest and where I thought we were all going to die.

We follow it for three miles and at last we arrive at the lake that the sign had promised at the end of the track: Blanchard Lake. (Not to be confused with the one in what I call "The Lake District".) Perfect, I think. All the water we need, a tree to pee behind and so remote we shouldn't be disturbed or arrested. I have no idea whether it's legal to sleep in your car or in a place that is not a designated campsite when there is one, as I am sure there must be in Whitefish. People had obviously been here before us: there were the remains of a fire and some rubbish lying around.

We go back into town for supplies, including a torch, then I phone Lindy's house. A boy answers.

"Is your Mom in?"

"No."

"Is your Dad there?"

"No."

"Do you know when they'll be back?"

"No"

"Could you tell them David Addison called please?"

"All right."

"Thanks. Bye."

"Bye."

So that was that. I am used to monosyllabic teenagers. It would have been nice to have spent a bit of time with Lindy, even just to see what she was like. It's going to be a long evening at Blanchard Lake. I hope it's also not going to be an endless night.

* * *

We get the kids into their sleeping suits and settle down for the night. With the back seat folded down, the Plymouth could be transformed into a hearse if you wanted and it's in the body space that Iona and Hélène hope to sleep the sleep of the dead with a blanket below them as a mattress and a sleeping bag over them as a quilt. George lies at their feet while I am in a sleeping bag in the front seat and in a happy set of circumstances, the bench seat happens to be so wide and I am so short, I can stretch straight out too. Surprisingly George settles down without protest. Hélène is a bit more restless but at last she too succumbs to sleep. Ah, the sleep of the innocent!

Not so for Iona and me. Sleep just will not come. We are abed much earlier than usual for one thing and in unusual circumstances for another. Time hangs heavy and when you lie there unable to sleep, your mind gets to thinking and what I can't stop thinking about is that this wasn't such a smart idea at all, especially when car headlights rake the windscreen. It is only 8.45. Maybe a courting couple. But what if it's not? With the state awash with guns, it would only take one maniac to wipe us out before melting into the anonymous darkness again. "Family from Scotland Massacred". I can just see tomorrow's headlines.

An hour later it happens again and the heart beats faster but after a while that vehicle too goes away. I've no idea who or what it was. I keep my head down, knowing that I'll freak out if a face should suddenly appear at the window. If it were the cops coming to tell us to move on, that would be the least of my worries. A relief even. Sometime later I think I hear a radio and loud voices but there are no lights and this time I do risk a peep. I'm sure I didn't imagine it but there was nothing to be seen or heard. That's even odder because it's a long walk out here. I could have used the torch but I didn't. If they haven't spotted us, though it's hard to imagine how they could not, I am definitely not going to advertise our presence to them.

I try to settle down again but I don't even feel drowsy. I am too hyped up - on my guard for something happening but what I could possibly do about it if it did, I haven't a clue. The best I can console myself with is that any potential attacker would see the Missoula licence plate and assume that whoever was dossing down in the Plymouth Station Wagon would be from there, not an Innocent from Scotland who doesn't even have one gun, let alone an arsenal to defend himself, like any self-respecting Montanan.

Time passes and I begin to relax as there are no more interruptions and eventually I doze off.

I am not sure if I was asleep or if it were the lights that woke me up. A glimpse at my watch tells me it is 2.15. My heart really begins to pound this time and my mouth suddenly grows dry. I don't have a good feeling about this. Who could it be? And what could they possibly be up to here, in a place like this, at this time in the morning? It surely can't be anything good.

There is nothing I can do but wait and see what happens next and reflect that if I had not slept very much so far this night, in a few moments I might well be sleeping the Big Sleep. Whilst that may be very peaceful, I was more than a little worried that before I got to this unwakeable state I might have to go through a very painful transition stage as I saw my life's blood pour out of me like a pepper pot. But what worried me even more was that he, or they, would kill Iona and the kids too and on the balance of probability that seemed likely. Why should they stop with me when the blood lust was upon them? I deserve to die for my parsimony, have only myself to blame, but they don't. Too late I realise I should have booked into a motel even though I could ill afford the $20 it would cost. It would have been a small price to pay for a combined estimate of more than two hundred years of life. Let us live, I hear myself saying inside my head, and I'll never be so mean again.

They must have heard me, or Someone did, for the prayer is answered and whoever it was drives away after a matter of a few heart-stopping moments and I am able to breathe again. I can't tell you how good that feels. But it's only a brief respite. I start worrying that they'll come back. Or if they don't, someone else will.

At last I doze off, counting not sheep, but racks of rifles.

* * *

There's one good thing about what the French call *camping sauvage* - you are up with the lark and you see things that you would never have done if you had been tucked up in a warm, cosy bed in a motel. The sky has a rosy tint to it and mist is beginning to evaporate off the lake. If it were a painting, with the trees on the turn, the sedge-hemmed lake and upside-down mountains reflected in the still waters, I would hang it on the wall.

I go down to wash at the lake when all of a sudden this perfect picture is disturbed by a V-shaped ripple. Something has emerged from the sedge. What could it be? Could it be what I hope it is? Then I see the pointy, sleek head ploughing through the water. It is! It is! It's a beaver!

I alert Iona and rush back to get Hélène to show her something that she would never see in Scotland unless in a zoo but by the time I get her, the furry fellow has gone and stubbornly refuses to show himself again. That's my second beaver. The first one I had seen on a fishing trip with Al who was vastly amused at my excitement.

"What, ain't you ever seen a beaver afore?" he had asked.

In my innocence, I had no idea it's what we call a "pussy" and I am not talking of a feline quadruped either. I should have known of course, that they do things much bigger over here.

The excitement over, I commence my ablutions. If I am feeling a bit washed out after last night, there is nothing like cold water from a lake on your face to stimulate the nerve cells, only I never expected it to be that cold. For some reason Iona does not follow my example, even when I tell her how lovely it is and how she would benefit from it and how good it must be for the complexion. I suspect I involuntarily gave the game away with my reaction, ironically like a scalded cat, when this life-restorative water first hit my face.

Breakfast is a simple, uncooked affair and then we are ready to hit the highway. There is nothing to show we had ever been there. What I realise I should have done last night was to light a fire, drink a few beers and gaze at the stars before going to bed. I am sure I would have slept a lot better. I am a long way from being a Montanan yet.

Chapter Thirteen

Going-to-the-Sun and back.

I don't like the look of the sky. It's an ugly, gunmetal grey. It does not bode well for seeing the tops of the mountains. Heading slightly south to begin with, we take Route 40 to Columbia Falls and then the 206 north to Hungry Horse. Now there's a name! It has a fine Indian ring to it and such a place deserves to be visited. But as a matter of fact it turns out that the unusual name has nothing to do with the Native Americans at all, but only dates back to 1900 when there was a severe storm and two horses used for logging, Tex and Jerry, became separated from their owners and were found a month later, skeletal thin but alive and hungry enough to eat ⁄ well, a horse. Luckily they did not resort to cannibalism.

There's not a lot to see here, but it does have more of those quaint frontier buildings that I am such a sucker for. But not that much of a sucker, since I don't buy anything. Nevertheless it does give me that Wild West sort of feeling again, even if I know perfectly well that the buildings are not authentic. I saw the real thing at Garnet not so long ago ⁄ a real Wild West ghost town. Only, disappointingly, it turned out that the place had not really been wild at all. All the same, the spirits were lifted by the fact that it was a real ghost town, that was good enough for me.

Just about the time Garnet was abandoned, Hungry Horse's outstanding attraction ⁄ a dam ⁄ was begun in 1948 and finished in 1953. At that time, at 564 feet, it was the second-highest concrete dam in the world and the third largest. What it dams is the South Fork Flathead River. That's quite a name too. You can walk along the dam though there is not a great deal to see as the parapet is so high you can't see over the top. And all you can see, if you look the other way, is the lake. It's the dam that's extraordinary, but being on the top doesn't give you a sense of its enormous scale: you need to be below it, looking up.

And so on to Glacier National Park which was founded in 1910 and just after the entrance at West Glacier, we stop at Apgar because there is a viewing point where you can observe that icon of the United States, the bald eagle. A pair are nesting in a distant tree. Fortunately Marnie had not taken her binoculars to Scotland and we can see these magnificent birds quite clearly through them. The two parents, masters of all they survey, are content to cling with crooked claw to the tree but their two youngsters, rejoicing in their new-found skill, are happy to put on a flying display for our delectation and a handful of other spectators.

A beaver and four bald eagles in one day, not to mention a dead skunk yesterday. Whatever else happens, it won't be a wasted day, but I fear they may turn out to be the highlights. The fine drizzle that had begun to sprinkle from a leaden sky at Hungry Horse has now become a fine rain as we head back to the car.

Our next stop is at Lake McDonald, the largest lake in the Park, to have a picnic. In the distance, at the end of the lake, across the grey and ruffled waters and in a monochrome landscape, we can see the massive bulk of a mountain rearing into the sky but its peak is shrouded by clouds. Then, suddenly, the heavens open and the gods pelt us with everything wintry in their repertoire: hail, sleet and snow.

Nevertheless, ever hopeful, we set off on the ironically named Going-to-the-Sun Road. Actually, it does stop snowing, but on the other hand, it doesn't look as if it is going to clear up either, but we may as well see what happens, see how far we get. At 6,640 feet, will Logan Pass be open? It seems unlikely. And indeed, that turns out to be the case. By the time we get to the finger sign pointing to Heavens [sic] Peak (8,987 feet), big, white feathery flakes are beginning to tumble from the sky and turning the road white. Do we go on? Another scary journey in the Big Blue Mean Machine I can do without thank you very much. But before we have gone much further the decision is unexpectedly taken out of our hands. A barrier has been placed across the road and a car is parked at the other side of it. I get out to see what's going on.

"You gotta turn back," the park ranger says, winding down his window. "Road blocked up at the pass. Snow ploughs are workin' up there."

It's a disappointment but also a relief. Knowing me, I probably would have gone on until forced to turn back or even worse, got stuck and perished or starved to death even after having been forced to eat poor George in the hope he would keep us going until we were rescued.

There *is* a decision we have to make however. Do we make it third time lucky and try to contact Lindy again? We decide not to. It's a long way back to Missoula and after the sleep deprivations of last night, the idea of our own bed and a long lie-in in the morning is very appealing. A long-lie in for me that is. As ever, Iona will get up and attend to the kids. It's only right. It's her the kids want after all and she doesn't mind mornings, unlike me. I've never been very good at them.

No debate required which side of Flathead Lake we will go down. We had already decided that we would take the western side back. It's astonishing the number of fruit trees there are. If Missoula is the Garden City, this must be the Garden of Montana, or should be. We must come back in the spring when the blossom is out. Glacier Park, however, will have to wait until the summer. I've been told that once the snow comes, the Going-to-the-Sun road will be closed until then. And we so nearly made it!

It was a pity we had not been able to see more, but like watching the Dance of the Seven Veils we had had a tantalising glimpse of what lay behind the clouds. We have already seen some stupendous scenery, the best I have seen outside Austria and Switzerland, but the glimpses we *had* seen today promise to surpass even that.

It's a long, long time to summer. It will be worth waiting for I am sure, and maybe all the better for that, the appetite having been whetted. In the meantime, the environs of Missoula certainly knock the cooling towers of Grangemouth's petrochemical industry into a cocked hat any day. After the initial doubts and fears that I had made a terrible mistake, compounded by the setback with the troublesome parents amongst other things, I am now convinced that coming to Montana will turn out to be the best decision I ever made in my life.

Apart from persuading Iona to marry me of course.

Chapter Fourteen

In which Mrs Bates makes her best effort yet to kill us.

We are going to have a special Sunday lunch today. To be honest, I never thought we would ever get round to eating what is on the menu. Some time ago, Steve, whom I call "The Birdman of Emerson", had brought me three of his victims. They were far from oven-ready. He was not to know I have a feather phobia. I couldn't bear to touch them, let alone cut off the wings (the worst part), pluck them and gut them. Especially gruesome was the alternative way Steve had of dealing with the smallest bird. He made a slit, and with some sleight of hand, somehow turned the bird inside out, peeling off the skin in one deft movement. But it was the sight of his hand and forearm, glistening red, as he disembowelled the bird that really made me feel sick and I had to confess there and that I could never do that, not even to save my life.

So Steve had had to do all the grisly work himself and when the job was finally done, they were put in the freezer and there I thought they would stay, a present for Marnie when she got back. But now Iona has decided that one of the birds, some sort of grouse, was going to be dinner. But of course, she had not seen what I had seen.

To go with this special repast we are going to have special roast potatoes, à la Miss Thomson. She was my landlady in my first year of teaching, a real character and rather unsanitary (and whom I have immortalised elsewhere) and despite her best efforts to poison me, I somehow managed to survive. But there was one good thing about my stay there, the *only* good thing - her roast potatoes. Her method was to parboil them first and then deep-fry them. It's not a method that Iona entirely approves of but today I am in for a treat as long as I do not break my teeth on any lead pellets: she has agreed to submit the tatties to the Miss Thomson method.

Picture the scene. It's a peaceful late Sunday morning. Iona is in the kitchen. I am keeping an eye on the kids and at the same time reading the *Missoulian* and drinking a cup of coffee sweetened with honey, a trick I had picked up at Daphne's Diner the time Al took me on his night shift. Who said that men can't multi-task? It was the calm before the storm.

Suddenly, from the Black Hole of Calcutta (which is what we not so affectionately call Marnie's dark galley kitchen with the light that doesn't work, the black linoleum and the small square window overshadowed by an enormous fir tree), comes a panicky shriek that has my heart racing and my hair standing on end.

"Oh my God! Help! David! David! Come here at once!"

I am already there and I don't need to ask what the matter is. Flames two-feet high are shooting from a saucepan on the stove. I'm struck dumb with shock; rooted to the spot in horror.

"Do something!" Fiona has stepped back from the conflagration, apparently frozen into immobility after that instinctive, life-preserving reaction.

"Where's the bloody lid?" It's a rhetorical question really as my eyes are already raking the kitchen and I spot what I assume must be it before I have even completed the sentence.

Now the initial shock has worn off, I am galvanised into action. Having your own house burn down around your ears is bad enough, but having to tell someone else that there is nothing left of their pride and joy but a heap of ashes is something else entirely. Just how would I break the news to Marnie?

"Out my way!" Seizing what I take to be the lid, I gingerly approach the fiery pan. The flames are too high to simply drop the lid on the top - it's got to be from the side, deflecting the flames like a heat shield until I can drop the lid on it. Phew! Disaster averted. Thank God the flames hadn't set light to anything else, or me, for that matter. Though if it had, perishing in the flames would have been the cowardly (and possibly preferable) solution to my Marnie problem.

Seeing the fire apparently safely contained, Iona is restored to life and breathes again.

"Oh, thank God!"

But is it really safe? For although I had removed the pan from the heat of course, what if, like a volcano, the heat blew the lid off and the flames shot into the air again?

"Open the doors!" I say urgently, at the same time taking a firm grip of the handle.

Iona opens the door into the porch, then the back door and I follow with both hands wrapped round the saucepan handle tighter than any boa constrictor's grip on its prey. I set it down gently on the grass, well away from anything. Safe at last! Thank God!

I take a few moments to reflect on what might have been and realise my hand is shaking. What next? I think I'd better make sure the flames are out, not just leave the pan out there. At arm's length, I slowly and carefully begin to ease the lid off. All seems well. The lid is fully off now. I am just about to take a peek inside when there is a WHOOSH and the flames leap a couple of feet into the air, just as high as they were in the kitchen. Hastily, I drop the lid back on. Phew! That was scary!

Hours later I go back and gingerly lift the lid off, this time prepared for the flames, and stepping back as soon as I have the lid off. A moment later there is a POP and the flames leap to life again as soon as the oxygen gets to the oil, not as high or as fiercely as before, but it astonishes me and scares me that even after all this time, that saucepan is still lethal.

Good try, Mrs Bates. You have tried several times to kill us, mainly by electrocution, but aided by Miss Thomson, this is your best attempt yet. We've not been in this house for two months yet. What's worrying me is that you may get us yet before we leave. After all, you have plenty of time.

It wasn't long before she made her next attempt.

Chapter Fifteen

*In which I have financial problems, Mrs Bates continues
her campaign to kill us and I get a fright.*

Back to school. It's been a successful long weekend for
Blake and Steve. Blake, whose shadow scarcely darkens
a butcher's door, has killed three elk and Steve has
dispatched two pheasants.

I am happy to tell him that we had eaten his grouse
and thus it did not die in vain, but I think it better not to
mention the roast potatoes to him, or anyone, especially Terri.
When Marnie comes back and finds a new saucepan, she will
just have to wonder what happened to the old one, for it was
as sooty as if it had come from hell's kitchen itself, and there
was nothing for it but to destroy the evidence.

I didn't think to ask Blake what his tally had been so
far this season but I could never have eaten *one* elk in a year,
let alone three, even with friends and family to help. His great
ambition is to kill a moose. Not being so thick on the ground
as elk, you have to enter a lottery to be allowed to bag one.
He hasn't been lucky in the draw yet, but say he did, I would
like to have asked, would that give the elks a break? To eat
your way through a moose must be the equivalent of eating a
horse, and surely he couldn't be as hungry as Tex and Jerry?

My third colleague, Nat, has the much more genteel
hobby of restoring furniture which he sells afterwards, so it's
also a supplement to the teacher's salary. I didn't ask him, but
I hope he managed to resurrect a table or two, but I've no

idea how long that Lazarus-like operation takes, so maybe he didn't have time to do even one.

I'm not on friendly enough terms with Matt to ask how he got on. I have never been invited to his house again after that pre-school gathering for the staff. Apart from his fundamental Christian beliefs, he is also a rabid tee-totaller and thus we could never be bosom buddies. That doesn't bother me but it does worry me slightly that as we passed in the hall today, he greeted me as "Mr Addison".

From the first moment I had met him, even during and after I had caused him all that trouble and grief with the pestilential parent, he had called me "Dave". Just another example of the informal way they go about doing things here that I had found so culturally shocking at first, so this sudden formality, it seems to me, could mark a possible deterioration in our relationship. Had his spy informed him about my early departure on Friday?

But as far as Ms Monk is concerned perhaps she is more of a guardian than an avenging angel. If we *had* left earlier, we might well have pressed on over the pass and camped in Glacier or in Waterton Lakes National Park in Canada which adjoins it. Together they form the Glacier-Waterton International Peace Park. And what if we had not been able to get back through the pass the next morning? It would have involved a detour of hundreds of miles.

* * *

There is one thing that *really* is worrying me - my salary has still not come from Scotland. I have not been paid since August and this is now the end of October. However pure the air is here compared to Grangemouth, we can't live on that alone, so at lunchtime I pop round the corner and visit my bank.

To my dismay there is no sign of a sympathetic ear on the friendly face of the First Bank of Missoula, in other words, my pal Fran, an expatriate Scottish lady who hails from Elgin, not a million miles from my own place of origin. Apart from being practically struck dumb by a sort of *Casablanca* effect: that of all the banks in this town that I should walk into, in the very first, I should meet someone from my own neck of the woods.

I was also struck by how it was more like the foyer of some swanky hotel than a bank. I was accustomed to tellers being installed behind a high counter with a metal grille extending to the ceiling but here, in the land of the gun, I found it staggering that there appeared to be nothing at all to stop Joe Doe just coming in off the street, waving his automatic rifle about and persuading the cashiers to hand over all the dough in the bank.

I am directed by another receptionist to a man I can see seated behind a desk at the other side of the potted-palmed, marble-floored foyer. The nameplate affirms that he is indeed the man I seek, Mr Nortman, a vice-president of the bank, no less. I am impressed by such a high-ranking individual attending to the needs of an impecunious little punter like me. Vice-presidents, you would think, would be handling the accounts of millionaires.

As I expected, Mr Nortman is all concern and would-be helpfulness personified. Unfortunately it turns out he can't, much. He can't send a telex to my bank in Scotland (as had happened when we had had money supply problems once before in France). He can offer me some money on account, but he would have to charge me interest. His best advice is I write to my bank in Scotland to find out the reason for the delay. How about if he phoned them instead? No he couldn't do that but I could phone *them* daily to find out if the money had arrived. The interview is at an end. We part the best of friends. We must be, because we shake hands and he calls me "Dave" and wishes me the best of luck. Thanks a lot, Mr Nortman. You've been a great help.

* * *

When I get home, I fire off a letter to my bank and later that evening I make a fire using the offcuts from Rustic Inc. They are very reluctant to burn, a very desirable feature in a log cabin admittedly, but far from ideal when you want them to burn merrily in your fireplace. They generate a great deal of smoke before the first flame flickers into life, the waiting and watching for which, I have discovered, is something akin to watching paint dry, only less captivating.

Therefore, as soon as I see a fair amount of smoke appear, I leave it to get on with it and take the kids upstairs to bath them before putting them to bed. I am, of course, a thoroughly modern father and not unaccustomed to doing my share of parenting and tonight, as usual on Monday nights, I am home alone with the kids. Entirely my own fault. Iona is at her Sweet Adelines and the reason she is there is because I had spotted an advert in the *Missoulian* looking for would-be *chanteuses* and had drawn Iona's attention to it. She had auditioned and been accepted, which came as no surprise to me as she can hold a pretty tune and play the French horn, not to mention understanding what all those tadpoles on those telephone wires mean.

It was the smell that first alerted me as I was taking the kids, washed, dried and dressed in their pyjamas, along the hall to their bedroom. Smoke! I hurriedly abandon my charges and rush downstairs, my heart pounding, dreading what I might see, hoping that I might yet be in time to deal with the flames. That was my instinct, to deal with the fire first, not to carry the kids down *towards* the fire and outside to safety. And as I rush down the stairs, as well as noticing how the smoke is definitely getting thicker, I can't help but think how the gods love to sport with us. Yesterday I had saved the house from a conflagration and the very next day, along comes another fire emergency.

There is no doubt where the smoke is coming from. It is so thick in the family room that I can scarcely see across to the other side of the room. There is no sign of any flames thank God and the source of the problem is immediately apparent too, for there do not appear to be any flames where I want them either, in the fireplace, just masses of smoke billowing out into the room instead of disappearing up the chimney. But why? The answer soon becomes clear. The damper is fully shut. I must have given it a dunt when I chucked in a log.

It is going to take some time for the room to clear. The one window in the room has a sofa and a net curtain in front of it. Not the easiest of things to get to. Besides, it's a sash window and it doesn't look as if it has been opened in an age. The only thing to do is to leave the front door open and use a log as a stopper to pin back the flyscreen. Having done that, I go up to read the bedtime stories and tuck the kids in bed.

What's that? I have just taken a couple of steps downstairs when I think I hear something down below. I freeze and listen hard. Yes, there it goes again ⸴ a sort of shuffling, scuffling noise. There is definitely someone down there. Or *something*. For one mad moment the notion swims into my mind that Mrs Bates has been smoked out of the cellar and has had to surface for some air. Or it could be an opportunistic thief who had found the open front door an irresistible invitation, but as I tread warily downstairs, I am hoping it's just an animal of some sort. I wish there was something near to hand, like a poker, to protect myself but there is nothing.

Nothing or nobody at the bottom of the stairs where smoke is gently wafting its way through the open door. Nothing to be seen in the family room where the smoke has now thinned sufficiently to permit a view across to the fireplace. Maybe I just imagined it and I begin to breathe a bit more easily as I enter the room - only for my heart to leap into my mouth and a moment later to begin thudding against my ribs. In the Black Hole of Calcutta, through the smoke dimly, I can see a shadowy figure with its back towards me.

I start edging towards the poker in the fireplace when, like the smoke in the room, the fog in the brain begins to clear. There is something familiar about that stooping figure and it is he, rather than me, who gets the fright of his life when I speak to him. That's because of his deafness, despite his hearing aid. It's only Grandpa Hertz bringing back the Anglepoise lamp he had taken away to fix after I had reported it wasn't working again. He was an electrician to trade in the year oatcake. No point in him calling out to ask if anyone was at home, he wouldn't have heard any answer.

He has bad news. The light is working perfectly well. The problem is the socket which has no power coming into it at all. No wonder the lamp wasn't working, though it did before - up to a point - its head hanging down like a drunk's and illuminating a circle of light at its base. Any attempt to make it shed light anywhere useful resulted in a display of pyrotechnics, which if they didn't quite manage to shock you in the electrical sense, they certainly looked impressive enough to set the whole damned house on fire.

It was our only source of illumination in the kitchen until Grandpa fixed the overhead light but now we are no longer dependent on the Anglepoise I tell him it doesn't matter. It sounds to me as if it could be a big job and I had better get Marnie's permission before I have it done and more importantly, make sure she is going to pay for it, though I don't tell Grandpa that.

An ineffably sad figure, he shuffles out again, taking with him this time *Hoover erectus*, as I call it: Marnie's prototype of a hoover, dilapidated and dangerous. On its one and only outing, when it too alarmingly showered us with sparks, we had interred it at the back of the cupboard beneath the stairs which is where it had remained ever since.

Now let's see if I can get this damned fire to light. Hard luck, Mrs Bates. That attempt to smoke us to death didn't work out too well for you, did it? I hope you don't have better luck next time, whenever that is.

Chapter Sixteen

In which I am invited out to lunch, we go out to dinner and I am impressed by the American way of life.

It was the last football game of the season. Just as well. Emerson was dumped 26 - 0 by Rattlesnake, their worst defeat yet. They don't have to worry about next week's game; they can lick their wounds and go into hibernation. As for me, I find it impossible to get even mildly excited by the Americans' passion for this perpetual stop-start game, but I do have a position of responsibility which stops me from terminal boredom - I run the chains, which means I hold one end of the pole to which a chain is attached and which measures how much territory has been gained by a team. In the case of Emerson, not much.

The real reason I attend the games is I enjoy going for a beer afterwards with Art and Sam, though Sam has the good sense to avoid the hors d'oeuvres and just joins us later for the main course. Art is Marnie's "special friend" as he had been described to me by Marnie herself, while Sam is Matt's special "pain in the ass". The quotation marks are mine, but I would be very surprised if I were wide of the mark, for Sam is a real thorn in Matt's side, if nowhere else. He is not afraid to challenge Matt with his wishy-washy management decisions and if Matt does indeed regard Sam as the fundamental pain above, for his part, Sam's description of Matt as a "dildo" is to my mind, even more insulting.

As for Art and me, we have not been seeing eye to eye recently, especially on matters pedagogical but today, unusually a Wednesday rather than a Friday, and also unusually, in the Golden Pheasant, we seem to be getting on very well indeed, with Art pumping me for information about Scotland. I am always happy to be an ambassador for Scotland, but today I am in my element, for the topic is Robert Burns, our national poet, and I regale him with a recitation of one of his most famous poems, *Tam O' Shanter*, or at least as much of it as I can remember (fortunately for Art, not a great deal, as I can see Scots is as far removed from his English as Anglo-Saxon is from mine).

Just then one of Art's ex-pupils comes in, and now one of mine, a nice kid called Nicky. He has come in to shine shoes. I doubt if he would be allowed to do that back home, especially in licensed premises. That's American enterprise for you. Of course, being his teacher, there is no escape for Art, he must give him some custom and, ever the ambassador, I feel I must too, to slay the dragon of the Scots' legendary meanness. Whilst it may give my footwear the shock of its life, it is hardly going to break the bank at 50 cents a shine, except in my case, it might just, since my money still has not arrived but my letter should, at this moment, be winging its way to Scotland. Hopefully.

I had popped in to the bank at lunchtime to speak to my pal, Fran, from Elgin. Contrary to what Mr Nortman said, she tells me that they could send a telex but it would cost $14. That's a lot of money for a man who has none.

"No thanks," I tell her. "I could probably phone for less than that. I'll wait and see what joy I get from my letter. Besides, the money might arrive tomorrow, who knows?"

My optimistic words must have belied the look on my face.

"Cheer up," Fran says. "I'm sure it'll come soon. Listen, we must go out for lunch sometime. Barbara would like to meet you so you can tell her all about Scotland." She nods in the direction of the attractive brunette at the next desk. If Fran is good-looking, Barbara is drop-dead gorgeous. Imagine me dining out with two stunners like this! I like being an ambassador for Scotland even more. It's a pity they weren't after my body, but if it's my mind they want, I don't mind that in the slightest.

It's great to dine out on the strength of being a rare and exotic species but this proposed lunch date will have to wait until my pay arrives. At the moment I am getting free lunches in return for supervising the kids, even although it does involve putting the tables away and wiping the floor clean with a mop which the custodian, or "janitor", as I would call him, kindly lends me and watches to make sure I am doing it right. But once that is done, I don't really have to do anything, as although they bring their own lunches, Blake and Steve are always there too to organise a game of scatterball and sometimes Nat stays too, if he has nothing better to do.

In the meantime, if my salary does not arrive soon, I can see I might have to go into the shoe-shining business. Nicky tells me he usually makes $10 a night.

* * *

That damned boy!

It's my son and heir to nothing I am talking about. As I said before, George is forever taking out his hearing aid and even worse, hiding it somewhere. In Scotland they had warned us that at his age (eight months) we would never be able to make him wear it and were reluctant to issue an aid. If they were right about that, we were vindicated by the Hearing Impaired Unit here at the university who said it was important to get him to hear *any* sounds we possibly could. Furthermore, they had tested the aid and found it wasn't working so we had bought one whilst the one from the NHS was sent off for repair.

This is the aid in question and this time we don't have to go hunting for it. Iona saw him post it into the demister vent in the car like a letter through a pillarbox. But even if she hadn't, we would know where it was, we can hear it – an irritating high-pitched whistling that will get on everyone's nerves, except of course the architect of this grand design to be rid of the aid forever. And a very good job he has made of it this time.

Contorting my body into a shape I would never have thought possible, with my head lower than my hips, causing not a rush of blood to the head exactly as I have been in this position for what seems hours, it nevertheless does nothing to improve my temper. I have unscrewed the screws from the dashboard facia and from fiddly clips and hoses, and now at last, I can see where it is. The problem is it's behind the air-conditioning unit and there is only a narrow space in which I can insert my hand and wrist as far as it will go but which immediately blocks off my sight. Frustratingly, I can just touch it with the tips of my fingers but try as I might, I just can't get enough of a grip of it to bring it back into the light of day.

With one desperate attempt, I force my spine into one further agonising twist, make an even tighter tourniquet of my wrist as my blind fingers grope for the elusive aid, trying to bring it that millimetre nearer so I can get a hold of it...Damn! All I've succeeded in doing is to push it further away. Now I can't even touch it with a fingernail let alone see it. It's gone forever. Money down the drain. In fact I wish he *had* just chucked it down a drain then I wouldn't have wasted three bloody hours trying to retrieve it.

Now I'm going to have to put the whole damned facia back together to the tune of that irritating whistling sound. That will be its tomb when the battery eventually gives out, and the sooner the better.

* * *

I'm not in the best of moods therefore, just after the reassembly, when we set off for the Andrew residence somewhere up the Rattlesnake, so far up the creek, you might say, that the tarred road ends and we continue up a track. But, as it happens, we are on the right track, and we find the house quite easily, or we think we do. But the instant we see through the screen door into the living room, all doubts are erased: we know without any shadow of doubt that we have arrived at our destination, the HQ of the Scottish Heritage Society ⁄ for the whole place is festooned with tartan, thus confirming what I had heard before, that Americans of Scottish descent are more Scottish than the Scots.

Gloria is just as warm and effusive as she had sounded on the phone. She apologises for her husband not being there at the moment. He will be back presently. He's taking his elder son on his first date. To the rendezvous I presume, rather than to act as a chaperone. The son in question is David H. Andrew IV. His father, is of course, David H. Andrew III and if young David ever has a son, you can bet your bottom dollar what his name will be, unless of course, his younger brother Ross, beats him to it.

It makes it sound like a dynasty and as if to emphasise the point, there are portraits on the walls of the ancestors, like you see in stately homes. I stop in front of one whiskery gent.

"That's Dave's great-grandfather, provost Coutts of Banff," Gloria says proudly.

"Coutts you say?"

"Yes."

"Well how extraordinary! One of my ancestors is a Coutts too!"

"Oh, my Lord!"

"Wouldn't it be amazing if it turned out we were related in some way!"

Of course, after that, we get on like a house on fire. I am sure we would have anyway, but there were certainly no awkward silences. Gloria tells me she is writing a book about Dave's ancestors and she shows me her file, all the documents and photos neatly arranged and indexed. I am very impressed and would never have shown her my amateurish dabblings in genealogy out of shame, but I was glad I had made a start as that was how I knew about the Coutts connection, one of my grandfathers or great-grandfathers being married to one of that ilk.

"You should go to the Mormon Church on South, David. They can get you all the records you want from Register House in Edinboro. And it's totally free!"

Isn't that an amazing thing! When I went there, it cost £5 for the day, to say nothing of the train fare in and back. And I had spent most of the time guddling about as it was so confusing, until some kind, professional genealogist took me under her wing and showed me how to find what I was looking for and how to put the microfiches into the machine. Now it seems I can do it much more conveniently from five thousand miles away and it wouldn't cost me a cent! This is the best piece of news I've had since I discovered the happy hour and half-price beer and free food to go with it. What a country! What an inspired decision of mine to apply for the exchange! All that stress and worry, the fear of the unknown was certainly worth it! If only I had some money...that's a worry.

If that was a pleasant surprise, it was another surprise altogether to see Gloria's husband for the first time when he walked through the door. A bear of a man, with a handshake like a vice, and not having given it the remotest thought before, it came as a bit of a shock to see how old he looked, much older than Gloria. It must have shown on my face or Iona's, or quite likely on both of us.

"I married my teacher," Gloria says with an easy laugh, not in the least put out.

I'm not sure how old she is but old enough to have a boy old enough to go out on a date, maybe fifteen or sixteen, while Dave is planning to retire next year. He teaches Speech and Drama at Sentinel, one of the three high schools in Missoula, and like a lot of teachers, he also has a second job, which if I understand him correctly, he manages a medical practice at the Community Hospital. How he manages to do that when he is teaching during the day, I can't begin to imagine, so maybe I got that wrong.

Apart from the Banff connection and the common interest in genealogy, and the mutual friend or acquaintance in the shape of George Clark from Portsoy, Dave and I have a common interest too - in making our own wine. But just as I would never dream of letting Gloria see my first stumbling steps down the trail of the family past, likewise I would be ashamed to let Dave see my humble attempts at wine-making. I am a mere amateur compared to him.

He takes me down to his basement, a real cellar, another thing that impresses me about the American way of life. Every house has one whereas I have yet to see one in Scotland or in the entire United Kingdom for that matter. Such a waste of space. But maybe it has something to do with the water table or something and I do know that Montana has long dry summers and that if you want to have a nice, green lawn in Missoula you have to install a sprinkler system. "I'd rather have a cellar than a sprinkler system. Yes I would, yes, I really would", as I am sure Simon and Garfunkel would sing if ever faced with the choice.

I had thought I was pretty productive in that department since I reckoned I had quite a stock of wine but with no basement and no cellar to store it, we had had to have some farewell parties before we left, and now my cellar is dry, so to speak. When I get back I will have to start all over again and since my name is not Jesus and flavoured water cannot be turned into wine overnight, I foresee months and months of alcohol-free days ahead on our return.

That is a thought on which I would rather not dwell, but here in the present, there is more wine than I could possibly drink in many, many evenings, let alone one, though I make a pretty good stab at it. Dave is as good a host as Al is when it comes to the matter of dispensing the cup that cheers and inebriates, and of course, I must try different varieties, as many as Mr Heinz has it seems - exotic-sounding potions such as huckleberry and blueberry, not native to our shores.

I blush to think of the paucity of my range from bramble (which is definitely my best) to elderberry and elderflower, to oak leaf (the smell of which made Iona feel sick, but she was pregnant at the time and women tend to be a bit funny about such things when they are in that condition), to rose petal (which my brother-in-law rudely called 'Rose and Dettol' and did not even have the grace to swallow, but unashamedly ran to the sink to spit out). I will say though, that my birch sap was delicious, even if I do say so myself. But getting the trees to give up their sap was rather difficult and I only ever managed to make one gallon of it. Dave, by contrast, never makes less than five gallons of anything in one batch, something I have never done, so no wonder he is swimming in the stuff.

And when it comes to the culinary department, Gloria is no slouch either. In fact that is another of her writing projects - she is writing a cookbook. It's to be entitled *Gloria's Glorious Gourmet Cookbook* (which is a very fine title indeed) and the idea is that as well as her own favourite recipes in which she will describe their provenance as well as adding some brief anecdotal notes, her friends and family are also requested to make contributions to which Gloria will append a few words about the contributor. Naturally Iona agrees to donate a couple of entries and thus become immortalised, her oatmeal gingerbread and oatcakes destined to be legendary in the State of Montana and beyond.

It goes without saying that we had a very pleasant evening indeed with so much in common, such excellent conversation, such excellent food and such excellent wine to wash it down with. They even offered to lend me some cash until mine arrived! And they have only just met us! Once again, I am touched by the kindness and generosity of Americans. I thank them profusely but say I hope it won't be necessary.

They had planned to show us their slides but we were having such a good time there just wasn't time. Hopefully we will be invited back and we'll see them then. I hope it won't make me homesick.

We are approaching the witching hour. People here tend to go to bed a lot earlier than we do, normally about the time parties or gatherings are just getting into their stride in Scotland. I'm not sure if rates go up after midnight or not, but I am mindful that time is money over here and according to the Babysitters' Union of America, the going rate is 75 cents an hour but we are paying Rob a dollar, partly for convenience and partly because he is the son of a friend. At home our friends do it for nothing, or rather for a few libations of my homemade wine after we get back.

That's going to be another problem when we get back, now I come to think of it: how am I going to be able to "pay" the babysitter? But I am not going to start thinking about that, not now that I am enjoying myself here so much.

Little I did I know that was just about to change in the space of just a few more hours. Oh, how the gods love to toy with us for their sport.

Chapter Seventeen

*In which I go logging again and receive an
unexpected gift.*

"Hey, Dave, you wanna go an' get some wood?"

It's Al at the other end of the line. The question is of course, rhetorical. I am holding the receiver away from my ear but I can hear him perfectly. I *would* like some wood, but not right now. To tell you the truth I have a bit of a headache and my mouth feels like the bottom of a parrot's cage. As I should have known from my own brew, homemade wine can pack a powerful punch.

"Give me five minutes," I tell him.

I was drinking a cup of tea at the moment and my plan had been to go back to bed and sleep off the hangover. Fat chance of that now. Never did I feel less inclined to go logging and I know exactly what is in store for me this time. I swallow the last two aspirins in the bottle, have a bite of breakfast and go upstairs to get into my old clothes as quickly as I can. It wouldn't do to keep Al waiting. His middle name is not Patience.

As he had promised the other day, we are heading for Pattee Canyon, where the wood is allegedly "lighter" and easier to get out, but first we have to pick up Grandpa. We just walk straight into his house without ringing the bell or knocking. Right enough, he wouldn't hear it.

"Hey, Pops! Pops! You ready to go?"

No answer.

"Hey, Pops!" Al bellows louder than before and when there is still no answer, "Goddammit! Where is he? Pops!" This last trumpet sound making the veins on Al's neck stand out and my ears hurt.

He marches into the kitchen, opens the fridge and hands me a beer. I know better than to refuse, even if it is only a little after nine o'clock in the morning. It saves time Al insisting that I have to have one. Beer is to Al as oxygen is to ordinary mortals. Besides, I convince myself, a hair of the dog might be just the pick-up I require, and as for the adage that you should never mix the grain and the grape, since the latter was nowhere near any of the wine I had drunk last night, I reckon I was alright on that count too.

And by the looks of it, it is going to be a scorcher of a day, albeit we are just a nudge off November, and I should take on board all the fluids I can because there is one thing I know for sure - I am going to be sweating like a pig before very much longer. Yes, I tell myself, Al is right, as usual. He *does* know best.

Al opens the back door and goes into what we would call the "garden" but Americans call the "yard". As it happens, the old man actually is in the garden because he is tending to his vegetables and that is what the Americans mean by a "garden" the place where they grow that mysterious thing known as "prodoos".

"Hey, Pops!" Al roars. "Ain't you ready yet? You forgotten that we are supposed to be goin' loggin' this mornin'?" This with an exasperated shake of the head at me and a "Goddammit!" scarcely less loud but which I doubt if the old man was able to hear, mercifully.

I also doubt very much if Grandpa had forgotten the slavery in store today. You don't forget a thing like that, more likely to have nightmares about it, and a moment later I am sure he had remembered. Had he just heard his son, or was it just coincidence that he had finished his task? Anyway, he straightens up at that moment and in his hand he has a couple of zucchini (courgettes) which he had been harvesting for me, knowing that I was coming. I've often wondered if his perpetual air of bewilderment was due to his wondering if Al really is his son, that two boy babies had somehow got mixed up at the hospital and he is wondering where the real one could be.

Before we go we have to take the camper off the truck. Another great American idea. A general purpose vehicle, so useful for "hauling" anything and everything, is transformed without a great deal of effort into a place to sleep out in the wilds without the tiresome business of having to erect a tent. And whilst I have camped all over Europe, but mainly in France, and love sleeping out in the great outdoors, I never felt in danger of being devoured by predatory wildlife such as bears or mountain lions whose gastric juices had been whetted once they had got a whiff of my socks. But out here it is different, and to me a camper sounds like an eminently desirable accoutrement to sleeping in the great outdoors.

The track to the Pattee Canyon site is very, very bumpy. Just what you don't need when you have just had your breakfast and your head is splitting. Poor Grandpa, who is on the outside, gets the worst of it, one moment squashed up against the door, the next lurching into me, but stoically making no complaint. Al has the best of it, with the wheel to hang on to. The track is very new, the caterpillar tracks deep and fresh and unnavigable without four-wheel drive. Finally we come to a clearing where we find the massive machine that created this track at rest from its labours.

Ours are just about to begin, alas. The wood is charred as before, and as before, Grandpa measures the logs, Al cuts them into eight foot lengths and who do you suppose gets the job of picking them up and lifting them into the truck, which of course gets progressively harder the higher they become, until I need Grandpa to help me. And then when that becomes impossible for us, Al has to take time off from cutting to hoist the logs up what must be ten or twelve feet as he has put iron rods into the side of the truck which more than doubles its capacity. And once that is done, it is time to fill up the trailer which holds even more wood than the truck.

I am getting off lightly this time however. The wood *is* lighter, just as Al said, because the tree trunks are thinner. Why didn't I think of that? I should never have doubted him. I am, however, just as black as before and just as exhausted after labouring under a merciless sun. But this time I know better to keep my shirt on, thus preventing a severe case of sunburn to add to my breaking back.

Back then (no pun intended) on that first logging expedition, I was not acclimatised, in both senses of the word, to Montana. I come from a land where, when the temperature climbs into the seventies for three consecutive days, it is called a heatwave and becomes headline news. People stop scowling at each other and begin smiling instead. Everyone strips off and takes this chance to address their Vitamin D deficiency while they can. Now that I know the sun shines in Missoula nearly every day, there is no urgency to expose my body to the rays. And I also know that I am right in my belief that the climate influences our outlook as I often catch perfect strangers smiling at me in the street here. I thought to begin with that they were amused by some perceived eccentricity in my appearance but then I came to realise that the Missoulians just have a naturally friendly outlook on life.

The whole operation takes three hours, as many as I had spent trying to retrieve George's hearing aid from the car, and although I am as black as Al Jolson and my back feels it must be broken in seven places, I'd far rather be doing this than that, even if I know that the job is only half done, that next comes the cutting up into fireside-sized pieces, and then the stacking.

In the event, this turns out to be not nearly so bad as I had feared, for this time we have a helper in the shape of Rob. The cutting is done by a saw powered by a 1928 Ford tractor engine. My job is to manhandle the logs to Lou and Grandpa who feed them into the saw, then Lou tosses the logs to Rob who stacks them neatly against what I heard first as the "wreck" room. My mind ran riot as I imagined either a very dilapidated building or some sort of therapy room where the kids were allowed to get rid of their tempers by throwing china at the wall. In fact "wreck" turned out to be short for "recreation" though "room" was a misnomer, for there were two of them in a two-storey detached building at the bottom of the garden, or rather yard, where the kids could go, or are put, to get them out of their parents' hair.

That's another great American institution, though I doubt if every home has one. Al's is at least as big as our humble semi-detached house or "duplex" as they call it, back home.

This is thirsty work of course, all that black sawdust flying about like snow from hell, the remedy being to take a slug of beer whenever I can find the time, which isn't often. I can't help but feel I have the hardest job, but on the other hand, knowing how machines and I don't get on, I am sure Al is right to keep me well away from the blade so I retain a hand at the end of each arm.

And if it is music to my ears that Al is now satisfied that he has enough wood to last him through the winter, it strikes a bit of a discordant note to hear that the plan is to go back to the canyon for my wood tomorrow.

"Thanks, Al," I hear myself saying, "but we won't need the trailer. I'm sure a truckload will be plenty for us." It's true. There is always a roaring fire at Al's place, regardless of how warm the weather.

To my relief, Al does not argue the point and says we won't need the Ford engine again either as we will cut my logs to size *in situ*. This *is* music to my ears and so it and the trailer are taken back to Grandpa's where, naturally, we have another beer and take our leave of him ⁃ for the present, for this evening we are all invited to one of Al's famous Italian dinners consisting of meatballs, spaghetti, fried chicken and of course, his legendary hot sauce. I also know that it will involve a great deal of alcohol. If there is to be no rest from the logging, there's none for the liver either.

"Thanks, Al," I say as we return to Lincoln. "See you later."

"Where y'goin', man? You gotta come in an' have a drink!"

"Well, no, I think I'd better go back and ⁃"

"Aw, Jees, you gotta come in an' have a drink, Dave. There's this French brandy you should try. It's sooo smooth."

And he brings the conversation to an end by turning his back on me and striding towards his door, leaving me standing dumbstruck beside BIG AL. Naturally there is nothing else I can do but follow him in. Besides that brandy sounds good. It might even be a cognac if I am lucky. And it will be very good for my back. Don't they say that it has medicinal qualities? The Swiss even put it in barrels round St Bernards' necks to revive people trapped in avalanches, or they used to so it *must* be good for you.

* * *

Hours later, full of food and swilling with brandy and beer, we take our fond farewells. I speak for myself naturally. Iona has only had two glasses of white wine, much to Al's disgust, who just can't get his head around the idea that anyone could drink so *little*. Hélène has been over at Sandi's all day and it is long past her bedtime, to say nothing of George's. As a matter of fact he has fallen asleep on the sofa, so Iona makes that the excuse or rather the reason to leave, and my reason too, as George is too heavy for her to carry although it is only a few hundred yards.

"You come right on over once you get the kids to bed." Naturally Al is addressing me. He knows one of us has to babysit and there's no point in Iona coming back to drink anything.

"Yes, well, eh...I'll see how it goes." I know if I go back, Iona will be more than angry - she'll be furious and will point out that I've been with Al most of the day and besides, I've had quite enough to drink. Apart from seeing him as leading me astray, she is not much enamoured of the Hertz lax attitude to children's bedtimes either. And neither am I if the truth be told. And if the truth be further told, much as I have enjoyed the food, the beer, the brandy and the blether, I am beginning to lag and the idea of just rolling into bed and having a good night's sleep is very appealing indeed. Especially with more logging to be done tomorrow.

It is spitting with rain as we walk the few hundred yards to the house from *Psycho*. As we draw nearer, we can see, through the dark, a huge pile of something lying on the grass at the front of the house. What could it be? We have grown accustomed to coming back and finding deposits of vegetables from kind colleagues determined to poison us by a surfeit of their "prodoos", but they come in paper bags or sacks (which they are called over here and which make them sound much bigger than they actually are). This is something much, much bigger and whatever it is, there are a lot of them. It has to be the work of Mrs Bates. Probably bodies.

But all it turns out to be is a pile of logs. A note posted through the letterbox explains. It is from Nat. How extremely kind. The kindness of Missoulians keeps on surprising me, although by now I should be used to it. I hope my fellow Scots are looking after Marnie just as well.

And just another of the gods' little jokes ⁃ the timing is immaculate. Not just that it seems to be raining wood all of a sudden, but because it *is* raining, I had better get the wood into the yard and stacked up if I want them to burn and not send smoke signals all over the state.

Luckily Marnie has a wheelbarrow and leaving Iona to deal with the kids, I set about wheeling the logs to the site I have chosen, the nearest convenient wall, the one that has the skull of what I take to be something bovine artistically framed in a rusty hoop from a barrel. I have nearly finished when Iona comes to lend a hand and thankfully the really heavy rain holds off to let us finish the task.

I have a good excuse, or reason rather, to give Al tomorrow when we go back for more wood, my wood. Unless of course, he uses that as an excuse for saying we don't need to bother going any more. And maybe we don't.

Chapter Eighteen

*In which I go logging again, receive another gift,
and an ultimatum.*

It is the last Sunday of October and so the clocks went back last night. Unfortunately we had forgotten to tell the kids, so it was business as usual for us. It had rained heavily in the night so I was glad that I had stacked Nat's wood, though I had not felt like it at the time. I phone him to thank him and then I phone Gloria and Dave. It came to me in a sudden flash, when I wasn't thinking about anything in particular, that I was mistaken about my ancestor called "Coutts". She was actually a Coull. Gloria sounds devastated to hear it.

I am eating my porridge like a good Scotsman when the phone goes. I need to build up my strength for the slavery ahead. It is Al telling me to be ready in ten minutes, which I am. He comes bearing a gift.

"I got somethin' for you, Dave. But you ain't got to wear it here, right. That would be an offence."

It's an old shirt of his. It's not that he thinks I am in need of clothes although he is well aware of my money problems. And the offence is not on grounds of sartorial taste. No, it's because it's a police shirt. Since it fits me perfectly, it must be a very old shirt indeed as Al has a chest measurement that would make Dolly Parton jealous.

"Gee, thanks, Al. That's great! Really great! Thanks a lot!"

This really is a souvenir worth having. It's grey with badges on the shoulders and one on the chest bearing the legend "Missoula City Police Department" and incorporating the state badge. I really am chuffed. Though what I really must get before I leave is a cowboy hat. Not that they would go together of course.

No reference is made to my non-appearance of last night and I don't mention the wood I got from Nat either.

We pick up Grandpa, the truck, but not the trailer, and the chainsaw. What a difference a day makes! The sky is cloudy and so chilly I am wearing a sweater. There is snow on Lolo Peak and when we arrive at the Canyon, it has been snowing there too. Winter is certainly on its way.

"Goddammit, what's wrong with this Goddamned saw?" Al wants to know. It is reluctant to burst into life and when it does, it just peters out again with a whimper. "Damned thing!"

"Maybe it's out of gas," I suggest helpfully.

"Aw, shit!"

This a moment later from Al, for this is indeed the cause of the problem. With a few more curses since he has also forgotten to bring a can of gas, there is nothing else for it but to make that bone-shaking, innards-shoogling journey back to Grandpa's. And while we are there, to my dismay, Al decides we may as well hitch up the trailer. Now we are going to cut wood for Grandpa as well. Which is fair enough. And it's not going to be fireside pieces any more either, but the usual eight-foot lengths. Just as I feared.

So it's back to Pattee Canyon for almost another three hours' back-breaking stint. Almost I say, not because we were working faster and harder, but because we are not piling the truck and the trailer quite so high. Despite the cold and a flurry of snow, it is warm work. Beneath my sweater, I am dripping with perspiration. I suppose that is why they call it a "sweater".

We just dump the wood at Grandpa's. It will be cut up another day into fire-size logs. Al can't tell me when that will be, but says he'll deliver them when it's done. While it is nice to learn that I appear not to be required for this operation, I would rather have had them now. A log in the fireplace is better than an eight-foot length at Grandpa's. But for that churlish chainsaw being out of gas I probably would have had hundreds of logs. Now I am left wondering if I will ever see the results of my labours before the snow starts in earnest. I certainly hope it will be before Nat's wood is finished, not to mention Rustic Inc's.

At Grandpa's I have to stay for a brandy. I have to, otherwise how would I get back to Lincoln? It's quite a long walk and there is no public transport to speak of. I have seen the odd Mountain Line bus (it's a pun) going about, but how frequent the service is or where it goes, I haven't the faintest. Neither do many other people, I bet. In the land of the gas-guzzling automobile, where they practically give gas away, this is a very new institution and it wouldn't surprise me if the end of the line was just around the corner.

"What you doin' tonight?" says Al, pouring another slosh of Grandpa's brandy into my glass, just because his is finished although mine isn't nearly.

"Well, you know, just kicking back and relaxing." I am quite proud of the way my American is coming along.

"Aw, shit! You don't wanna be doin' that. That's so Goddamn boring! Come on over to my place an' have a drink."

"That's really neat of you to ask us, Al, but we were at your place last night and I know Iona plans to cook some chicken."

I know Iona will kill me if I go back and tell her we are going round to Al's again, tonight.

Al sees this as an obstacle of not the slightest significance. "Just tell her to bring the chicken over and we'll cook it at my place."

Oh my God! I am in for it now. How can you say no to such a modest proposal? I haven't the faintest idea.

"I'll see what Iona says," I prevaricate, like the wimp I am. Iona can tell him. After all, she's the one who doesn't want to go.

In Scotland I had wearied of boring weekends with no money to go out and with nothing to do. That was how I had got into wine-making and was one of the reasons I had applied for the exchange, never expecting that we would be inundated with invitations, rarely a weekend going past when we are not invited somewhere. And when we were not doing that, we were out exploring in the Big Blue Mean Machine, when it was not suffering from some mechanical fault or other that is, and although it's a guzzler, gas is only 70 cents a gallon.

But the gods will have their little joke. I leave in fear and trembling, wondering how I am going to break the news to Iona, only for her to tell *me* where we are going this evening. What a relief! Terri had come over to see Iona when we were logging and she had already invited her over there.

* * *

A long time later, after a soak in the bath to ease my aching back, then a shower to wash off the dirt, I head over to the

Hertz household. Iona has preceded me with the chicken and the kids while I took the car to the liquor store to pick up a gallon of Bacardi.

This tribute is received by Al with more matter of factness than I would have hoped at my apparent generosity, particularly in view of the bank situation. Thank God I hadn't just bought a litre bottle. Al doesn't do litres and despite its size, I know I won't be taking it back although potluck etiquette permits what is not consumed of your contribution can be taken away again. And I don't grudge leaving behind what will remain of it at all, which is likely to be precious little, providing that is what we will be drinking tonight. God knows I have drunk enough of Al's alcohol (and Grandpa's) to float a battleship.

"Do you want some of this, Eeeona?" Al asks hopefully, only to be disappointed again. Bemusedly, he shakes his head as armed with a couple of glasses, he goes to the fridge. He's never met such a weird broad as this in his life, ever.

I am very impressed with the Hertz fridge. It has an ice compartment and ice as clear as crystal just tumbles into a glass at the press of a lever. You don't even have to open the door. I had never seen such a thing before but I have discovered that over here ice is a staple of life. You see bags of it for sale outside the supermarkets and yet when we went on our first expeditions in the Plymouth, it never occurred to us to buy a bag to put in Marnie's cooler to keep our drinks cool. In fact, we never even thought to take drinks with us. It just doesn't get that hot in Scotland.

I find the kids installed behind the kitchen counter having the time of their lives dipping some French fries that Terri has just made, into a bowl of tomato sauce. George's face is smeared from ear to ear and he has cottoned on to the idea that he doesn't need to eat, just dip. Iona has had a glass of white wine pressed upon her.

Al has another present for me - a cowboy hat. It's a bit shabby, but it is what I've been wanting for a long time - and it fits. I am effusive in my thanks. I am so lucky to have a pal like Al who is kitting me out like a real Montanan and also giving me a taste of Montanan life away from school. Not to mention all the alcohol I have tasted of course. And like a proper Montana man, I keep my hat on at the bar as I drink my Bacardi and Coke, and also at the table, as I have my meal. It is perfectly acceptable to keep your titfer on indoors, whether that be in a bar or at home.

For afters, there's a sweet I have never had before. I have Terri to thank for this. Instead of ice, you put in two scoops of ice cream, slug in some Bacardi and mix it all together. I've never had ice cream with a kick before. Delicious. I really am picking up some good ideas on this cultural exchange. What with keeping my hat on indoors as I dine and being introduced to new desserts, I feel I am becoming much more cultured.

Terri has another great idea. She has a sister who lives in Los Angeles whose husband works at Disneyland. His job is to make Peter Pan fly.

"Before you set off on your trip, I'll give them a call and I'm sure he'll show you around behind the scenes - if they are still together by then," she adds, dashing my hopes at a stroke.

I have good reason not to be optimistic. Divorce and separation are a way of life here. But I have reason to be grateful: if it had not been for Marnie's quick-fire divorce I would not be here now. In fact, Terri and Al have been separated themselves ⸱ twice! Looks like they can't live with each other and can't live apart either.

This truth I only discover a lot (and after a lot more Bacardi) later. Iona has long since left to put the kids to bed. Unusually, Al has passed out on the sofa and is dead to the world. But then of course, he had probably been carrying on with the brandy from the moment he got back home, not to mention Grandpa's before that and he has certainly been outpacing us on the Bacardi ever since.

It's not talking behind his back exactly, as he is there right in front of us, snoring happily away to himself. Terri tells me he was brought up by a doting mother and grandmother, an only child and spoiled rotten. That was why everything had to be done his way, at the jump. That was also why he did not do parenting: that was women's work. His job finished with the conception. Nice work if you can get it.

She also tells me some stuff about Al's mother who sounds a real terror, checking all the time that Terri was looking after her boy properly and not hesitating to tell her when she thought she wasn't. It was Al who ran home to mother when things weren't going too well between them, and of course, the doting mother took Al's side every time.

The phone goes for the third time and Terri's platitudes and promises won't wash this time. Iona insists on speaking to me personally (though I am sure the voice over the red-hot wire is loud enough for Terri to hear too) commanding me to get home that very minute. And thus Terri's tales of the Terror and other stories from the confessional are unwontedly cut short and like *Kubla Khan,* I fear they will never be completed, the drink being in Terri and Al being out for the count and the opportunity never likely to present itself again, especially if Iona has anything to do with it.

I get a hard time the moment the flyscreen door slams shut behind me. The fly has just walked into the spider's parlour.

"And about time too! And you can take that hat off for a start! And if you think you are going to be wearing that thing in the house, you have another thought coming."

It does no good at all to explain that I hadn't been drinking with Al all this while but instead had been lending a sympathetic ear to Terri. I don't think history records how the "person from Porlock" felt about interrupting Coleridge's drug-induced slumbers and depriving the world of one its greatest poems, or at least severely reducing it, but the person in the house from *Psycho* is unrepentant about Terri's tales being similarly truncated.

Instead she gives me a lecture about my symbiotic relationship with Al. My problem is how to keep a low profile from him when he is just along the street and when he seems to be so desirous of my company. For one thing he'll be round with the wood sooner or later.

And sooner rather than later I think I may be given an ultimatum: Al or her. Talk about the horns of a dilemma. With the best intentions in the world, I don't see it's a choice I can possibly make. Somehow, I've got to keep both of them satisfied and at the moment I haven't a clue how I am going to do that.

Chapter Nineteen

In which I experience an American Hallowe'en in which clowns feature largely.

For weeks now the supermarkets have been trying to get us in the mood, festooning the stores with witches and all sorts of other things of a supposedly spooky nature. I am shocked at just how seriously everyone takes this festival which we call "Hallowe'en" but the Americans call "Trick or Treat".

All meant to be a bit of harmless fun. But I'm not so sure. The American idea is that you have to give the kids a treat or they'll play a trick on you ⸴ a license to commit some act of vandalism or other. It sounds more like blackmail to me, demanding candy with menaces, whereas with us, it is known as "guising".

As a lad, my friends and I used to go around the neighbours' houses, dressed up, or in disguise (hence "guising") and before we were given something, we were expected to sing for our supper so to speak, recite a poem or tell a joke. The householder would always give us some sweets or monkey nuts or a tangerine or an apple ⸴ or even money, as payment for this riveting entertainment, before sending us on our merry way to regale the next house.

At school, only the floor below mine, down in Art's room, it's more like a descent into some circle of hell. Art has spared no effort in decorating the room with orange-and-black crepe paper, skeletons and ghosts and ghouls, and paper lanterns in the shape of pumpkins. The kids themselves, not to be outdone, have entered fully into the spirit of the thing, painted their faces and dressed up, some even having gone to the expense of buying Spiderman and Dracula costumes, while others have homemade witches' outfits with cloaks and pointy hats.

I can't believe it. This is horror and the supernatural in spades, which makes my unit on writing a mystery or horror story pale into insignificance. So where is the "corrupting" of young minds now? If I had only known then what lengths they go to at Hallowe'en, I would have pointed that out to the parent from hell. But Matt knew and he hadn't pointed it out. Why hadn't he? I think Sam may have the answer.

Art's class had been making pumpkin lanterns when I called in on them, and later two of his pupils had arrived at my classroom bearing one each for Hélène and George. I may not be a fan of "Trick or Treat" as an institution, but I am of the pumpkin when it comes to the matter of hollowing one out to make into a lantern. In Scotland, the equivalent is the turnip, or neep, and trying to disembowel one of those, for those of you who have never tried it, let me tell you it's marginally easier than breaking stones with a plastic hammer.

Another thing to be said in favour of the pumpkin is with its innards you can make pumpkin pie and pumpkin jam and pumpkin soup and goodness knows what else besides and I wouldn't mind betting my new friend Dave Andrew, master vintner of Montana, has made a few gallons of pumpkin wine in his time. Neep wine and neep jam however, have still to take the Scottish culinary scene by storm. There is nothing you can do with a neep but use it as an ingredient for Scotch Broth or mash it and serve it up with haggis ‐ a condemned foodstuff in Montana. Even back in Scotland, you might be forgiven for thinking the humble vegetable is a condemned foodstuff, for it is most commonly seen as a decoration on the sides of children's plates or more commonly, winter fodder for cattle. Poor and humble neep: few would weep if they never saw you again.

But Art is by no means the only teacher to be engaged in this celebration of Trick or Treat day. Only we sophisticates on the top floor, the 7th and 8th grade teachers, have nothing to do with this nonsense. But we cannot escape completely. We are treated to a parade of the entire school passing by our door so we can admire the efforts of the little un's to frighten us to death.

It's hopeless trying to do any work today: it's bad enough getting them to do any at the best of times. And they know there is going to be a party in the afternoon. It's being held in my room because it's the biggest. The kids have brought in cupcakes and Kool-Aid, a sort of flat lemonade in luminous colours. They don't bother to dress up too much, but some have painted their faces to look like ghoulies and ghosties.

There is an old Scottish prayer that goes like this:

From ghoulies and ghosties
And long-leggedy beasties
And things that go bump in the night,
Good Lord, deliver us!

I have a prayer of my own. God deliver me from kids' parties! Nat and I are perched on my desk near the door, wishing we were on the other side of it, eyeing the clock, willing it to move round to the time when the long yellow bus will come to deliver us by taking the kids away. But perversely, it moves slower than ever, scarcely having moved at all from the last time I looked at it.

Being friendly and chatty with the students does not come easily to me. At teacher training college it had been dinned into us that trying to be all palsy-walsy with your pupils by getting down to their level was a cardinal sin - they would take advantage of you and once that was done, it was impossible to put the genie back in the bottle.

Methinks Nat would fit quite easily into the Scottish classroom situation. He's much more formal than Steve and Blake. Like me, he would far rather be teaching right now, whereas they are in their element, laughing and joking with the kids, the best of pals. They are even dancing with them, the worst of nightmares for me, as you know.

And then the nightmare gets worse.

"Laura Gleischman wants to know if you would dance with her." The speaker is Tina, a little blonde who is not backward in coming forward, as most of the kids are here, but unusually it seems there is one youngster in the school so eaten up with embarrassment that she hasn't the bottle to ask me herself.

"Tell Laura I'm sorry, but I couldn't do that. My wife wouldn't like it," and the little blonde goes off gaily to impart the bad news.

If the girl had asked me herself, then of course, I would not have refused. But the moment Tina turned away, I realise that is exactly what I have done - refused her by proxy. And then another moment later, the enormity of what I have done hits me like a truck. I break out into a cold sweat as I realise that if anyone else asks me to dance, I am going to have to refuse them as well. I suppose what I should have done, in hindsight, was to pretend that I had been joking and asked *her* to dance. But by the time this face-saving solution occurred to me, it was too late. Further thought also told me if I asked one to dance, I had better ask others too. But apart from that, it was just too much of sacrifice, just too embarrassing for words - all those eyes upon me, all that sniggering behind my back at my pathetic efforts to follow the beat, for I have no sense of rhythm.

It is one thing to lose your pupils' respect by being too friendly, trying to be one of them. It is a different matter entirely to make a complete fool of yourself by dancing with them and in front of them like an elephant with two left feet.

* * *

After school, to see if he can do something about solving my desperate need for funds, Steve introduces me to his friend Jack Svensen, who is vice-president of another bank, the Missoula Bank of Montana. Are all the bankers in this place of Scandinavian ancestry?

Now I discover that vice-presidents are two-a-penny and it was just another example of that tendency amongst Americans to aggrandise everything. Thus a stone with us becomes a "rock" and instead of leaving secondary school, they "graduate" from high school. Under our system, you can only "graduate" if you pass your exams after a minimum of three years at university, something like 5% of the population. Under theirs, the whole country is overrun with graduates. No wonder they have put a man on the moon and we haven't.

I might have been forgiven for thinking I had strolled into the wrong place, but what sort of place it was exactly would be hard to say. Like my "old" bank, it is open-plan and

I can see the entire staff, though I suppose there must be some high heid yins in ivory towers somewhere. The first girl I notice, or rather can't help but see, is dressed in chest-high waders and a fisherman's hat. Another (how come I didn't see her first?) is wearing a dressing gown with her hair in rollers and her face painted green. The rest of the women obviously had made a pact to come as clowns, with silk, spotty costumes and the traditional make-up, only each and everyone is wearing a pink wig. Utter madness!

But then I have to remember this is Hallowe'en and the USA seems to enter into the spirit of it wholeheartedly even if the spirits are clowns.

Fortunately Jack is much more soberly attired, which is still pretty casual (since he isn't sporting a tie and suit) and once he has doffed his clown wig, I feel a little more reassured that his status might be what the nameplate says on his desk and he is someone in whom I can put an absolute trust to be the person in charge of my finances and not some clown.

He listens to my tale of woe with a totally straight-faced, clown-smile-free face and probably for the second time too as I am sure Steve will have already alerted him to my problem or else I would not be here.

"No problem, Dave, we'll soon have you sorted. Just fill in this form," and he tells me what to write. Taking it from me he explains: "This is an instruction to your bank in Scotland to instruct the Midland Bank in London to instruct the Western Bank in St Paul, Minneapolis, to pay your salary into your account here. In future you should have your money in three to four days."

So it's as simple as that no matter how complicated it sounds!

"Wow! Three to four days! That's fantastic!"

"It won't happen till November's cheque, Dave," he cautions.

"No, no, I realise that. Thanks very much indeed."

But as I shake hands with him as I leave, I can't help wondering if I can really trust my finances to a bunch of clowns like this.

* * *

As soon as I get back, we set off to John and Carolyn's. Hélène is wearing a clown costume (clowns are taking over the planet) donated by Amy, Sandi's daughter, not that I imagine Amy had much say in the matter. Later Sandi is going to take the two girls Treat-or-Tricking. Gloria had introduced Iona to a fabric shop yesterday and she had made some additions to it. She's pretty nifty with the needles. It's good Iona should have another female friend, and good for me that I should have another outwith the teaching fraternity too.

Naturally Hélène has her face painted like a clown's but George just goes as himself, as do we. I should, I suppose, have been prepared for the unexpected when an old hag answers the door, but I wasn't. She is dressed completely in black with a pointy hat. Her hair is white, her face is green and her eyes are red.

"Come in, my dears!" she croaks, giving us a smile which reveals a mouth with a single, solitary tooth in the front, then she gives vent to a spine-tingling gale of cackling laughter. Hélène squeezes her mother's hand even tighter and looks away, not quite sure what to make of this apparition. I must admit I get a bit of a fright myself but George takes it all in his stride, as if he were accustomed to seeing scary women like this every day of his life.

When we are admitted to the witch's den, we find John dressed-up as a hillbilly with a red-checked shirt, blue dungarees and a hat that looks as if it has been trampled by a herd of buffalo. To complete the picture, he is sucking on a stubby little pipe. And when he smiles, there are black gaps where his teeth ought to be. He didn't need to grow the beard as he has that already and the glasses are real too. Although he looks initially the less intimidating of the two, as anyone who has seen *Deliverance* knows, he is potentially far more scary. And if I hadn't known better, I *would* have been scared, as behind the glasses John has put on what we call a "glaikit" look, as if he was not all there.

We are invited to sample a witches' brew, which is actually much tastier than its lurid green appearance might have suggested and packs quite a punch, which of course, is what it is and not primeval swamp water at all, as we had been told. There is Kool-Aid and candy for the kids, but like the good dentist he is, John takes the opportunity to do a bit of proselytising and gives them a toothbrush each to take away.

But he really should do something about his own teeth and those of that witch he is living with.

Chapter Twenty

In which I get into trouble at school again.

"You know, Dave," says Blake, apparently apropos of nothing as he, Steve and I watch our students file into their homerooms, "you oughta have danced with Laura Gleischman yesterday."

Nat isn't there, already ensconced behind his desk as usual, ready for the off, the moment the students come in. He reminds me of one of my old Maths teachers who never tired of reminding us, like a mantra ⸍ "the lost second can never be regained". We three musketeers, by contrast, tend to start the day by having a chat and cracking jokes as we supervise the students as they come along the hall. Someone's got to do it, so it might as well be us.

Eh? Did I hear him right? What kind of a joke is that? How did he know anyway? Nat and I had been standing by the door wishing that we had been on the other side of it while he and Steve had been dancing in the thick of it. Besides, it was tiny Tina who had done the asking. And Laura doesn't seem to be here today. Unless…Oh, my God! I feel a hot flush wave over me then my blood turns to ice as the enormity of what I've done dawns on me. Is that why she's off ⸍ so upset at this rejection that she couldn't face her fellow students today. But surely not! That would be preposterous.

"Yeah," chips in Steve. "He's right. You shouldha', Dave."

"It's not very polite," Blake pursues, "to turn down a lady." This is uttered with his habitual deadpan expression so I can't tell if it is another of his jokes or whether he is being deadly serious. It's no good turning to Steve for help: they are a real comedy duo, Steve acting as Blake's stooge.

"But she didn't ask me," I protest. "I mean if she had, of course I would have danced with her. But she didn't. She got someone else to ask. Maybe it was all a joke, she didn't really want to dance with me at all, it was just Tina winding her up, to embarrass her. Yeah, I think that probably was it."

Whilst it sounds convincing to me I am conscious of the fact that to Blake and Steve I must sound like the lady within the play in *Hamlet* whom the discomfited Queen Gertrude observed did "protest too much". Was this the reaction they had hoped to provoke? If so, they must be laughing so hard inside that their guts must be hurting like hell, for if there is anyone who is embarrassed now, it is me. Or are they being perfectly serious? The last time Blake had used the word "polite" was when I had gone behind Matt's back to seek an interview with our boss. He was serious then and maybe he is serious now.

I wouldn't worry so much, only like Queen Gertrude, I have a guilty conscience. If there had been sackcloth I would have worn it and if there had been a bucket of ashes, I would have dumped it over my head. But surely to God no-one would stay off school, heart-broken, because her teacher had refused to dance with her (by proxy) would they? No, that would be just too much of an overreaction, to say nothing of making me too conceited by far.

That's my consoling thought as I enter my classroom to begin the day. Steve and Blake *must* have been joking. Somehow they had got wind of my refusal and when Blake had noticed it, that's why he had brought up the subject. Unless it was the talk of the school... Was it?

That is why, as I close my classroom door behind me, it sounds like the doors of Cawdor Castle slamming shut with the entire school agin' me. Little did I know that by the end of the school day I was going to be under attack from another quarter also.

* * *

When I first saw the lists of my new pupils, apart from being intrigued at the surnames, it was a source of some amusement for us both, as I showed them to Iona, with some of the names at least, to speculate which were male and which were female. We both got "Loren" wrong.

The boy, Loren, has been very good recently, coming in on time for the fourth day running, but when he resorted to habit, coming in late again on the fifth, I felt I had to ask him the reason for this relapse.

"My mom couldn't be bothered," he said with a shrug of his shoulders and what I would call a helpless smile of resignation. I might have taken that for insolence once, but I know Loren well enough by now to know he's not that sort of a boy. He has a point: it may not be his fault. I've no idea where he lives. He might have to be driven miles to catch the school bus. He may even live in a place so remote he may not be on the bus route and is totally dependent on his mom for a lift to school.

Loren doesn't seem to be fretting in the least about this loss to his education. If you add up all the times he has been late and the amount of minutes that can never be regained, it all adds up to a substantial loss of tuition. And not just any tuition either: my pearls of wisdom actually, the homeroom class (register class) being the first of the day. I wouldn't say it if it weren't true, but Language Arts is the most important subject of all (as most people realise) since it is the foundation of all the others, and the only one that the students will really, really need in their voyage through life's troubled waters unless they are going to be teachers of Math and Science and History. Which is why they need to know things like what a metaphor is and when to use it.

"Thanks, Dave, for tellin' me this," Matt gulps. "I'll phone the parent."

I had thought after this latest excuse, this cheeky remark, not from Loren, but his mother, it was high time to involve Matt. His job, not mine, to persuade the mother of the importance of what I have just written above. I got the feeling, and I was sure I was not mistaken, since I know him better now too, that as I sailed out of Matt's office, he would rather I had just let sleeping dogs lie – or Loren, if the truth was that he just couldn't haul himself out of bed in the mornings, a state of affairs with which I had a great deal of sympathy. While I didn't think Matt was thinking "who will rid me of this troublesome teacher" exactly, since he had called me "Dave" again, he hardly looked over the moon at the prospect of phoning Loren's mother. I wondered why, since he had the high moral ground here. It was her parental responsibility to make sure Loren got to school on time, no question about it.

Now, at the end of the school day, I am just about to find out why Matt had something of the look of the condemned man about him when I broke the news. We all have to write up the following day's lessons plans in case a substitute teacher has to take our classes, regardless of how perfectly hale and hearty we are feeling. You just never know when an unforeseen incident might arise, like being murdered by your wife, which could happen to me if I go drinking with Al again anytime soon.

So that's what I am doing when I am aware of a thin, careworn-looking woman standing in front of my desk. I can tell by her body language she has not popped in to have a friendly chat. I wish they wouldn't do that, parents just popping in without so much as a by-your-leave. It's most disconcerting. But then, I seem to be the only one it happens to. I haven't a clue who she is or what she wants, but I am not to be kept in the dark for much longer.

"I'm Cynthia Van der Bosen, Loren's stepmom," she says without preamble. "Am I to understand that you have been complaining about Loren coming late to school?"

That is an impressive-sounding handle. It's not Loren's surname but I am quite accustomed by now to the kids having different surnames from their parents.

"Er, um…" For the second time today, I know I am blushing furiously, instantly coming up like a beacon proclaiming Guilty! Guilty! Guilty! in the eyes of the beholder. If everyone was like me, the country could save millions by dispensing with a judge and jury system. But in reality, I'd probably be a bit like Iona - I'd blush at the very thought of being accused of something I hadn't done.

"Well, for your information, just let me tell you this," the lady ploughs on. "I get up at 6 am and before I take Loren to school, I got to get another one to another school." She pauses to let that sink in before picking up the cudgels again, "And I'll get him here just as damned soon as I can." Pause. "You got that?"

I nod, the power of speech still not having returned. I hope I don't look too much like a startled rabbit caught in headlights but that's exactly how I feel ⸱ paralysed. It seems to satisfy the lady however, as she now seems somewhat less aggressive. Having said what she came to say, she continues, though her tone is hardly less sharp, "And, since I am here, what are his grades like?"

"Er...um..." I know what they are really but it might sound like I was just making up good ones out of fear, so I reach for my file to read them out to her, all professional-like. I know I am in smoother waters now, for, thank God, Loren is one of the brightest kids in the class, practically a straight A student.

"That's all right then, isn't it?"

"Well, yes. He's a smart boy." Crawler. But it doesn't impress her. Of course he's not really her son.

"There you are then. Good day to you."

And with that she flounces out of the room. I don't know if Mrs Van der Bosen has any Latin or not, Montana being one of places the Romans never got to, though you might well be forgiven for thinking they had once you see how straight the roads are. If she did she might well have said, "Quod erat demonstrandum" but what her body language actually said was, "So in future, you can stick Loren's late-coming up your ass!"

Once she has gone, when I am left, like Wordsworth, in solitary reflection to contemplate in tranquillity on what had just happened, wondering if it really had as it had all been over so quickly, I wonder if she had given Matt a piece of her mind too before she came storming into my room like a whirlwind. If so, he had done nothing to stop her, or at least come up to mediate between us. He must certainly have phoned her. I imagine the conversation going something like this:

"Mrs Van der Bosen... ahrrum... I am sorry to have to tell you that... ahrrum... well you see, Loren's been kinda comin' late into school recently "

"Who said that? Who's been complaining?"

"Well, ahrrum "

"Was it that Scotsman, Adderson or some such reptile like that? His homeroom teacher? It would be, wouldn't it? Well, we'll see about that!"

And then the line would have gone dead. What's a poor principal to do? He wasn't to know that she'd come tearing up to my room and tear strips off me. No point in warning me in advance that she was on the warpath. No point in worrying about something that might never happen, Matt would have thought. Or was he just too scared of her to do anything? Like he did the time before last when a parent wanted my guts for garters.

When I tell Steve and Blake all about this latest escapade, once they have stopped laughing, they really get me worried. I'm not worried in the slightest about Loren's mom or stepmom, as she appears to be. Loren can be as late as he likes as often as he likes from now on for all I care.

"Just wait till you meet Mrs Apachito, Dave," says Blake, as expressionless as ever.

"You bet, Dave!" agrees Steve. His eyes, above his walrus moustache, are animated. "Just wait until you meet her! Boy, are you in for some fun!"

I have an uneasy feeling that they are the ones who will be having the fun when I tell them all about it later, but when I press them for some more information about her, they will not be drawn, only increase my anxiety by saying, "Wait

and see, Dave. Wait and see. She is somethin' else. Oh, boy!"
And they walk away, shaking their heads, chuckling at the
prospect.

Unbelievably there is going to be another parents' day
in a week's time, on Hélène's third birthday, as it happens,
and then there's going to be another long weekend. We
should finish at noon on Thursday and are not due back in
school until Monday morning. We are going to Vancouver,
just a wee skip and a hop over the Rockies, to meet the
relatives, as we had hoped to do at the last long weekend.

And so, as the day of fear draws nearer, my anxiety
grows in proportion. Blake and Steve might just be winding
me up of course, that she's not so terrifying as they would
have me believe, but I have met three scary moms already and
there must be something in it, no smoke without fire.

At least they seem to have forgotten or forgiven me for
not dancing with Laura. Unless this is their idea of putting me
through purgatory. If so, it is working very well indeed.

Chapter Twenty-one

In which I have a near-death experience.

Friday evening and we are invited to Sam's for a meal and beer. Art is there of course and also a great number of Sam's cousins, as well as Chris, his lawyer friend, and his wife Mary Jo, a teacher, whom we had met once before in the Holding Company, a Mexican Restaurant.

I get talking to Chris about politics. Election day is on November 8th, Hélène's birthday. As well as voting for members for the national and state senate, they will also be voting for a whole raft of other matters which they call "propositions", some of which can be quite controversial. Sometimes the list can be as long as your arm. It sounds pretty democratic to me, more so than our system, where once you have elected your representative, they are left to get on with the decision-making. And as often as not, because of our first-past-the-post system, you end up with someone you never voted for and a lot of policies you never wanted.

Sam is always interested to know what I have been getting up to with Al and thus my latest logging expedition comes to light.

"Pattee Canyon, eh, David?"

"Yes. They seem to have just opened it up."

And so it is arranged that Sam will give me a call, I'll show him where it is and I'll help him cut some logs tomorrow afternoon. He has a wood-burning stove. I'm glad to be able to return the favour after he had done the brakes on the Big Blue Mean Machine for me recently.

One of the cousins tells me that she is going to Seattle for the weekend.

"As long as I can get through of course," she adds.

"What do you mean?"

"Well the road may not be clear. You just can never tell for sure at this time of year."

Great! Something else to worry about as well as Mrs Apachito.

* * *

It's Saturday morning when the summons comes, too early to be Sam, but as soon as the phone rings, I know instinctively it is for me. Iona gives me a meaningful look as I go to answer it. Sure enough, it is Al.

"You wanna come an' workout with me at the Elks?"

Right from the start, I had made up my mind that I was going to make the most of this year and I was not going to turn any experience down - within reason. Working out in a gym is not my idea of a good time but I was intrigued by the Elks, had been ever since I saw Fred Flintstone in his furry hat with the horns attending a meeting of the Loyal Order of Water Buffaloes. And what was that, if not based on the Elks or The Benevolent and Protective Order of Elks, to give them their full title? I have visions of them all wearing antler hats as they indulge in strange cabalistic rituals.

I can't remember if Fred actually attained the honour of being Grand Pooh-Bah of the Bedrock Water Buffaloes, but knowing Fred, he probably did. Certainly at one time, Al had been the leader of his lodge, the so-called Exalted Ruler. You just can't take a name like that seriously, but I am sure Al managed to live up to it. Now this is my chance to enter its hallowed portals, maybe uncover some of its secrets. The lure of this outweighs the complete lack of desire to indulge in a workout ⁓ and the fear of telling Iona that I was going to be meeting Al in ten minutes. I was right to be frightened.

"Oh no! I was looking forward to doing something together this weekend, just us! You were with Al *all* last weekend for God's sake!" Bang goes a plate down on the table, there goes another one. Iona is laying the table for breakfast, not very quietly.

"Not *all* weekend…"

Sometimes silence is more powerful than words especially when it is accompanied by a look that could kill. This is one of those times.

"Where are you going *this* time?" she says at last.

"Just to the Elks. We're going to workout."

"Huh! What's that supposed to mean anyway?"

"Well you know, lifting weights and things like that."

"Glasses of whisky more like!"

"No! No! Nothing like that at all!"

"Huh!"

* * *

If the Elks turns out to be a disappointment, the workout turns out to be hell. All I saw of the Lodge was the logo over the door. We go straight to the gym. I could have been anywhere.

We begin with lifting weights. Al takes some weights off a bar and puts lighter ones on for me.

"Try this for starters, Dave."

I am lying on my back and the idea is to lift the bar off my chest then gradually lower it and raise it and lower it and so on. I take a deep breath, a firm grip, grit my teeth and lift the bar ⸱ a few inches.

"Push up, Dave! Push up! Straighten your arms for Chris' sake!"

"I can't! I can't!" I have barely the strength to get the words out.

Al takes the weights from me with one hand as if they were made of polystyrene.

"They too heavy for you, Dave? Jeez!" His moustache bristles as if on the point of saying something but thinking better of it, confines himself to a shake of the head in a bemused sort of way instead and sets about fitting on some lighter weights. It's a terrible cross he has to bear, being surrounded by lesser mortals all the time.

While I get on with lifting my new (feather) weights, Al lifts his own, his biceps bulging and the veins sticking out like cords, not just in his arms either. I am scared he's going to burst a blood vessel in his temples. To think some people do this for fun! And Al does it nearly every day. No doubt that's why his biceps are as thick as my thighs. Maybe he feels he has to have them, being a cop. Some of the blokes I have seen Al having to deal with, like bikers, are very scary indeed, with muscles at least the equal of his. Can you imagine if I were a cop, coming up to them and saying: "Say, guys, er, but would you mind not revving your engines like that? Please?" My best hope, my only weapon of self-defence, would be if they were too weak with helpless laughter to snap my neck like a chicken.

No need then for me to build up my biceps, so pretty soon I stop doing that and turn to something I do know how to do ⁄ ride a bike. If you were to count all the miles I've cycled ever since I was a boy, it would probably stretch across this continent from sea to shining sea. Only this bike, no matter how hard I pedal, isn't going to get me anywhere. But at least I feel no-one will laugh at me, pedalling futilely into the future.

After a while I get tired of doing that (as well as feeling tired) and go back on the weights for some non-light relief. I've only lifted a couple when I suddenly feel very strange indeed, very lightheaded. I am trying to let the weights down under control before they smash into my face.

"Al... I don't feel too good..."

Amazingly, despite his concentrating fiercely on his task in hand, he sees something is wrong at once, takes the weights, helps me sit up, tells me to put my head between my knees and switches on an electric fan. The world fades to black, then my feet swim into focus again before a black shutter comes down and blocks them out again. I expect the next blackout to be the last one. So this is what it feels like to die. It's not a very pleasant feeling, but at least it's not painful. I wish I could think of some memorable last words to say rather than "I wish I had never come here" but I can't think of anything. So much for those famous last witty words some are said to have trotted out while *in extremis*. But I suppose there are many different types of death.

But after a few moments I think I might make it. The black fades to grey and eventually my feet stay in focus. Al is standing over me, looking concerned. It seems to me I have been dying for a long time.

"You oughta go to the bathroom, Dave, an' splash some cold water on your face."

When I think my legs will support me, that's what I do and I feel a whole lot better for that. But what this near-death experience proves to me is, far from being good for you, as the fitness fanatics would have you believe, exercise can be seriously bad for your health. Even kill you. Had not one of my colleagues died not so long ago, waiting for a bus after a game of squash? He wasn't even forty.

There is a steam room and a Jacuzzi, which was another thing I had never heard of before I came here. I was, of course, familiar with a "bathroom" but in the American sense it is a very grand description for a place which contains any amount of urinals and toilets, but nothing at all for the total immersion of the body for the purposes of ablution. While Al continues to pump iron and lose a great deal of sweat, I lose a great deal of the same thing by doing nothing more strenuous than contemplating my navel in the steam room. This is the way to do it. Then when that gets a bit too hot and boring, I slip into the Jacuzzi and let the bubbles massage the muscles without me having to do a thing.

Al had said to bring my shaving things. "Your skin will be as smooth as a baby's after you've been in the steam room an' Jacuzzi."

I don't know about that but it is certainly a red and sweaty face that stares back at me in the mirror. And to think I must have been as pale as a ghost not so long ago! In fact I very nearly was one.

Chapter Twenty-two

In which I receive some good news.

"You gotta come over an' have a drink, Dave," says Al when we get back from the Elks. "I got this Canadian whisky you gotta try. It's called Black Velvet. It's sooo smooth."

And so it should be with a name like that. I know it's hopeless to refuse but I dare not stay.

"I'll come in but it's got to be just for just a minute," I warn him. "I'm going to help Sam cut some wood."

Al says nothing but wastes no time in going straight to the fridge to liberate the Black Velvet. I don't think it's got anything to do with what I said however.

"Dave nearly passed out at the Elks," he tells Terri as she joins us in the kitchen. He doesn't make it sound like I nearly died at all.

Terri takes this in her stride, the customary shrug of the shoulders and a spread of the hands. "Oh well!" I always get the feeling that if a man came on the radio and announced the end of the world in ten minutes, she would react in precisely the same way.

"Ain't that smooth?" Al asks, standing over me, waiting for my reaction to the Black Velvet. I may be a wimp when it comes to lifting weights but Al has great faith in me as a connoisseur of whisky, as he thinks I should be, coming from Scotland. Little does he know that I am punching well above my weight in that respect.

It doesn't take a mind reader to know what sort of answer is expected. Just as long he does not ask me for tasting notes which might challenge my powers of creativity as I think it is pretty much run-of-the-distillery, so to speak. But what do I know? When I pronounce that it is very smooth indeed, Al is as pleased as if it were a punch he had made himself. You see, he can spot a good whisky as well as any Scotsman.

Some hopes of getting away after one swift whisky. Terri, bless her, but she wasn't to know of my ban, has started making lunch, tacos in fact and it's assumed that I am staying. That had been another great thing about the exchange. I had never been exposed to Mexican food before coming here and I am much taken with it. In fact, I think I may take it up when I get home. I am not allowed to go until I've eaten at least one taco and in the meantime of course, my glass has been replenished.

When the phone rings, I have a nasty feeling it is for me. After all, if Iona wanted to know if we were back yet all she would have to do is stick her head out the door and see if BIG AL was sitting outside or not.

The telephone cord is so long I don't need to come and get the receiver. It can go from the back of the kitchen right to the front door so you can walk around just about the entire ground floor, especially as it is open plan. There are a few preliminary exchanges between Terri and Iona, then she hands her over to me. This is going to be acutely embarrassing, being given a dressing down in front of my friend and for the very reason that I was with him again, sitting right across the bar from him in fact. Nor does she need any imagination to know exactly what sort of exercise I am engaged in at the moment. But it is not at all what I had expected.

"There's a letter here for you from the bank in Scotland."

"Really! Great! Go on and open it!" This is unexpected as surely there has not been enough time for my letter to have arrived, let alone for them to act on it, but my heart is hopeful. The suspense is infectious and tangible, for Terri has suspended what she was doing and even Al has forgotten to take a draught of whisky as they wait for my next utterance.

"It says that $1,022 has been deposited in your account." Iona's words come over the wire.

"Wow! Really! At last!"

"It goes on to say," she continues, "that they made a mistake and apologise for any inconvenience."

"Wow!" It sounds like a lot of money. Much more than I am accustomed to in pounds. Apart from the exchange rate, good old Uncle Sam, in his wisdom, has said that I don't need to pay him any tax. I am rich! Rich!

So it *was* my bank's fault all along! The gods of course, had delayed the arrival of this letter until I had changed banks. Probably about the time I was doing that, they were sorting out the error. Now they are going to have to cancel that arrangement and set up the new account. And what if they get that wrong this time too? And what is my friend Fran from Elgin going to think about my defection? It wouldn't surprise me if that was the end of a beautiful relationship.

But that is in the future. This is a moment for celebration. I break off to tell Al and Terri the news. Terri says, "Well, congratulations!" Al tops up my glass. This is a special occasion after all. In fact it's even better than it seems, for without this good news, only the gods know what sort of strife I'd be getting from my wife at the moment.

"Has Sam phoned?"

"Yes, just five minutes ago."

"I'll be right over. (Just as soon as I finish this Black Velvet)."

* * *

"I don't know, David," says Sam. He's the only one here who calls me "David" and I like him all the more because of that.

He has stopped his truck at the entrance to the track up to Pattee Canyon. He has seen a sign that says "No Trespassing".

"It didn't bother Al," I tell him, "and we've been here twice. Nobody bothered us. And I mean, that's what it's for isn't it, all this burnt wood? They want it cleared out don't they? Why they drove in this track?"

But Sam is not so sure. To me it looked no different from the place we went to on our very first logging expedition, the dead and charred trees felled and bulldozed to the side of the track - only here the tree trunks were thinner and easier to get out which Al does by means of looping a chain round them and hauling them out with the truck.

Sam won't be persuaded, so we drive on to somewhere else. It's a bit higher up and it starts to snow while we are there. The wood here is not so easy to get out as it is further from the track, but on the other hand, we cut it into more manageable lengths, ones we are able to carry to the truck. I also get the chance to work the chainsaw, the first time I have ever used one. And we stop from time to time to have a beer that Sam has brought.

It's very strange but Al doesn't drink when he's logging. Drinking and driving, no problem, but not when logging, apart from the time I took some beer on that never-to-be-forgotten first expedition. When you see what that saw can do to a tree trunk, it doesn't bear thinking what it could do to a human limb. But Sam doesn't need to think about that. He knows. He only has one leg after an accident in a sawmill.

* * *

I'm glad to see there is no snow in Missoula, but it is a reminder to me, as if I needed any, the difference a few feet can make when it comes to turning rain to snow and we have to cross the Rockies...

Meanwhile it's great to have money, and Iona, who wanted to do something with me today, now finds we are doing something neither of us expected - we are going on a shopping expedition. Naturally there is no doubt about where we'll go, my favourite store - K-Mart.

Boots are the main purchase: cute cowboy boots for my six-month-old nephew, US size 6. Obviously he can't walk yet, but by the time we get home, he should be able to; cute cowboy boots for George; a cowboy belt for Iona's brother which should arrive in time for his birthday; likewise for me, to go with my cowboy hat, and a woollen hat for me too. I'm going to need that for cycling to school when the snow starts. The cowboy hat just wouldn't do. Well, have you ever seen anyone wearing a cowboy hat riding a bike? I have no intention of making an exhibition of myself. I also buy a pair of boots ($12, sale price). Not cowboy boots alas, I'll get them later, but boots for cycling in the snow. Total bill $59. Easy come, easy go.

We don't get anything for Iona and Hélène, but their time will come. And Iona did get that leather coat of great price, and a very fine coat it is too and will do her very nicely when the snow comes.

But there is one item of pure indulgence that I can now afford to buy, now that I am so rich. I had set my heart on it and coveted it from the moment I saw it. Love at first sight. Hoping that it will still be there, we head forthwith to the Little Professor Bookshop on Higgins, the best little bookshop in the West, only it's not so little and far superior to any bookshop near my home in Scotland. I'd have to go to Glasgow or Edinburgh to find the equivalent. That's the beauty of living in a university town I suppose.

And just what is this must-have book? It's a handsomely-bound volume of *The Complete Sherlock Holmes Treasury* but that's not what's so special about it - it's because the stories are printed just as they originally appeared in *The Strand Magazine*, in the same font, in columns and with Sidney Paget's original illustrations. And to make my cup of happiness complete, not only is it still on the shelf, it is now reduced from $10 to $5. The gods are surely smiling on me now. The irony of it! A few hours ago I thought I would be meeting them face-to-face.

But of course the day was not nearly over yet. Things were just about to take a different turn...

Chapter Twenty-three

In which we spend an unusual Saturday night, so unlike our own dear homelife.

Al is on the phone again. I'll swear he has extra-sensory hearing for he seems to know the instant I get back in the Plymouth.

"You gotta come over, Dave, we're havin' a celebration. The Grizzlies beat the Bobcats 24-8!"

Seemingly, when we were out shopping, we had missed the game of the season, a football game between those two arch-rivals, the Montana State University at Bozeman and the University of Montana, here in Missoula. The Bobcats belong to Bozeman while the Grizzlies, of course, are the local team. You would expect a Grizzly to beat a Bobcat any day of the week, but it seems when it comes to college football, the Bobcats usually vanquish the Grizzlies, so this is a cause for a celebration indeed, especially since it was by such a huge margin. Al sounds very pleased indeed, whereas I of course, despite my allegiance to Missoula, can't see what all the fuss is about. It's a boring game to start with and only between two college teams after all. It's not like they are professionals or anything.

"Oh...well, I'd like to Al, but the thing is you see...Iona and the kids ⸚"

"Bring them over."

"Yes... well... erm... the thing is, Al, we haven't eaten yet."

"Neither have we. I'm gonna send out for double front fried chicken."

"Are you sure that's all right?" It's as feeble a question as I ever could ask. It's just something to say whilst my mind tries to dredge up a possible reason for refusing but it is paralysed by a fear of what Al will say if I refuse and a fear of what Iona will say if I accept. I'm caught in the middle between two opposing fronts and what on earth could a "double front fried chicken" be? Two breasts? But surely all chickens have two don't they? At least I never heard of a chicken having a mastectomy. Maybe they fry them on both sides. I'm no cordon bleu chef, or even much of a cook, since I have a resident one of my own, but that's what I would do if I were frying chicken and not even think of mentioning that I had done anything special with them.

Bang goes The Teacher's Saturday Night once again, to paraphrase Burns's romanticised depiction of blissful domesticity in *The Cotter's Saturday Night.* It was never going to be that blissful anyway but stood zero chance when, with a heavy heart, I replace the receiver and go to break the news.

"Well?" The tone tells me she has already anticipated the news whilst my nervous demeanour is mute testimony to the fact. One benefit of living in someone else's house, even if it is the one from *Psycho*, is the crockery is not yours to fling about, nor the frying pan a blunt instrument of correction. The lashing of the tongue was severe, as I knew it would be. I hang my head in shame and say nothing to pour flames on the fire.

It turns out we're not the only guests, which I would normally be very happy about, another chance to meet more people who are not teachers, only it's obvious that they are all as drunk as skunks, too drunk to notice the ten degrees of permafrost that has suddenly appeared in the room as soon as Iona clocked this state of affairs, which was the moment we stepped over the threshold.

Putting his arm around me, our jovial host introduces me to Patti and Paul and Jean and Tony. "This is Dave. He's from Scotland an' what he don't know about whisky, ain't worth a gnat's piss."

But I'm not offered any Black Velvet on this occasion, or any other whisky for that matter. I imagine it had been consumed by the football spectators long ago. Although the actual amount of playing time is sixty minutes, these football games often go on for *three* hours, with all that starting and stopping. (Yawn!) And yet the Americans find it riveting. I'll never understand it, fear I'll never get to like it, keen though I am to embrace all aspects of American culture.

So, assuming that the guests came for a pre-game warm up, to get them in the mood, and the game itself, which would have been very thirsty work indeed since it was so exciting, and since I have no idea when the game stopped, but let's say an hour ago, I estimate they could have been drinking solidly for about five hours as Al is no slouch when it comes to dispensing alcoholic refreshment. And when the whisky and beer ran out and they changed to wine (never a good combination, mixing the grain and the grape), it's no wonder they are all afloat.

Tony takes an immediate liking to George.

"Aw, she's so cute!"

It's not the first time that George has been mistaken for a girl, though I suppose his hair *is* rather long. He is wearing his new cowboy boots and he does look rather cute, even if I say so myself. Then to my surprise, Tony swoops on him, picks him up and says, "Did anyone ever tell you how cute you are, sweetie? What's your name?"

"His name's George."

Tony is not in the least wrong-footed. "Hello, George, you *are* so cute, ain't you?"

"He won't hear you, I'm afraid. He's deaf."

"No! What a shame! Poor fella! Completely deaf?"

"As good as. He does have some hearing, enough to wear a hearing aid, but the little turkey usually manages to hide it somewhere, like down the air vent of the car."

Tony, finding this as hilarious as I had found it frustrating, throws his head back in a great drunken laugh before embarking on a kissing onslaught, which, fortunately, George doesn't seem to mind too much. I'm not sure about me though. It is one thing for complete strangers to admire your kids but it's another thing for them to go completely gaga over them, especially when it's a man and kiss them all over the face. I realise of course, that the Black Velvet or whatever, is largely to blame for Tony's excessive adoration, nevertheless, much to my relief, and I dare say Iona's, he sets George down gently with a "There you go, little fella. Go back to your mom." And then as he watches George toddle over to Iona more like John Wayne than ever in his brand new cowboy boots, "Darn if that ain't the cutest kid I ever saw."

"Huh! Never saw you make as much fuss over your own kids." It's Jean speaking. Or is it the Black Velvet? The tone is bitter, spoiling for a fight. Whisk(e)y affects some folk that way.

"Whaddya mean?" Tony's bonhomie and joviality have suddenly vanished. His face is thunderous and his tone aggressive.

"You know damn fine! You never showed your own kids half as much affection as you've just shown to that little kid!"

"You're a goddamn liar! You know that ain't true!"

"Huh! I know what I know!" Jean, sitting at the breakfast bar, her shoulders slumped, stares at the bottom of her glass as if to say that is the end of the matter, but if Tony would care to pursue it, she'd gladly enlighten him, and she didn't give a damn if the rest of us heard it all too.

We can all see Tony is itching to say something back but with a superhuman effort is managing to restrain himself. I get the feeling that the incident with George was not the sole reason for Jean's sniping remark, just the latest one. But how many more had there been before?

It's gone very quiet in the kitchen. No-one really knows where to look or what to say.

"Aw c'mon, honey!" says Terri giving Jean a hug, "it's been years since your kids were that high!"

Mercifully Jean says nothing, just scowls into her wine glass, which, fortunately, or unfortunately, is a very big one and very full.

"So, did you go loggin' with Sam?" Al asks and I was never so glad to have something to say.

"Yeah, but we didn't go to Pattee Canyon. Sam saw the notice about no trespassing."

"Aw, he didn't need to pay no attention to that shit. That's just 'cos they ain't got it prop'ly ready yet, see?"

I also see that Al's hand is unsteady for once as he splashes out a generous helping of wine into my and Iona's goldfish-bowl glasses without bothering to inquire about preference for colour first. Perhaps he doesn't have any red or perhaps he has remembered that white wine is the only alcoholic drink he has been able to force down Iona's neck.

That done, he is our jovial host again, throwing his head back at something extremely funny he has said which elicits an appreciative response from everyone except us and Jean who stares morosely and unseeingly into her glass. I can see Tony's laughter is hardly convincing but Iona is the only other person to notice. Normally the kitchen is the hub of any Hertz gathering but today we leave Jean to contemplate her sorrows alone and move through to the big room with the hairy carpet, where a log is burning merrily in the fireplace as usual and the TV is talking to itself.

What concerns Iona a lot and me not a little, is there is no sign of this mysterious double front chicken making an appearance anytime soon. Who needs food when you have plenty of wine and have consumed copious amounts of beer and whiskey? The present company certainly doesn't. There are nibbles on the table at the back of the room and like cattle, Iona and I and the kids gravitate up there in search of fodder, though chips, as the Americans call "crisps" (if *only* they were what we understand by the term, we'd feel less hungry) are not what Iona considers a suitable source of nutrition for the kids especially. She is rather keen on them (and us) having protein as if it were the sort of stuff that keeps body and soul together.

When Al tacks across the room on his way to the kitchen for more of the stuff that makes the world go round, to say nothing of some people's heads, I consider it would do no harm just to drop a hint about the chicken.

"Say, Al, just what *is* double front fried chicken exactly?"

Al drops anchor and comes to stop just as fast as a person afloat on a raft of alcohol possibly can. His eyes drift into focus and he looks at me as if I were some sort of congenital idiot, as if his ears had deceived him. He shakes his head to clear the fog of disbelief.

"Fried chicken from the Double Front restaurant, man. Jeez!" A further shake of the head. How could anyone be so stupid?

Of course! I have of course, heard of it. How prosaic! An image of well-endowed chickens barely able to move under the weight of prodigious chests pops out of my mind like a pricked balloon.

"C'mere, Dave," Al says sotto voce with a glance over his shoulder and a sideways inclination of the head in the other direction. I follow him into the kitchen where we are alone, Jean having come out of the sulks and rejoined the party some time ago. He reaches into the fridge and his fist emerges with a gallon jug of brandy and he pours out a slug for himself and one for me without as much as a by-your-leave. He drinks all of his off in one go and pours another then puts the brandy back in the fridge. It's obviously for those and such as those only.

"See that Paul?" Al continues with a nod towards the lounge and with a formidable bristling of the moustache. "Asshole. He's a goddamn asshole." At this foul word, Al feels the need to wash his mouth out with brandy again. "Goddamn hanger-on!"

What is he doing here then? There is no more generous host when it comes to doling out the booze than Al and his Italian dinners are legendary, so how come he has got so parsimonious all of a sudden?

"Damned sure I'm not gonna get a Double Front fried chicken for *him*," says Al, draining his glass and slapping it down on the workbench with such vehemence that I feared for its life. "Been tryin' to get ridda him fo'ages. Damned hanger-on!"

With that he seizes a gallon of wine from the fridge and lurches out of the kitchen leaving me alone and speechless with all hope of Double Front chicken abandoned. I go back to the party room to tell Iona the news.

She receives this with much better grace than I had expected. In fact "relief" may be semantically accurate. She gathers up the kids and leaves, ominously saying nothing. No-one sees her go apart from me. What am I to do? I search out Terri and explain as tactfully as I can that I have to go but before I get even as far as the door into the hall, I hear Al call after me.

"Aw, shit, you can't go yet, man. You jus' got here, for Chris' sake."

"It's the kids, you see, Al, they're hungry. And I haven't had anything to eat either."

Al blinks at me owlishly for a moment, his mouth hangs open then you can see the light going on.

"Come right back after you've eaten."

It is then that I make my fatal error. Instead of simply saying, "I will" like a bride, I tell him I can't leave Iona alone with the kids again.

"No problem. I'll send Rob over." And he goes back to join his warring guests and the friend he hates. Great! Now I am going to have to pay Rob so I can go to a party I'd rather not and dare not return to in the first place. And if I am not exactly over the moon about the idea you can imagine how Iona feels about it. Reader, I will leave to your imagination

wife to the beloved's bedside. Al can't: he's passed out on the floor.

We see this an appropriate opportunity to take our leave too. We say goodbye to Debbie and Sandi and Amy (who should be in bed), wave to the Daves, and head back to the house from *Psycho* which is now not as half as scary as some of the things we have seen today.

I give a wry smile. How ironic life is or how the gods love to pull our strings! Back home I had been starved of entertainment, one uneventful weekend rolling into another, with five days of repetitive work in between. Now we are struggling to find time to spend together as a family.

And whatever could be said of this weekend and this evening in particular, it certainly wasn't boring.

Chapter Twenty-four

*In which things go wrong and I meet
the parent from hell.*

There is nothing better to enliven a dreary Sunday afternoon than to go on a Great Hearing Aid expedition. The hearing aid which was only loaned to George on Friday by the university in lieu of the one he posted down the heating vent of the car, is lost. After a search upstairs and downstairs and in my lady's chamber, we come to the conclusion that since the last place he had got rid of the accursed aid was so effective, the little turkey probably thought the central heating vents would be just as good.

Despite what I might find lurking down there, in Mrs Bates' denizen, I take my courage in both hands and venture into the basement. Down there, amidst what we Scots call "stoor" and what Sassenachs (or the English) call "dust", I can see the gleaming aluminium pipes (what the Americans call "aluminum", pronounced "aloominum") which convey the hot air from the furnace to the floors above.

Even for someone with my limited technobility, to coin a word, it *should* be a simple enough job to undo the clips of those gleaming heating entrails - if, in the first place, I could get up to them and had I the tools. Which I do not, but there is sure to be someone who has the means and the way. But of course, it might all be a wild goose chase anyway, as to mix my ornithological metaphors, the little turkey may have hidden the aid somewhere completely different altogether.

I decide I'll be like Mr Micawber and wait and see if it turns up first before I go to all that effort.

* * *

Someone once said, and it has become a household saying ever since, "There is no such thing as a free lunch". Well, I have news for that someone: there is. I have just had it. It was an antelope steak, donated by one of my pupils, Tony Zweig, shot by his own fair hand and what's more, washed down with a bottle of his huckleberry wine. Or maybe that was his dad's. I didn't think it was polite to ask, since he can be no more than fourteen at the very oldest.

I was very touched by these gifts actually. In the unlikely event that such a thing should ever happen in Scotland, I would be most suspicious indeed and assume that it was a not very subtle attempt to poison me and would closely observe the pupil the next day looking for signs of surprise that I was still alive or in the hope and expectation of seeing me writhing around the floor in agony.

The next day I tell Tony that I had enjoyed the steak enormously. To be honest I hadn't particularly. The meat was very dark. I suppose it was akin to venison really and I am not that fond of venison if the truth be told. I consider it too strong and gamey. But the wine was delicious and I was able to enthuse on that without calling on my skills as a thespian, if they be any.

Tony grinned from ear to ear, well chuffed at the compliment. Nice kid, Tony.

* * *

After school, I cycle round to the university. It's on the way home anyway, albeit not a direct route. I am worried about how much the lost hearing aid will cost. Mike Wynne, who is one of the team looking after George, tells me that it will be $50.

"But, you know, Dave, I think you should think about getting a phonic ear for him. We tested him with one and he said three intelligible words."

"Three! Wow!" It doesn't sound much but every long journey starts with a few steps. "Phonic ear? What's that exactly?"

"It's a radio aid. The speaker has a microphone and the receiver is a box that fits on the chest, with straps. The advantage is that it cuts out all other sounds so that only the voice goes in the ears. And there are two earpieces, so the sound goes in both ears."

"Sounds good," I say with no pun intended. "And the little turkey won't be able to chuck it down the nearest available heating system either."

Mike laughs, as I intended, but then I get serious.

"How much are they?"

"Well...I reckon about $115."

Mike must have seen the shock on my face. "Well, that's just a guess. I'll look into some prices for you. Maybe it would be possible for you to rent one."

That sounds like a better idea and of course we want to do the best we can for George if we can possibly afford it. When we get back to Scotland, we might be able to persuade the audiology department at our local hospital to get one for him, which would, of course, be free to us under our National Health system. And they might just be persuaded if Mike were to furnish us with the evidence that that was what he needed...

When I get back and tell Iona the news, she has news for me too.

"After I took Hélène to Margaret's the bloody car wouldn't start again."

"Oh God! Not again! What did you do?"

Margaret is the professional babysitter who looks after Hélène when George goes to my school for his signing class.

"I called out the Triple A. They diagnosed a fault with the automatic choke. They showed me where it was and how to wiggle it if it happens again."

"Show me."

But when we lift that vast expanse of blue, what we call a "bonnet" and the Americans call a "hood" and gaze into that mass of wires and cables beneath, she confesses she hasn't a clue.

"I think it was over there somewhere. It looked very simple, what he did."

I haven't a clue either. Maybe if it does happen again, a wee tweak of all the wires in that area might just do the trick. But in the meantime, there is the problem of the hearing aid. I phone Al but it is Terri who answers.

"The little monkey! I'll send Al round to have a look."

"Thanks. That would be great. How's Tony?"

"Well he's got a smashed kneecap, lacerations to his face and quite a few bruises, but he's gonna be OK. He'll live. And he'll be able to walk again, so he's quite lucky really."

So he is. Extreme measure it may have been, but I imagine the accident has brought about a peace between him and Jean. Or a temporary truce at least. It will certainly put paid to him running anywhere for a while, never mind after a whore.

* * *

It's November 8th and Hélène's third birthday. It's also the start of the parents' conferences which makes them sound much grander and more important than our "parents' evenings". That's when we have them, in the evening, but the system here is that the kids are sent home from school at midday and we are available for parents all afternoon until normal school closing time, then in the evening again from six until nine and then the next day until lunch time, which makes it a very long drawn out and protracted affair, especially when I have so few students here by comparison anyway. What's worse in my view, is that there are no scheduled appointments, so you don't know when or if a parent is going to show up and worst of all, an interview could potentially last indefinitely because you can't say, if you have a troublesome parent like the dreaded Mrs Apachito, "I'm sorry, but I'm afraid I'm going to have to terminate this interview because I've got another parent waiting outside."

I go back at lunchtime so I can see Hélène open her presents. We have given her a doll's house which opens up into three parts like a triptych. We know she likes it because she shows not the slightest interest in any of the other presents that have come all the way from Scotland. It's all too brief a time before I have to go back to school and my appointment with doom - the conference with Mrs Apachito. Possibly. Maybe. That's part of the trouble, it may not be this afternoon at all - she might keep me living in fear and dread until tomorrow.

185

In the event, it is 3.30 when she shows up. That's the time the kids would normally be released from school and we are technically free to go, though Matt thinks it creates a bad impression if we leave at the same time as them so we have to hang around for a while even if there is nothing to do. On this day, especially, I was going to leave the minute I heard the bell ring. But as Robert Burns knew only too well - *the best laid plans o' mice an' men/gang aft agley.*

A shadow falls over my desk. It is the angel of gloom and doom herself.

"I'm Mrs Apachito." There was no need for her to introduce herself actually. Her features are unmistakably Native American, and Helen, her daughter, is the only Native American I teach. I was thrilled, at the beginning, to have her in my class, since I am a great fan of the Native Americans and the Plains Indians in particular. But that was before I heard about her mother...

Without further ado, she plonks her bum with what I would describe as hostile intent on the chair I have provided next to my desk. The body language says, "Right go ahead. Tell me about Helen's grades and I'm tellin' you now they better be good because if they are not, I'm gonna want to know why you are such a goddamn awful teacher and what you're gonna do to improve them."

At the precise moment her posterior hits the chair, the bell rings which would normally be the sound that would release me from my labours. Now it sounds like the first round in some sort of pugilistic encounter. Seconds out. I'm all alone with her and I have a feeling that each second is going to feel like a minute and there are going to be quite a few of them...

Even if I had not been pre-warned about her, knew nothing about her at all, I always knew it would be a difficult interview, because just how do you explain to a parent that their pride and joy is what we call "as thick as mince", or "ground beef" in American? That's bad enough, but the trouble with Mrs Apachito is that she suffers from delusions: the delusion that her daughter is a budding genius and drop-dead gorgeous to boot. Regrettably, although Helen is a nice kid, she has got nothing going for her at all. Beauty is in the eye of the beholder and fortunately there is no accounting for taste, otherwise the future of the human race would be in jeopardy except in the country of the blind. Hopefully there is someone for Helen out there somewhere, but when it comes to the matter of brains, there's just nothing can be done. Poor Helen was just not blessed with them whatever other hidden talents she may have and hopefully does.

It has been my experience as a teacher, that some people, while they may not have an aptitude in certain areas of the curriculum, are red-hot in others, like cricket is divided broadly into those who can bat and those who can bowl, with a smattering of all-rounders. So the world is divided into those for whom languages and the arts come naturally, whilst maths and the sciences remain much of a closed book, and vice-versa, with a few lucky all-rounders who can do both.

Fortunately for me, Helen falls into the category of not being able to do anything in either category. We have all given her Fs because she fails everything we give her to do, I might say, spectacularly. It must be very demoralising for her, though she doesn't seem to show it, and try as I might, I find it impossible to find anything at all in her work which I could offer as a crumb of encouragement.

Also fortunately, for us all, Blake had arranged a reading test to be done with the psychologist. After the results came out, Mrs Apachito lowered her sights and no longer expected Helen to get As but Cs instead which is still insanely wide of the mark, so to speak.

"Good afternoon, Mrs Apachito. Nice to meet you," I say with faux cheeriness and with complete disregard for the truth.

The parent from hell disregards this opening gambit completely.

"Just tell me how Helen is getting on."

"Yes... We'll... erm... let me see... she's very attentive in class. Does everything I ask her to do. I never have to tell her off for talking to the others or -"

"Yes, yes. But what are her grades like?"

I find it impossible to imagine that she doesn't know the answer to this already, the very reason why she has come with such a hostile attitude. Had Helen managed to get a D one day, she would certainly have rushed home in a lather of excitement to divulge this earth-shaking news.

"Well, erm... you see... the fact is that Helen... erm... I mean, she tries *very* hard indeed. *Very* hard indeed, but you see, erm... she is finding the work very hard. But she is giving it her best shot. Yes, she always gives it her best shot..."

Mrs Apachito gives me a look that curdles my blood and makes my mouth go dry.

"I've got all her papers here, if you'd like to see them."

I am already handing them over so she can see for herself just how dire Helen's work is. One of the problems about being an English teacher is the vexed question of subjectivity but there's no question of that being the reason for these low grades. They are "dittoed" tests from the textbook that Marnie uses, brain-numbingly boring exercises that test (and are meant to teach) grammatical matters like punctuation, the correct use of relative pronouns, the difference between "their" and "there" and "they're" and other matters. And just in case the teacher can't do them either, the answers are written in blue at the back of the teacher's copy. Although I disapprove and dislike having to do them almost as much as the students, regarding them as almost a complete waste of time, I am heartily glad of them now. The evidence is plain to see. Surely Mrs Apachito couldn't argue with that?

There are also some pieces of extended writing or there would be if Helen had managed to get past fifty words instead of the desired three hundred. Well that was the aim. My pupils back home regularly produce such an amount and more, but getting the students here to write half as much is like getting the proverbial blood out of the stone. Until I arrived and imposed this slavery over a pencil, it seems they weren't expected to write more than a sentence. You can imagine how well that went down with my charges.

Mrs Apachito looks through the papers. Her face is impassive.

"Must be the teachin'," she pronounces at last.

There could be a great deal of truth in that. Just *how* do you teach kids who haven't got it, can't see anything wrong - how to put a full stop or "period" as they prefer to call it here, in the right place? And as for the apostrophe - ye gods! If I'd had a dollar for every time I've seen a misused or omitted apostrophe I don't know where I'd be but I'd not be here that's for sure. I'd probably be cruising in my yacht in the Caribbean or somewhere else warm.

I overlook the insult and pretend Mrs A has made a serious pedagogical point.

"You're quite right, Mrs Apachito, it is an enormously hard thing to teach. One of the best ways I know is to read and read regularly. When you see sentences and grammar being used correctly, it sort of gets imprinted in your mind. You get familiar with it. Know what I mean?" And then as if it had just occurred to me and although I know the answer perfectly well, I add, "Does Helen do much reading?"

"Naw, she ain't got much time for book-readin'. An' neither do I," she adds unnecessarily.

"Well, you see, Mrs Apachito, I'm afraid that means we're rather up against it. If you want to see an improvement in Helen's grades, I strongly encourage you to persuade her to start reading."

"What good's that gonna do? It's your job to teach her, not hers to teach herself by readin' books. That's never gonna work. Sounds like a cop-out to me."

"Well, actually it *will* help, Mrs Apachito," I say patiently, resisting the urge to shout at her, like I did at another parent not so long ago: "And who do you think *you* are, a woman off the streets, to tell *me*, a qualified teacher what will or won't work?"

Snort of derision. Plainly Mrs Apachito does not believe me and never will be convinced. "Naw. *If* (and there is a heavy emphasis on the word) Helen's grades are as bad as you say they are, there's gotta be an explanation. It's not like she is dumb or anythin', is it?"

"Well, no, erm, I mean to say..."

"So there's gotta be some explanation ain't there?"

She's got me there. I don't know what to say. But Mrs Apachito has a helpful suggestion.

"Maybe you just added them up wrong, huh?"

"No, no, Mrs Apachito. That's just not possible. Not with all these papers. They couldn't all be wrong!"

The idea is so preposterous I want to laugh in her face, the rising tide of anger within me somewhat defused. The woman is completely insane. But how *do* you reason with a mad woman?

"So if that's not it, it's gotta be the teachin'." She pauses dramatically before dealing the *coup de grâce*. "So what you gonna do about it, huh? How are you gonna get her grades up?" Another ominous pause. "Or do you not know how to?"

Oh God! How am I going to get out of this? We are going round in circles. And how am I ever going to get away except by pretending to have a heart attack? Come to think of it, I may not need to have to pretend.

"Well, you see, Mrs Apachito, I'm afraid it's a two-way process. Helen's got to meet me half way and here's another thing you should understand too ⁓ there's no quick cure. It's going to take a long time, and it's going to take a lot of hard work on Helen's part. But if she sticks at it, you should see an improvement ⁓ over time."

Mrs Apachito mulls this over for a moment. "Yeah, but what are *you* gonna do?"

"Well I can give her as much practice as you like. I can give her exercises until they are coming out her ears. Practice makes perfect you know," I add in a light-hearted tone that I don't feel.

Mrs Apachito seems to be mulling that over too, but says nothing. I take advantage of the silence to leap in.

"That's the best I can do I'm afraid, Mrs Apachito. And like I said, if you could persuade her to start reading…

Now, if you don't mind, it's way past school closing time and it's my little daughter's birthday today." And then, in the hope of changing the subject, disentangling myself from this Gordian knot I am entangled in oh, so tightly, I go on ⸱ "She's three and I've got to be back here at six, so if you don't mind, I'd like to get going." And in an attempt to create empathy ⸱ "She's almost got the same name as your daughter, you know. Her name's Hélène."

The response is as swift as it is brutal.

"I don't care nuttin' about that. I stomp an' trample on teachers. It's your job to be here an' teach kids and it's your job to be here now an' talk to me an' explain why Helen's grades are so low. And," she adds chillingly, "I'm not leavin' until I get a satisfactory answer."

A long time later, after retreading the same ground over and over again, I do manage to get away. I don't meet anyone else as I leave the building. It seems deserted. It is pouring with freezing rain as I mount my bike. When the gods have it in for you, they really put the boot in.

I was just about to find out they hadn't finished with me yet.

Chapter Twenty-five

In which we set out on the Great Canadian Expedition and encounter some setbacks.

It's madness really. Who would be mad enough, at the onset of winter, to drive a twelve-hundred mile round trip over the 4,725 foot high Lookout Pass, to name but one, through the mighty Rockies to Vancouver - just for a weekend? Well we are. Canada, here we come at last! The Canadian relatives are expecting us again, and this time, I have told them, we *will* come.

It is Thursday and school will close at noon and not reopen until Monday morning. I see a few parents which helps while away the time and mercifully, not one was in the least troublesome - but all the time I keep a weather eye open on the door, petrified that through it would appear Mrs Apachito on the warpath again.

Once I was rid of that turbulent parent yesterday, I was able to spend some time as an honoured guest at Hélène's birthday party, along with Fritz who was making a rare appearance at his former home. He was absolutely no trouble apart from repossessing the sofa and going to sleep on it which meant that there was not a lot of seating left for the humans. Other guests were Amy and baby Benjamin, their mother, Sandi, and grandmother, Terri, as well as John and Carolyn and most honoured of all, Jock, the brother of Jack, the Snively's pet sock monkey. Hélène had taken a great shine to Jack as Carolyn regaled her with tales of what that mischievous and naughty simian got up to. Now they have kindly passed Jock on to Hélène for adoption. I hope he is better behaved than his brother.

However, I am happy to say that on this occasion Jack behaved impeccably and did not lead his younger brother astray, at least not when I was there. But after Mr Strict left, who's to know what those couple of cheeky monkeys got up to? It seems to me that John and Carolyn are rather lax keepers and Jack could have done with a good spanking. Iona had made a cake with lots of pink icing on the top, and for all I know, they might have started flinging it at each other and about the room for good measure. Just the sort of thing Jack would have done if he thought he could get off with it.

Hélène was looking beautiful in a pale blue dress that her clever mother made herself and to set it all off, she is wearing her "jewellery" - the bangle we gave her for her first birthday. And when I got to school, would you believe it - I had not a single parent to relieve the boredom. Typical! They really need to find a better system.

Between my intermittent Thursday morning parents, I spend the rest of the time making up worksheets on a book called *A Boy Called Hopeless*. It seems like an omen if you substitute "Trip" for "Boy". I wouldn't have thought there could be anything worse than Mrs Apachito, but there is. It starts snowing heavily, huge flakes whipped at the whim of a wind which seems to have blown up out of nowhere. No sky can be seen, just masses of tumbling white flakes. It looks as if it might snow forever. To my despair, as I look out my classroom window, I can no longer see the familiar M on Mt Jumbo or even the mountain itself. It has been completely blotted out. Apart from objects in the immediate vicinity, all is white.

Whilst there is comfort that this might well deter Mrs Apachito from darkening my door, this sudden appearance of snow worries me a lot more than even hers would. Then the word reaches me that several of my colleagues who had been intending to go to Spokane (pronounced Spokann) had decided to cancel their trip. A mere hop compared to my journey over the Rockies to Spokane, Seattle and beyond, an infinitely longer and much more hazardous journey. To not instantly dismiss such a thing but still actively contemplate it, you might conclude we *were* mad, but when you also take into account the transport we are relying on - The Big Blue Mean Machine, and that we are accompanied by two small children - you might conclude we were completely barking.

I am in constant communication with Iona thanks to the phone at the end of the hall and she has been checking weather and road reports but the last time she phoned all she got was a recorded message which she could make neither head nor tail of. So should we go or should we stay?

To my enormous relief, by noon, the snow stops. But that doesn't mean it's stopped for good. Steve says I'll have to buy snow tyres or chains. Tyres are much dearer but once they are on, all you have to do is drive. Chains are cheaper by far, but the big disadvantage is I'd have to put them on, something I have never done before and I don't trust my ability to do this in the snow, in the dark, with frozen fingers. I am going to put my trust in providence instead and hope I'm not going to need them at all.

Then Steve tells me that the Highway Patrol will not allow us over the pass if they reckon the conditions are too bad, snow tyres and chains notwithstanding. Another reason not to travel. Just think of it - to come hundreds of miles through God knows what horrible conditions, only to be turned back at the final hurdle. Having said that, that is good in a way, as the decision whether to risk attempting the pass or not (with or without chains) would be taken out of my hands. But we wouldn't know what conditions were like until we got there. Decisions. Decisions.

I make the executive decision to go and will take our chances. After all, is this not the driver who negotiated the Skalkaho Pass and lived to tell the tale? Besides, the allure of meeting my Canadian relatives is an irresistible magnet. I might never get another chance.

"I got some chains," Steve informs me. "Why don't you come round an' see if they fit?"

I don't need a second invitation, but then the next minute I get a phone call from Iona to say that the car won't start again and she's waiting for the AAA.

"Watch what he does this time, for God's sake!"

But of course it may not be the choke this time but something completely different…

* * *

If it was a bit of luck that it *was* the automatic choke to blame for the Plymouth's refusal to start again (with Iona watching the man as closely as the keenest hawk), at Steve's I am not so lucky. His chains do not fit. In fact, they don't even come close, both in length and width.

"You're gonna have to go to Wood's Second-hand Store. Bound to be a set there that'll fit."

I am grateful for that, yet my heart sinks at this further delay. It had been my intention to be Canada-bound the minute school closed and but for this snowstorm, I would already have been happily on my way. But now I see that to have rushed away like that would have been incredibly foolish. But you know what they say about fools rushing in where angels fear to tread. The snowstorm has probably been a blessing in disguise, though my excitement and eagerness about the trip has now been replaced by an awful anxiety about the sort of weather we might expect to encounter.

The man at Wood's looks at the big, fat tyres and shakes his head doubtfully. Although he has more chains than a chain store, he's not sure if has any that will fit. It seems that the tyres on the Big Blue Mean Machine are exceptionally wide. Just another reason why I should never have bought it. I was just about to find out another.

Because it is easier to put chains on a tyre when it is not attached to the car, the man takes the spare out of the trunk. It's as bald as the proverbial coot. He finally finds a set of chains that fit, but when he tries to fit it on one of the tyres on the car, it just won't go.

For a moment Mr Wood is non-plussed, then the reason becomes clear.

"See here," he points out. "This tyre here is a radial. The spare is a cross-ply." And just in case I didn't know, he adds, "You didn't oughta mix 'em, you know."

Brilliant! So now I have to worry about getting a puncture as well as everything else. The good news is that all the tyres actually on the car are radials, so as long as I don't get a puncture, which isn't likely to happen, it really doesn't matter that much.

Just then, Steve surprisingly and very kindly, turns up to see how I am getting on. His eyes open wide and his walrus moustache seems to spread even wider at the news.

"Boy, you sure do know how to pick 'em, don't you!" he says, shaking his head more in admiration at my incompetency than in sympathy.

Mr Woods has an idea. He cannibalises another set of chains to make two pairs for me. He says one pair on the front might do but where I am going, two would be better. I ask him to make four chains. Reader, you can imagine how this fills me with tons of confidence for the forthcoming journey. Then he and Steve show me how to fit them. Well, they try.

"I reckon that's good enough," says Steve after my third failed attempt. "You get the idea anyhows."

If I can't even put one on in daylight in the dry, how am I ever going to manage to do four in the dark in the teeth of a blizzard and with fingers like frozen sausages? I just hope I won't have to. Why do I get the feeling that as Steve says goodbye and wishes me luck, he is looking at me as if it might be for the last time?

"Oh," he calls after me. "Watch your speed as you go through Washington. Those highway patrol cops are red hot."

* * *

The road is wide and straight and best of all, bare and black, apart from the bridges where it is white. Because I have a promise to keep and miles and miles to go before we sleep, as that wintry-sounding poet, Robert Frost, almost said in his celebrated wintry poem, we have agreed that as long as these good conditions persist and as long as the snow stays off, Iona will do the driving and I will save myself for the night driving and the snow, if necessary.

It's all a bit of a skoosh really, easy-peasy. I am metaphorically hugging myself at just how easy it has been. A big fuss about nothing. My feartie colleagues could easily have made it to Spokane. Why, we are nearly in Idaho already, with just its narrow panhandle to be crossed and after that there's only Washington and the border to be crossed. Did the gods read my thoughts? Is that why they decided a little bit of hubris was in order?

I had failed to take into account, forgotten about, Lookout Pass. Well not forgotten exactly, but the big Plymouth is purring effortlessly onwards and upwards, taking the gradually increasing gradient in its stride and so it comes as something of a surprise to see after a while, the trees which had been green are now white and the road, which had been black, was now also white and not with freshly-fallen snow either. It looks deep and packed hard where countless cars have compacted it.

Iona is driving, when as we approach the summit, the snow begins to fall and worse, at the summit itself, it is blowing a blizzard. We do not stop to change drivers. For one thing it is not very convenient and besides, who would want to go out into weather like that? But most of all, if we stop, perhaps we might not be able to get going again. No, better by far to keep pressing on, despite Iona's lack of experience in driving in snow, unlike me, where every winter I was accustomed to driving on the ice-slick roads of Banffshire, even found it exciting and exhilarating, such was the folly of youth.

At the summit (and for some time before) we are higher than it's possible to be in Scotland and still have your feet on terra firma. Only out there somewhere in that snowscape, snow-capped peaks are rising even higher but it's impossible to see just how much higher. Things can only get better, as from now on, it's downhill all the way. Precisely.

It all happens so suddenly. Without any warning, we are in a skid and sliding irresistibly towards a concrete barrier and Iona is screaming, "What do I do? David! David! What do I do?"

I'm struck dumb, too terrified to utter a word, never mind instructions. I know that the theory is not to brake, however counter-instinctive that feels and you also are supposed to steer into the skid, which seems to me just as counter-instinctive. Is that what I did in Banffshire all those years ago? Did I really keep my head, or did I just do what seemed the right thing to do and trust to luck?

By the time I find my voice, before I hear myself screaming back, "I don't know! I don't know!" - it's probably too late anyway. No doubt Iona has had the brake pedal to the floor the moment she felt the car go out of control and also closed her eyes as she saw the barrier coming inexorably closer and closer.

The awful thing about it is you are completely helpless. You are in the lap of the gods and all you can do is hope that once they have had a good laugh as you panic, they will be merciful. This time they are.

The Plymouth skids to a halt. For the moment I am not sure if we are facing in the right direction or not but I do know we are on the wrong side of the road. I have the sensation of breathing again. I must have been holding my breath all this time, however long that was. Probably seconds rather than minutes, yet it had seemed endless. It crossed my mind that I might die, yet my whole life did not flash before me. For that to happen I believe you have to experience a falling sensation. If we had somehow crashed through the concrete barrier into the ravine below I might have been able to tell you ⁃ if I survived to tell the tale, as the saying has it.

I breathe, therefore I am, as Descartes might have put it. And since we have not hit anything, I presume everyone else is alive too. A quick glance at the other occupants of the car confirms the truth of this and a moment later my ears confirm it: Hélène begins crying. Although she does not know what is wrong, she instinctively knows something is not right as if she has absorbed our fear by some sort of osmosis. Or maybe it was just the way Iona and I were screaming at each other. Ironically, now the danger is over, there is no need for tears.

Phew! We owe our survival, or lack of injury, to the road, the I-90. Despite it being a pass in these parts, it is as wide as ever. There were two cars behind us which managed to stop and whose occupants presumably stared (W.H. Davies would most certainly approve) as we put on this impromptu mechanical ballet as we pirouetted over both carriageways ⁃ and by good luck there were no vehicles coming *up* the pass which we would have been extremely lucky to have avoided, given the whimsical and erratic nature of our trajectory.

We change places. I am the driver now while Iona gets into the back to comfort Hélène. As for me, I derive a great deal of comfort from the fact that once we come down into the plain it's a different world, not a flake of snow to be seen. We've also gained an hour since Idaho is in the Pacific Time Zone but despite this, it soon becomes apparent that we are never going to make Canada tonight. The light is beginning to fail and a great part of the pleasure of the trip was to enjoy the scenery. It was not in the plan, but we are going to have to stop somewhere for the night. Where exactly will depend on what progress we make and how soon it gets too dark to see the scenery.

We still have two more passes to negotiate - the 4th July Pass, 3,081 feet at the other side of the panhandle, and Snoqualmie Pass, 3,022 feet through the Cascades in Washington. Though about 2,000 feet lower than Lookout Pass, I would expect there to be snow on both. I might even have to fit the chains and I definitely don't want to do that in the bitter-cold dark.

Then just before Coeur d'Alene, something very strange happens.

I pass a car only for it to overtake me a few minutes later. Nothing particularly strange about that, but what *is* strange is that having done so, the driver immediately slows down again so I have to brake.

"What's that turkey playing at?" I mutter irritably, mainly to myself, but loud enough for Iona to hear, as I draw out to overtake him again.

"He's making some sort of sign to you," Iona tells me after I have completed this manoeuvre.

"What kind of a sign?"

I have a vision of a gesture involving only two fingers, though on reflection, over here they prefer to use a middle finger. But then the Americans never had an army of archers who fought the French and taunted them by waving the two digits they required to fire their arrows at them to show they still had them intact. Had they been unlucky enough to have been captured, those digits of mass destruction would have been chopped off so they could never fire another arrow in anger.

As for me, it's not like I cut him up or anything or had been driving too closely behind, so what's his game? If he's some idiot wanting to challenge me to a race, he's out of luck. Maybe that's it, for here he comes again. His indicator is on showing he's going to overtake.

As he draws level, I draw him a dirty look. Iona's right. He *is* making a sign. Seems to be pointing at something. Something on the car? Low down. What does it mean? Doesn't look as if he is mad at me anyhow and he doesn't look like he's going to beat me up, or pull a gun on me and turn my brains to mince, so when he pulls up in front of me, I draw up behind him. All the same, I stay in the car as he gets out and strolls towards us. I lower the window but keep my finger on the switch, not that that thin pane of glass would make any difference if he's concealing a gun.

"You gotta flat," he says.

I have been living here long enough to know that what we call a "flat" they call an apartment and a "flat" to them means a puncture.

I get out to have a look. Sure enough, the rear offside tyre is almost completely flat. I groan inwardly. How did that happen? Was it something to do with the skid? But what an extraordinary thing to happen! In thirteen years of driving I have never had a puncture before, ever. And it has to be now and it has to be when I know that the spare is a bald cross-ply and I should not be mixing it with radials! I can practically hear the laughter in heaven.

I thank my benefactor profusely but wait until he is out of sight to make him think that I am changing the wheel right there and then, but actually I have no intention of subjecting my bum to the risk of being shaved by a passing truck as I bend over that damned wheel. It's not far to Coeur d'Alene, I reason. I'll change it somewhere safer and where's there's more light.

That light is the glare coming the forecourt lights of a filling station. We're not even halfway to our destination and now I've got to continue with this apology of a tyre. I'll get it fixed tomorrow, somewhere. Not now. I'm not going to tour Coeur d'Alene looking for a garage that's still open and wait until it is done, all the time itching to get a bit closer to Canada whilst this good weather lasts. God knows what it might be like tomorrow.

Whilst I have been working out where to put the jack, then wrestling with the nuts and cursing that stupid tyre for getting a hole in it, Iona has not been idle. She has been consulting the AAA book. These books are marvellous. Not only do they tell you the population of all the cities and towns in the state as well as a bit of their history if it is big enough or important enough, but most importantly of all, from our point of view, it lists all the hotels and motels with their prices so we don't need to go shopping around for the best bargain. It's a great saving on time, never mind money.

What a brilliant decision of mine it was to join this organisation (though they must already be heartily regretting I did). It would have been a "far, far better thing" if, as Sidney Carton remarked before his noble demise, I had not bought the Big Blue Mean Machine in the first place, but I am stuck with it now.

The AAA is not going to make any money out of me, that's for sure ⁓ I am going to cost *them* money if it continues to behave as badly as it has been doing. I am going to be nine months more in this country, including a transcontinental journey, not to mention the south-to-north trip. How many states is that we will pass through? The books alone must be worth the membership fee.

Iona has decided that Moses Lake would be a good place to stop for the night. She reckons that it is halfway to Vancouver and there is a motel called "The Interstate" which sounds good and also cheap at $25 for the night. Maybe that's because it is equidistant from the two major centres of population in Washington - Spokane and Seattle. I would have said in the "middle of nowhere" but I don't want to alienate my legions of fans in Moses Lake, population, according to my bible, of 10,471 good souls, and who might (rightfully) regard it as the centre of the universe. After all, if it was good enough for Moses, it can't be that bad.

Spokane is just a hop over the Idaho border now. We're in Washington State and I must be vigilant for the traffic cops. It is sprawling, seems to go on forever, but we ignore its welcoming lights and press on towards the promised land of repose - Moses Lake.

It's dark on the highway. The cruise control is set at 57 mph, a scandalous two above the legal limit. The headlights stab the darkness revealing the road ahead built after the Roman model without a hint of a curve to add a bit of interest and as empty as an impecunious elephant's pockets. Such a ridiculously slow speed where the biggest danger to life and limb is through boredom, an irresistible urge to fall asleep, so relentless is the sameness. When a car does pass you coming from the opposite direction, you want to flag it down, like a ship upon an ocean, at the joy of the discovery that you and your family are not the only ones on the planet.

This snail speed is intensely frustrating, makes it seem as if you are hardly moving at all and I can't help thinking about those hundreds of miles ahead of me. How tempting to put the foot down and gobble them up. Without the cruise control, it would have been more than I could have resisted, but I remember well Steve's last words to me and resist the urge to disengage it.

Besides, for some time now, there has been a car behind me, its headlights, like two burning eyes burning into my rear view mirror. I am dazzled by the light. All I can see are the two twin globes as they follow me for mile upon mile through this pancake-flat terrain. Could it possibly be the cops, or is it just another law-abiding motorist obeying this ridiculous law?

Eventually I have my answer. How long he had been behind me, I couldn't say for sure, maybe half an hour, when I first noticed he was on my tail. Finally, he loses patience and in a sudden burst of speed, spurts past me. It *was* a cop car. Now he'll break the speed limit massively until he catches up with another car and sit on its tail, hoping to catch it out.

And what if he had stopped me? What if he had examined the car and seen the baldy tyre and also spotted it was different from the others? That could have been another fine mess I had got us into. Would I at least, be spending the night in a police cell instead of the Interstate Motel, Moses Lake, had I been issued with a pay-on-the-spot fine which I would have been unable to stump up?

No-one ever heard of offering the cops a cheque in lieu, but in any case, as I know by experience, a cheque in this country is no good outwith the town where your bank is. Isn't that an amazing thing? This incredible country can land a man on the moon 239,000 miles away, but hasn't yet been able to figure out how to cash a cheque in the next town, never mind two states away.

Chapter Twenty-six

In which we come across a terribly strange bed, a terribly strange forest and some other terrible things happen.

Wow! What an amazing place! It's my first experience of an American motel and it must be tons better than a police cell. Thank God for Steve and his timely warning, only added as an afterthought.

The carpet is brown and thick. There are two huge beds with mattresses so thick I would defy any princess to detect a walnut never mind a pea beneath them, and so wide that two elephants could sleep together and not be within a trunk's-length of putting the other off a good night's sleep.

I won't bother to mention the power shower and the coffee-making facilities, nor the ice machine in the hall, nor the huge colour TV which, I discover, receives programmes from Canada, and which I have to say, are mercifully free of adverts and canned laughter, and are of the sort of quality I associate with our dearly loved and sorely-missed BBC. And to think this is the cheapest motel in the AAA book!

I phone Canada from the phone in the room. Mae, my cousin John's wife, answers. She sounds very welcoming despite the fact that two perfect strangers are about to be descending on her a good few hours later than expected, and for all she knows, with two squawking kids who might keep her up all night. She understands the reasons for our delay and is looking forward to seeing us tomorrow.

We have a humble meal which Fiona had prepared before we left, kept cool in Marnie's coolbox. We are seasoned travellers now and know that you never set out in these parts without at least a drink. Pity we had not realised this during the summer with the temperatures in the 90s but we were Innocents then.

According to the TV news, there is a great deal of snow in Montana but on the other side of the Rockies where we now are, there are merely flurries, though the wind is bitter. The forecast for tomorrow looks good. It looks like we are going to make it.

We bathe and bed the kids (who go out like lights in one of the king-size beds) and after attending to our own ablutions, we hit the sack. We are pretty bushed. What better idea therefore than to invest a quarter by putting it in the slot in the bed, which it assures us, will gently rock us to sleep, like *Rock a Bye Baby*? What's a quarter in the grand scheme of things? After all, do we not deserve it, after all the stresses of the day?

The deed is done. I'll never see that quarter again. Iona and I lie feet apart (far too tired for any of *that* nonsense) and wait for it to happen. It begins slowly, a gentle rocking that is at first quite soothing, but then it gathers momentum and soon we find ourselves on a seasick-making swell on this vast ocean of a bed. Even worse, it is accompanied by the sort of buzzing that I associate with the dentist's drill of my boyhood, a sound that filled me with dread, as it did lots of others, adults included.

We lie waiting for it to stop, expecting it to any minute, long for it to when it doesn't. At last, by unspoken mutual agreement, resenting the loss of sleeping time, we get up. It must work by electricity somehow. But how? There are no visible signs of connection to the mains. If there had been, I would have cut off its life support, but instead we are reduced to standing by the bed, looking in consternation at this latter-day demonic device, like something the Spanish Inquisition might have cunningly devised to exhort confessions through sleep deprivation if only they had had the power.

Half an hour later, feeling not a little irritable that we should get such good value for our quarter, when the bronco stops bucking, we tumble gratefully into a bed that stays still like a bed ought to do.

* * *

Everyone else seems to have slept like logs. I would have laid me down to sleep like a babe too once that infernal machine had finally run out of money, but I know that the gods like to kick you in the teeth at the slightest hint of an optimistic thought, and I also know that the way to appease them is to lie tossing and turning, worrying about what might be. By this method the gods get a jolly good laugh at you fretting, and to ensure they have the last laugh, never allow your fears to materialise. Accordingly I worry, despite the weather forecast, about snow and seven-foot high snowdrifts and another puncture (without a spare to put on) and having to put on the chains in a blizzard before venturing the crossing of the Cascades, the last hurdle before Canada.

Or maybe I just couldn't sleep with the excitement of it all, of seeing more magnificent scenery, more Rockies, and at the end of it all, finally getting to meet the relatives.

While I try, belatedly, to get a wink of sleep, Iona attends to the kids, then they leave to go next door for breakfast, to Perkins Cake and Steak Restaurant. It may be a nice rhyme but it sounds a distinctly unappetising combination to me. Hopefully they don't put them on the same plate together though I wouldn't put any bets against it. The thought of having either at breakfast makes me feel so nauseous I prefer to remain in bed. But presumably there are other things to eat and when sleep refuses to come, I give up, drag myself up and have the longest, hottest, most luxurious shower I have ever had. Then I go over to Perkins.

I find the children happily drinking orange juice and eating cereal, but catch out their mother tucking into a stack of six pancakes smothered in blackcurrant sauce. That sounds sickening enough, but you should have seen the pancakes! The mother and father of pancakes, the size of dinner plates, stacked six inches high! I elect to have the same as the kids with the addition of the bottomless cup of coffee, an institution to which I am now accustomed but which had first astounded me and I can't help thinking about how astounded Marnie must have been when she first went into a café and found she had to pay for the second one. Was it that which finally brought home to her that she'd made a dreadful mistake: classes twice the size of hers; more than twice as much correction or "grading"; "gas" twice as expensive and our pokey house only half the size of hers and worst of all, nothing in it older than three years.

Finally, we are on our way, with Iona at the wheel. My fretting was not wasted: the weather is bright and sunny, at least for the moment, so she may as well take the first stint since my snow-driving credentials may be needed later. And since there is no sign of a tyre place or a garage, we decide to press on and if we see one we'll stop, but we won't actively seek one out since the Plymouth seems to be driving as smoothly as ever. I have to say, after all the unflattering things I have said about it, when it *does* go, it goes like a dream and I love its roominess, its silent, effortless power where, once you have switched on the cruise control, it drives itself, apart from just a couple of lazy fingers on the wheel to keep you on the straight and wide.

And this, what we are looking at now, is wide, impressively wide. We have only come forty miles or so, but this below us, has come a lot further from its source somewhere in the Rockies of Canada. From the observation point, we are gazing in awe at the gorge of the mighty Columbia at a point somewhere along its 1,243 mile-long meandering way south to the Pacific Ocean - so the AAA book informs us. It also tells us the gorge is 4,000 feet at its deepest point and 80 miles long, which makes it, in my book, a sort of mini Grand Canyon, only not so colourful, according to the photographs I have seen of that. That's another thrill in store. If this gorge impresses, just think what it's going to be like when we see the Grand Canyon for real, in the summer!

I am surprised, when only after a few moments of gazing at awe in this spectacle, I notice Iona beating a hasty retreat to the car without saying a word. As a former Geography teacher, I would have expected her to have stayed much longer to admire the sort of scene she could never see on our little island, or on the European continent either for that matter.

"It's freezing out there, isn't it?" I remark as I climb into the driver's seat. "Not surprised you couldn't stand it." I feel as if I have done a round with a heavyweight boxer, so strong was the wind.

"It's not that. Didn't you see the sign?"

"No. What sign?"

"The one that said 'Beware of Rattlesnakes'."

"Oh really?" I say, disappointed. Had I known, I would have had kept a close look out for one. Not out of fear, but out of desire to see one at close range. The expression "You dirty snake" that I had heard so often on the likes of *The Lone Ranger* and other TV cowboy shows that I devoured in my boyhood, for me meant only one of member of that form of reptilian lowlife - a rattlesnake. "And did you see one?"

"No fears!"

Well thank God for that! It would have been awful if she had been lucky enough to have seen one and I hadn't. But probably it was the snake (if there had been one), which would have been the really frightened one and scuttled off to safety, had it happened to see her.

And talking of being really, really frightened, at the other side of the river, we stop at the Gingko Petrified Forest Museum. These trees were scared rootless about 15.5 million years ago when they were covered in volcanic ash and turned to stone a long time later when minerals in the water replaced the trunks' soft tissue. There are some exhibits outside, a mini-forest, parts of trunks upstanding and some on their sides. Fantastic! So old and yet so beautiful, the grains of the wood, seen in cross-section, have an infinite variety of shapes and colours. And like Cleopatra, age will not wither them.

Just think, if we had got away at noon as I had hoped, we would have missed all this! The puncture had a role to play too and even Washington's rigorous policing of the speed limit, when you consider this is only forty miles away from where we happened to stop for the night. The gods move in mysterious ways and this time to our advantage.

And they haven't finished yet. They are so unpredictable! It's not of much interest to the kids, these specimens of different types of trees, with their different grains which, when polished, as some fragments are here, brings out even more the beauty of the patterns and the colours. As pieces of jewellery, transformed into a brooch for example, in my opinion, they would be far more desirable than any sparkly thing made of crystallised carbon atoms, aka diamonds.

It's while we are admiring these that we are practically turned to stone ourselves as a paralysing stench pervades our nostrils. It's not a skunk but it certainly smells as bad as one.

I take Richard into the men's to change him, while Iona takes Hélène into the ladies to change her. Most unusual for her: she has been toilet-trained for months. It can't be anything they ate, nothing out of the ordinary in that. No, it was simply the benevolent gods smiling on us again. If this had happened just a few moments later (for we were just on the point of leaving), we would have been on the road where it would have been much more difficult to change them. But what would have been much, much worse - we would have had to carry that stench with us until we found a bin somewhere. Thank you, ye gods!

But then, just to remind you of their whimsicality, there's a reversal of fortunes. Another forty miles on, at Ellensburg (pop 11,777), we stop for money and gas. We call on them in that order. The motel and the pancakes have all but cleaned us out. And then of course, we are going to need some Canadian dollars. The Pacific Bank is the lucky one to get my custom, or my bad luck to call in on *them*.

I stand in the queue or "line" as they call it for a long time and then, finally, when I get to the head of it, I am directed "over there" to another line, though frankly, I can't see the difference. Probably it has something to do with me being a difficult customer, wanting foreign currency. Why on earth would you want to venture north of the 49th parallel when you could get all the milk and honey you could possibly want on this side? The Pacific Bank, for all its name implies, certainly has a way of irritating me and we've only just met. Just as well that this is likely to be our one and only transaction. And it's then, in that line, that the real fun starts, as I somehow knew it would.

"I'll need to call your bank in Missoula, sir, in order to confirm that you have sufficient funds, sir."

"What's the matter with me? Do I look like a crook?" He can grovel as much as he likes with all that "sirring", but it doesn't cut any ice with me. I don't actually say it, as a matter of fact, I just convey the idea with a look, and look even filthier when he adds, "You do understand, don't you sir, that this call will have to be at your expense?"

Ye gods! Of course I do. In this country, they can't make it harder for you to get money out of your own account than if they had opened a branch on the moon. Robbing the bloody place would seem easier.

I nod my assent. Better to say nothing than something I may regret later. After all, he is only the messenger, but knowing how much it costs to make a long-distance phone call here, I wonder how much will be left in my account by the time he has finished it. It could even be the Missoula branch on the Moon he's talking to when you take into account the length of time he spends listening without saying a word. Finally I hear him say, "Have a nice day" and then after a long pause, "Thank you" and hangs up.

"Your bank has authorised the payment, sir. If you'll just give me a few moments, sir," and he stabs his calculator with such ferociousness and intensity with such a rigid digit that I wonder firstly what it could possibly have done to offend him, and secondly, with such speed that I cannot help but feel it is likely to result in a massive error and it won't be in my favour either.

"Here's your money, sir. I have debited one dollar for the call."

Oh excellent employee of the Pacific Bank! He certainly knows how to pacify the savage breast. I forgive him for not explaining there was a flat charge of $1 for the call, regardless of whether it was to Missoula or the moon.

And so on to the gas station. I need gas anyway, but better to fill up here than in Canada where prices are said to be higher. I put the hose in the nozzle and click it so that I can get on with doing something else, like reading a book, as it takes so long for this huge tank to guzzle its gas injection. I wasn't reading anything as it happens; maybe I just nodded off. I wasn't paying attention anyway - no need to with the automatic cut-off. Which just proves you should never put complete faith in gadgets (or the gods) for I suddenly become aware of a splooshing, splashing noise and to my horror, I see a Niagara of petrol issuing from the hose, still firmly *in situ*. The nozzle seems to be stuck and by the time I manage to wrestle it out and somehow make it stop, there are dollars and dollars of petrol swimming about on the forecourt and I am smelling like a refinery.

When I go to pay, the attendant is not impressed by my claim that due to technical failure I should not have to pay the full amount, though there's no way of telling just how many dollars were spewed on the ground.

"Ya shoulha' bin lookin' out for it," she says, unmoved, but she agrees to knock off a dollar, probably to get rid of me.

I can see I could argue this forever and not get anywhere so I throw in the towel. It would probably have been cheaper in Canada, I reflect ruefully. But I have learned a lesson. Never again will I trust that automatic shut-off contraption. From now on I am resolved to hold on to that ice-cold metal handle even if my fingers drop off with frostbite first.

Because Snoqualmie Pass is coming up, I am also resolved not to be caught out again and I take over the driving. The scenery had not been particularly interesting since Coeur d'Alene, but now it is with the jagged white-capped peaks of the Cascades serrating the distant sky. Stretching all the way from British Columbia to Northern California, these are what I think of as "The Rockies", not the grassy mounds that hem in Missoula. As a boy in Banffshire, I had admired them then, never ever dreamed I would be lucky enough to see them one day - and this is another of those days. I bless my lucky stars.

The pass is mercifully clear of snow and the next hurdle is the mighty Seattle metropolitan district of over two million souls and looming ever nearer at a steady fifty-five miles an hour. On this journey we have become so accustomed to empty roads and small places, we agree that the best policy through this potentially tricky part of the journey would be for us to stick to what we each do best: I will drive and Iona will navigate. Before we reach that point however, while we are still out in the boondocks, we stop at North Bend (pop 1695) to pick up a hamburger for lunch. I calculate we will not get to the relations until after 4 pm, assuming there are no hitches. It would save some time if I ate as I drove.

As usual, in this land of the fast food takeaway, it takes just a little longer to be presented with your order than it does to say, "Three regular hamburgers with fries, one barbequed beef sandwich with fries and four Cokes." Far too fast, as it happens, for only one bite is sufficient to tell me, from the mess down my front and the contents of my lap, that my sandwich is going to be impossible to eat on the move. It turns out to be like a Sloppy Joe - a hamburger with so much tomato sauce in it it's practically liquid and which makes eating it such an undignified sight it should only be done in private.

"Do you want to swap?" I ask Iona, offering her what has not landed on my lap. "So I can drive."

But she has already seen what has happened to me. She gives a slight shudder, pulls a face and adds unnecessarily, "You can keep it."

And so I have to, for miles and miles, by which time the sandwich is colder than a miner's butt, as Steve, from whom I have been picking up more colourful speech, would have said. And it turned out to be a lot more miles than it should have been. That's because we took a wrong turning in Seattle, as I always feared we might. Never, in all of our journeys, have we seen traffic remotely like this, not in the United States, nor back home, nor in some of Europe's capital cities - so many lanes, so much traffic and everything moving so fast, knowing precisely where it's bound.

We know we are bound for Canada and very soon it will be time to say goodbye to the I-90. If ever anyone could be said to be fond of a road, or more precisely, a highway, then I would admit to being very fond of this. So wide, so straight, so empty for the most part. But now no more nice I-90. It has morphed into a monster with five lanes of traffic all frenetically rushing eastward and westward. We are on the lookout for the 405, signed to Bellevue or Everett or Canada. Even just north would do.

It comes upon us unexpectedly, but there are *two* 405s. "Left or right?" I shout at Iona, who has the map for I must make a decision ⁓ and faster than a fast food outlet serves food.

"Left! Left!" she shouts back and then, "Which one's left?" she asks in panic, holding out both arms so I can see them. "Is it this one?" And she takes away one arm, so that only the right one is left, if you follow me.

You can't be married to someone for six years and not be unaware that she suffers from this affliction of not knowing her left from her right, but any witness in the car would have been forgiven for thinking there would not be another year in this marriage when, too late to take the other 405, we see signs to Tacoma and Portland and realise we are heading south. Great! Simply great! Lost in the largest city in the Pacific North West, with no idea how to get out of this endless tide of rushing traffic and turn ourselves around.

But it's not as bad as it seems.

"It's all right," says Iona, who has been studying the map in the meanwhile and stuffing cotton wool in her ears, or would have, had she had any to shut out my diatribe on people who don't know their lefts from their rights. "If we stay on this, after a place called Renton, we should hit the I-5, which we want, and that will take us to Everett. Seattle is built round a lake and this road will take us up the west side rather than the east side, that's all."

She looks a mightily-relieved woman, as am I. Except I'm a bloke.

But you can't be too careful. "So, when we get to this I-5. Which way do we turn?" I don't need a map to tell me. Common sense does.

"Right."

"And which one is right? Show me!"

And she does. And she's right! But how long will she remember?

Chapter Twenty-seven

In which we finally meet the relations.

This detour has added quite a few miles to our journey so it is quite a long time later when I am able to pull into the first rest area after we leave the built-up environs of Seattle behind and I am able to attend to the less than tepid mess that is my barbequed beef sandwich. I eat it outside, firstly so the family is not grossed out and secondly so that what misses my mouth does not end on the floor of the car looking like something the cat has sicked up.

There is some compensation though. Something I had seen pictures of and marvelled at. It so happens that this rest area features a massive cedar with a trunk so thick that you could drive your car through it if you wanted. The King of Norway once did but we resist the temptation. As soon as I have scoffed my anything-but-tempting sandwich, we're heading for something so thin it's invisible - that imaginary line, the 49th parallel.

At Bellingham, we leave the I-5 and take the 539 to Sumas. I buy a bottle of my national drink at the duty-free to take as a present to my relatives for the hospitality about to be received. I am lucky to be able to proffer such a convenient and universally accepted token of appreciation and they should thank their lucky stars that I am not English and they are not getting a box of tea bags instead.

The purchase made, I am told to go and wait in my vehicle. Someone will come and bring it to me presently. I don't doubt that they will, but wonder why. It comes a few moments later and they stand and watch as I drive off, making sure I do not execute a U-turn but drive straight across the border. If that seems an idiosyncratic piece of bureaucracy, it is at least better than what I can expect on my return, for as far as I can see, although there is a huge flag with a red maple leaf on it, flapping as if to say: "Come on! Come on! Canada this way!" There is no sign of a duty-free shop at all. Al would be very disappointed if he knew I had been intending to bring a bottle back with me to see in the New Year, since he was mainly responsible for disposing of the two litres I had brought when I arrived in Missoula.

No snags at Customs. The maple leaf is now waving us farewell: "Bye. See you again! Have a nice trip!" Thank you flag. You don't realise we will be back all too soon, unfortunately. But now the first leg of our epic journey is nearly over. It is just a skip and a hop from here to our destination - Abbotsford (pop 11,747). Indeed that has been our destination all along. We don't have to go through Vancouver at all, mercifully. Abbotsford is 40 miles to the east, close enough for those who have never heard of it, to say that Vancouver was where we were going to.

The only problem is that we don't know how to find our precise location so I pull in to the first available big parking place.

"Do you know where Arlington Street is?" I ask the first two people I meet.

"Don't know. Never heard of it." And they pass on by without hardly breaking step like the Levite in the parable.

I use a phone at the Fraser Valley Inn. A young male voice answers. It's my cousin's son, David. I ask for directions.

"Stay right there," he says, "and I'll come and get you."
I tell him where we are and to look for a blue Plymouth.

We sit and wait. And wait and wait. Surely to God it shouldn't take all this time, should it? Something *must* have gone wrong. I had noticed that it was 5 pm when we first arrived in Abbotsford and it's well after half-past now. I decide I'd better phone again. This time Debbie answers. David, it seems, had rushed out of the house without telling anyone where he was going, that is to say her, as she was the only other person in the house at the time. Maybe he was just so eager to see us, he couldn't wait. Or it could possibly be because he had just that week passed his driving test and this was his opportunity to get a shot of the car? That wasn't why we were left stranded however. Put it down to an excess of excitement if you will, but he somehow contrived to not only go somewhere completely different from where we were waiting, oh so patiently, but he was also looking for a white car. Or maybe it was my fault all along: he just was not accustomed to a Scottish accent.

This time Debbie comes to meet us which would have been a better idea all along, as I had met her once before, when she came over to Scotland about five years ago. She hasn't changed at all, physically, but I am glad to see that she has changed in another way. She is much more friendly and sociable. She had driven my mother batty when she stayed with her as she hardly said a word, having her nose perpetually in a book. And when we took her from my mother's house to stay with us for a few days down south, she read all the way in the car and during the stay. Even in the last minutes of our time together when we took her to the station in Dumfries where she was to start the next leg of her sojourn in the land of her ancestors, she still had her nose in a book as she needed to finish so she could give it back to me. Personally, I read into all this that she was just very shy, but I could be wrong about that as it seems at odds with the courage it must have taken to travel alone to and in a strange land where even your relations were total strangers.

She says her dad is at work ⁃ he's a pharmacist in a chain called "Shoppers' Drugstore" and won't be back before nine. Her mother should be back shortly, however. She is working in "Fat Albert's", a T-shirt franchise they manage. It seems to me that every breadwinner on this side of the Atlantic has a second job to supplement the main job, though I suppose for Mae, it is the main job. Debbie doesn't have a job at all, having given it up to study French. It's the sort of thing you could learn as you chewed your cornflakes in the morning, as by law, probably as a result of pressure from the Québécois, all packaging in Canada has to be written in French and English. David is a student too, but still at school.

Until Mae arrives, we chat over a cup of tea and coffee. Debbie has still retained the travel bug.

"I'd like to travel," she says, "but I'll probably end up married and have kids."

I would say this was said in something of a tone of regret, to say nothing of the "but" which had signalled this option was very much a second-best. Certainly she did not make a big fuss over our kids. It's not obligatory, but most people usually do, especially when they meet them for the first time.

When Mae arrives, she *does* make a fuss of them, and us. She supplies me with beer and I know I have got my feet under the table, so to speak, when she asks if I wouldn't mind lighting the fire whilst she gets on with cooking a ham. Later, Pat, her third child, appears. I am much taken with her good looks. I find myself thinking if there weren't nine years between us and not forgetting the slight matter that I am already married...

I won't be meeting Stanley, the firstborn, three years younger than me, born in Edmonton and where he still lives. He is in the RCAF. They are putting him through law school so he can do legal stuff like courts martial. Since only two were selected for this out of I don't know how many, but I presume quite a number, I also presume he must be something of a bright cookie. He and his wife are expecting a baby any day. It is already a week late.

A long time later, David is dispatched to bring his father back from work and a little later still, I hear the door open and voices getting louder as David and his father climb the stairs to the living room where we are waiting to receive them on the upper level. This arrangement could not have been better contrived to whet the so-long-waited-for moment of meeting with the distant cousin. Furthermore, from where I was sitting, his face appeared not in profile and all at once, but bit by bit as each step took him closer to our rendezvous.

I had seen a photograph of him but this gradual exposure meant that the first feature I saw was his eyes and it gave me quite a jolt to see my mother's eyes looking back at me, and then a moment later, when the nose and chin came into view, the effect and the resemblance was gone. I was happy it had happened that way. It gave me a feeling of connection with him, so that when he gave me a welcoming hug, it was very much reciprocated on my part. After six hundred miles and arriving in a country I had never set foot in before, I felt as if I really was amongst family.

Like the Walrus said, the time had come to talk of many things, and during the meal in which Debbie said not a lot and David said a great deal about things with technological-sounding names that meant nothing to me, nor, if the glazed expressions of the others were anything to go by, did they. And after the meal, by the fire, with beers to start with and whilst I drank Canadian whiskey (when in Rome) and John made inroads into the bottle I had brought, we talk about family matters.

"There is a tale that we Blythes are descended from one of the wives of William Faa, King of the Gypsies."

"Is that so?" I ask, interested. "Have you ever followed that up?"

"No," John sighs, taking a slug of whisky. "Maybe I will one day, when I'm retired, when I have more time."

"I hope you'll let me know," I tell him. I think there might well be some truth in it, might explain Debbie's wanderlust, the desire to go travelling outweighing by far the instinct to be domesticated, to settle down and have kids.

John shows me Aunt Mary's, his mother's, prayer book in which she has recorded some significant dates: her marriage in 1904 to John Daniel Blythe; the birth of their first son, Stanley in 1905 and sadly, his death six years later; the birth of their second son, John, in 1916, his marriage to Mae and the births of her four grandchildren. When her husband died in 1951, she emigrated to Canada in July of the following year and that is where she died ten years later, aged 81.

It means a lot to me to hold this in my hand and be reacquainted with her handwriting. I tell John how much I appreciated her Christmas presents, in particular, *Tom Sawyer* and the Davy Crockett hat. It was my designated task to write the thank you letters for both me and my sister. That's because she was illiterate. By the time she was old enough to be able to string some letters together, sadly Auntie

Mary had died. The firstborn of the family often has the thick end of the stick, not least in the fact that your parents practice on you first (and hopefully learn from their mistakes).

I ask John about my grandfather. My mother never had a kind word for him, not that she spoke much about him at all, but I was left in no doubt that he was a womaniser and an alcoholic with a fierce temper who, one occasion at least, tried to strangle my grandmother. My cousin however, the son of my mother's brother, had a different, and possibly male perspective on this, a point of view he could only have got from his father. He told me that my grandmother was a passionless sort of woman and of course with him being a ship's engineer and away from home so much, the marriage was semi-detached anyway. And when you consider that while at home he was probably drunk a great deal of the time, and if my granny did not respond to his amorous overtures, especially if he was two sheets to the wind - you could easily see why she might erroneously have been described as "passionless". Not that my grandfather necessarily went without. You know what everyone says about sailors and ports...

John confirms that he had heard that my grandparents fought like cat and dog, though he never saw any of it himself. To him my grandfather was a hero, someone who travelled the globe, a real adventurer. And then he has something surprising to tell me.

"It was my mother that he was courting at the beginning, you know, David."

"What! Auntie Mary!"

"None other! And then he met your granny."

"Really! I never heard that before! What happened exactly?"

"Don't know. Expect he thought she was better-looking."

I wish I had thought to ask how Auntie Mary had taken being dumped for the three-year-younger sister, if it affected the relationship between them, but I'm too taken aback by this revelation to say anything. Later I think they were stupid questions, so I am glad I did not ask them. Another stupid question occurs to me, however. Although she would have been upset at the time, did Auntie Mary later come to count her blessings and congratulate herself on her lucky escape? But of course that marriage might have been a totally different animal. We will never know.

We have both fallen silent. Whilst I have been staring into the fire and musing on the above, John has also been looking into the fire and thinking his own thoughts. We are alone with our respective bottles of whisky, everyone else having repaired to bed long ago.

At last John breaks the silence. It's as if he has been reading my thoughts, at least to some extent - the mystery of how one person finds someone attractive - and more attractive than someone else.

"Look at my daughters! All they seem to be interested in is retreads."

"Retreads?"

"Debbie is going out with a divorcee and Pat's bloke is ten years older than her and he's divorced too," he pronounces glumly.

Ten years! Why, that makes him just a year older than me! Maybe she finds older men attractive. That's not to say she'd be interested in me of course, but say, for sake of argument she was. And say that Pat and I had become attracted to each other that year when I was a student and looking at the possibility of going over there for the summer, only I didn't because I couldn't find the fare ⁄ it's a sobering thought that John might not have approved of me, even if he did completely overlook the fact (which is doubtful) that we were cousins, albeit twice removed.

It's time I removed myself to bed actually. It has been a long day. I'm glad now that I didn't go to Canada back then. I wouldn't have wanted to put my relationship with John at jeopardy. I've only just met him and already I feel very close to him, kindred spirits. And if the bear hug he gives me as we bid each other goodnight is anything to go by, I would have to say with all due modesty that he reciprocates the feeling.

Of course there is nothing like a few whiskies for casting aside a few inhibitions.

Chapter Twenty-eight

In which we acquire some new clothes, explore
Vancouver and get into a bit of a mess.

reakfast is bacon, the Canadian way, which is how we
are used to it but with the addition of lashings of maple
syrup, of which Iona approves heartily (unlike the
American style of bacon which is only one degree short of
total cremation and only possible to eat by picking it up with
your fingers as any attempt to stab it with your fork only
results in it being fragmented into small, hard shards.)

Despite the libations of the night before, my head is
mercifully painless and I am eager to begin the exploration of
Vancouver, but first I must get that puncture attended to.
John takes me to a garage and then to his work where he has
to drop off some keys, then it is on to Fat Albert's where Mae
has been slaving over a hot iron. She can iron any slogan you
like onto your T-shirt and shows me a few samples of the kind
of thing you can get, some of them far too risqué to repeat
here.

We can't come and not buy anything, so Iona picks a T-
shirt for George with a sort of homemade wooden sign on it
that says in rude lettering, "Kid for rent. Going cheap" and for
Hélène, a little girly thing of Holly Hobbie. I don't need a T-
shirt, but my attention is taken by a pewter buckle for my
belt. It is a Native American chief's head, in profile, in full
headdress. It would go very well with the design on the belt. I
am delighted to have it to further my American image and
more delighted still when John and Mae say instead of the $6

price tag, I can have it for $2.50 - cost price. To our surprise and delight, we get the T-shirts for nothing.

By now it is lunchtime and I am itching to get to Vancouver, but first John says we need to grab a sandwich. So we do, and when we finally set off for Vancouver, the traffic is solid and we are not going anywhere fast. It happens to be a Saturday afternoon. But we do arrive eventually and make first for the totem poles in Stanley Park.

They have been collected from various locations in BC but mainly Vancouver Island. Like a miniature forest from fairyland, they are tall and very gaily-coloured. Each one portrays an amazing number of figures. There is one with a projecting bill just at the right height to perch the kids on so they can have their photos taken. I'm not sure what it's meant to represent actually, probably some sort of bird. The whole area around his eyes is shaded sea green as if suffering from an excess of eye-shadow. His eyes are looking upwards, which, together with his very heavy, thick black eyebrows, set at a rakish angle, gives him an air of long-suffering forbearance. No doubt he has been accustomed to generations of kids doing this, at least since the pole was moved here.

It only occurs to me after the kids had their photo taken, that this was possibly a disrespectful thing to do. Certainly the figure above the one the kids were on looks not too pleased about it. He has the same thick black eyebrows but they are drawn together in a massive frown, his nostrils are red and flared and the lips are drawn back in a snarl to display a great set of shard-like teeth. On the other hand, that might just be because there is a mighty big black-and-white eagle sticking his talons into his scalp. Well it looks to me like a stylised eagle with his wings wrapped around him like a cloak, only the beak is all wrong - it sticks straight out like the snout of a bottle-nosed dolphin, only more elongated.

In his turn, his rather squashed head is due to the enormous figure squatting on *his* head. What he might represent, I couldn't possibly imagine, and on top of *his* head, something like a skunk (if the broad white stripe down the middle of his broad, black back is anything to go by) is pecking, if skunks could be said to peck, at the bridge of his nose, which no doubt goes some way to explaining why this figure has such an air of alarm, with popping eyes and teeth clenched in a grimace of utter anxiety. And so it goes on, up and up, but I won't go any further.

Utterly fascinating! What could it possibly mean? And so many others to gaze at in awe and wonder and admire the artistry of the carving! And the colours! And the designs! And should they be read from top to bottom, or the other way about? We could spend all day here if I had anything to do with it, but I mustn't. Besides, there is much more to Vancouver than totem poles. Time is pressing and I am aware of just how limited our time is here. It was madness to come all this way for such a short time, but we will be back in the summer, if not before, for we have been invited back for Christmas.

What better way than to spend Christmas with relations, especially ones as hospitable as these? A funny thought actually, for Christmas is notoriously a time fraught with family anxieties, quarrels and disputes, a time when people get together, not because they want to be, but because they feel they have to be. There is nothing I would like better than to come to Canada for Christmas - if it were not for the thought of Lookout Pass, and the others. In fact, the thought of it puts a bit of a dampener on the time I am having now, for I am starting to have an uneasy feeling in the pit of my stomach about the return journey...

We move on to the old town, Gastown, so named after "Gassy" Jack Deighton, who originally hailed from Yorkshire. There is a not-very-good bronze statue of him standing on what appears to be some sort of a barrel and a plaque which tells us about his short but interesting life. He died aged only 44 in 1875. He originally operated a steamship but ill health forced a change in career. He built a saloon. Location was everything. It was situated near a sawmill and the thirsty workers were his main customers, supplemented by sailors. He came to the place that now bears his name practically penniless, made a fortune, but lost it. Also interesting, at least to me, is he married a native lady whose dying wish was that he married her 12 year-old niece Qua-hail-ya.

But why was he called "Gassy"? Ever since John had told me about him, I had visions of a rather insanitary individual with people giving him a wide berth due to his flatulence. It turns out I was not too wide of the mark: the gas from Jack emanated from the other orifice so to speak. Jack could talk the hind legs off a donkey and wouldn't spoil a good story by sticking even approximately to the truth. That's not a bad attribute for a publican actually, engaging the customers in conversation, not that they probably needed much encouragement to spend their time, and wages, at his establishment which he called "The Globe".

That is long since gone, along with all but two buildings, in the Great Fire of 1886. But what *is* there is Gastown's most famous (but not oldest) landmark - the Steam Clock. Don't ask me to explain how it works, but it's got something to do with chains and balls, powered by steam, which drop into an escapement which operates a pendulum, at which point it becomes a conventional clock, apart from the whistles, which, with a great deal of literally letting off steam, also announces the hour. Very quaint, very cute and very clever.

Only it wasn't built as a tourist attraction. Its real purpose was to cover a steam gate, a valve for Vancouver's underground steam heating system. The city's founding fathers it seems, had little time for the homeless who, in cold weather, were camping around it. So they decided to clean up the streets and call time on the vagrants by building a steam clock on the site.

Time is our enemy too. That's our all too-brief tour of Vancouver done. We had seen, from Prospect Point where the totem poles were, the Burrard Inlet on which seaplanes and yachts bobbed happily together, the skyscrapers of the financial district, the Lion's Bridge and Grouse Mountain with the cable cars climbing to its summit. Now we are off to Debbie's bedsit, where she has kindly offered to give us a hot drink and a snack.

It all goes swimmingly - at first. I suppose you could say the blame for what happens next stops with George. He did another of his nasty nappies and Iona took him off to the toilet to change him. After a few minutes, there is a cry of alarm.

"Help! Help! Oh, my God! Help!"

We all rush in the direction of the panic-stricken voice to see a flood of Biblical proportions, or so it seems, in a room of such small proportions. Water is cascading from the toilet bowl onto the wooden floor which is swimming in water and as water has a habit of doing, it is spreading itself out and ever and ever closer to the door in a bid to flood the whole house.

It's all hands to the pumps, or as many as can get in the tiny space without getting in each other's way and mopping up the water with towels. It's obvious what has happened ⁃ the diaper, as they call it, should never have been put down the "pabby", as I call it. Of course we are horribly embarrassed, Iona and I, but the author of this catastrophe, George, is supremely unaware of the commotion he has unwittingly caused. All he did was a nasty poo, but as far as Debbie is concerned I wouldn't be surprised, if, long after we are gone, we have left a nasty smell behind us.

To her credit, she keeps insisting "It doesn't matter. It doesn't matter, don't worry about it," but we do and we can see that it *does* matter to her and I don't blame her either. Like Jesus, she suffers the little children, especially this one, who has come unto her and almost flooded the place.

The mopping up of the water is one thing. But there is another. Now Debbie has the unwanted problem of a blocked toilet, the unblocking of which is more of a challenge than the stemming of the flood, though less pressing. From somewhere, John comes back with a plunger and sets about plunging like a piston engine, and at last, the nasty sodden thing is persuaded gradually, piece by piece, to regurgitate itself from the pipes. When we think we have got it all out, it is time to try a test flush. Success! The water drains away. Debbie's drains are clear again, thank God!

It seems a good time for us to clear out too, so we do, with more profuse and abject apologies and Debbie is as charming and gracious as ever, but you can tell that she will be glad to have her bedsit back to herself, to the peace of a childless zone. I don't know how much travelling she will do in the future, but I have a feeling that first and foremost, it will be in the opposite direction of any bloke who is likely to give her babies.

Back at Abbotsford, another David has arrived - Pat's retread. He doesn't look anything like as good-looking as she is. Hard to see what she sees in him actually. I can begin to see why John is a bit disgruntled. Maybe it's the name she likes, as well as him being older…

Sometime later, I hear the sound of raised voices in the kitchen and then see Pat and Mae disappear into a bedroom. And there they are ensconced for a long time. I am engaged in copying the family tree, Iona is looking after the kids, David and John are making desultory conversation or having a really serious talk. I can't tell. Young David is out somewhere.

At last Pat emerges and says they are leaving. We make our farewells, say we hope we'll meet again some day, maybe at Christmas. Only after they have gone, does Mae emerge from the bedroom, looking slightly tearful. No-one says anything, certainly not me. I haven't a clue what to say. The silence is so oppressive it is Mae herself who feels the need to say something to break it.

"The trouble with being an old-fashioned mother," she says, trying to make light of what has obviously been a big thing. And that is all she says.

John doesn't say anything either. I suppose it's all to do with what they think of Pat's present choice of partner or maybe she or they don't approve of them living together, if indeed they are. I suspect, during our fireside chat last night, had it not been for the whisky, John wouldn't have taken me into his confidence as much as he did.

Whether they had been intending to stay longer or not, for a meal, I couldn't say, but John sends out for a pizza which we have with wine and very good it is indeed. Once again, we are invited to come for Christmas. Stan and his wife and new baby will be coming too. That is an incentive and a disincentive at the same time. It would mean that I would have met the whole family but that would be, it seems to me, at the cost of a great inconvenience to John and Mae, though they swear it would not be. As it is, we are all in one bedroom, the kids sleeping on a mattress on the floor. If we were to come, we'd have to sleep in the living room.

"It's very kind of you," I say, "we'd love to come, but I am rather worried about the driving conditions." There it goes again, that sinking feeling in the pit of my stomach. In only a few hours we will have to begin the long drive back. I calculate that by the time we get to Lookout Pass, it will be pitch black, unless it is a whiteout, of course.

"Maybe we could take the train, or a bus," Iona suggests hopefully. Whilst she does appreciate my relatives, their warmth and hospitality, I think I know what really lies behind her enthusiasm to come to Canada. After her spin in the snow and taking this journey as a whole, never having been a lover of snow in the first place, I would now say she is a fully-paid up member of the snow-phobic society and yet she wants to risk another journey at the height of a North American winter. There is no doubt in my mind that the reason for this is to put as much distance between me and Al at this festive season as possible. Never being short of an excuse for a party, I am sure she has visions of me being over at the Hertz household so often I'll suffer liver failure.

"Well, we'll see," I reply, "we'll see what the weather's like nearer the time." But I am thinking in my heart of hearts, it's not likely that we *will* be here. And there is another reason which I will go into when Iona and I are alone: I sincerely doubt if we could afford it ⁃ the petrol, the motel bills and not least, the presents.

"You'd be very welcome," they both assure us. But possibly they know themselves that it's not going to happen, for they get out the movie camera and put us on film. Thus Stan and his wife might well see us this Christmas, but I suspect we will not see *them*.

It is a very sore parting the next morning at 8.30 when we hug each other goodbye. But we will be back in the summer, that's for sure, even if we don't make it for Christmas. There's some comfort in that.

Chapter Twenty-nine

In which I receive a grave warning, receive some
contraband and we see a slide show.

It's 25 below freezing today. I know because of Marnie's
indoor/outdoor thermometer which I look at religiously
every day, like some people say prayers. It was at zero
yesterday, the day we got back from Canada. Eh? Wait a
minute! Can't possibly be! Stupid mercury. Must be some
mistake. It's gone mad, like the Mad Hatter in *Alice in
Wonderland*. Mercury did that to hatters. An occupational
hazard. Teaching kids can drive you daft too.

But the moment I step out into that crisp-white
snowscape I know something is drastically different. I take a
breath, as normal, as you tend to do when you are alive.
Instantly, I feel my lungs crackle as if they had been lit up like
the lights on a Christmas tree. Shocked, I tentatively take my
next breath, short and shallow, easy does it, filtered through
my scarf which I have taken the precaution of putting over
my mouth like a surgeon.

As I cross the bridge on Higgins a chill breeze is
funnelling down the Clark Fork, making my eyes water. I am
amazed to find the tears freeze on my cheeks. As I puff my
way like Stephenson's *Rocket*, only a lot more slowly, icicles
form on my scarf like stalactites. If I'd had the power to see
myself I might have been granted a vision of the future, me
with a snow-white beard, if I live that long of course - which I
might not.

"You oughta get off that bike an' walk across the bridge," Steve admonishes me sternly when I arrive at school. "If you fall off, you're dead."

That's a sobering thought. It's not only the wind that's funnelled over the bridge ⸲ so is the traffic. He had passed me in his pick-up although I hadn't noticed him. There were so many other things to concentrate on, like breathing the right way and keeping my slim pair of wheels on the straight and narrow on the icy surface. All the streets and roads are white with hard-packed snow and particularly slippery on the bridge. They don't put salt on the roads like we do ⸲ after all, Montana is a long, long way from the sea. It's up to the motorist to adapt to these conditions, to drive with winter tyres or take a chance with ordinary ones. No dilemma there as far as I am concerned. They are very expensive and although they last for years and years, I'd never get another winter out of them since I'll be gone in the summer, by which I mean from Missoula, not the planet, or so I trust.

I am reminded of the Scots saying "We never died a winter yet". It's a statement of indomitable determination to carry on in the teeth of any adversity the gods may care to throw at you, a declaration of indefatigable optimism. But now, methinks, if I fail to heed Steve's advice, this could be the way the world ends for me, with a bang and a whimper, mown down by a pick-up with Marnie's mangled bike on top of me. And how will she ever forgive me for the loss of her antique velocipede? And how ironic that I will be buried in a foreign field so far from home, in a land that I never, ever dreamt I would ever visit, let alone die in!

Yes, I will take his advice and walk over the bridge in future, even if it means I have to sacrifice precious minutes in bed. Better than having the tyre tracks of a two-ton truck tattooed upon my forehead.

* * *

Missoula and this part of Montana is a snowy place. It was only as we negotiated the panhandle of Idaho that we first came across snow lying on the ground but mercifully we were not treated to any fresh falls. We crossed Washington with the needle on the speedometer at an unwavering 57, as before, thanks to the cruise control. I reckoned that was just enough over the limit to get away with but even this paltry two miles per hour over such a long difference would add up to quite a saving in time.

It was dark by the time we reached Moses Lake and for mile after mile, a pair of lights burned in my rear-view mirror, urging me to go faster. I knew without a doubt to whom they belonged and at long last, running out of patience, the cop car swept past and sped off, many miles over the speed limit in the hope of finding a victim doing what he just did. No wonder some people, not only the ungodly, don't care much for cops.

It took us twelve hours, sharing the driving and Mae's sandwiches which we ate as we drove. The toilet we *had* to stop for - twice. We also had to stop a couple of times for petrol. I'm not a Scotsman for nothing and from near Aberdeen besides, where the buck is said to stop as far as the Scots' legendary canniness as far as money is concerned. We have another saying, "Tak' care o' the bawbees an' the pounds'll tak' care o' themsel's". In other words look after your cents and you will amass dollars. The price of petrol at the last place I stopped was an outrageous (in American terms) 78 cents, 10 cents more than in Missoula, so I only put in $5 thinking that would be enough to see us home. But with still some way to go, the petrol light came on and I thought it best to get some more in Frenchtown, whatever the price, some 18 miles short of safety. But to my dismay, the one and only gas station in the town and the very last before Missoula was closed and I had to nurse the guzzler home at fifty while the sweat stood out on my brow as I worried what I would do if we didn't make it. That's the price of parsimony: all that time I had gained by driving two miles per hour over the speed limit wiped out at a stroke.

Another worry is that we have now been in the state for more than 90 days and I'm not sure if my driving licence and therefore the car insurance is still valid. Not that it is a legal requirement to have such a thing. What some people do is take out insurance against being hit by an uninsured motorist. It seems a cack-handed way of going about things but that is the way it is here. I'm also aware how litigious a society this is and despite my enthusiasm to embrace most aspects of the culture, seeing the inside of the Montana State Penitentiary is not one of them. And that's where I would probably end up, having no money to pay for the damage, to say nothing of the lawyers' fees which I'm sure would be the most costly of all.

In order to obtain a Montana licence we're going to have to sit a driving test although both of us have been driving for years. In any case, a driving licence is a very handy thing to have as proof of your ID as when you want to cash a cheque, they always ask to see it.

It's something I had better see to sooner rather than later on account of these snowy streets and Iona's inexperience in driving in such conditions especially, as she's the one who uses the car most during the week, like yesterday when she took George to the university for another hearing test. The bad news is he will never hear sibilants, ever, which means his speaking voice is going to be severely impaired without a great deal of speech therapy. He would get that here, but in Scotland I'm not so sure...

On the doormat, two unwelcome bills to greet us ‹ a phone bill which we *are* responsible for and a bill for the sewer which Marnie should pay. The services in Scotland are already taken care of as part of the rates, paid monthly, by direct debit from my bank. Marnie should have seen to such things before she left, according to the advice handed out by the Central Bureau but she hadn't got round to it. She's a *que sera, sera* sort of person.

* * *

We've to be in school half an hour before classes start which seems a precious waste of time in bed as far as I am concerned or any other sort of time for that matter as there is nothing we can usefully do or at least I can't. Usually Blake and Steve perform their comedy duo act for my benefit while Nat gets on with writing hieroglyphs on the board or something else useful.

Yesterday Blake gave us a demonstration of his latest toy. It's a Heath Robinson sort of contraption which he slung from the top of his door and pulled on elastic handles. It's supposed to improve your pectorals. He confessed he had bought it for Diane, his wife, but she hadn't used it. I don't blame her. If I'd bought such a thing for Iona the only slinging she would have done was a right hook and quite possibly with a frying pan in her fist. It's good to see the device is not going to waste but having said that the last person who needs to improve his muscle tone is Blake. Indeed Montanans are hopelessly addicted to exercise. I've never met one yet who isn't. By contrast, they must think the Scots are a right bunch of slobs, if they regard me as typical.

Despite being such a fit specimen, Blake doesn't keep very well. Maybe he's pulled a pectoral. He's off school again today and we have a substitute, another one I've never met before. He tells me he works nearly every day which tells *me* Blake is not the only one who suffers from ill health despite all that healthy exercise, whilst ironically, slobby me can't remember the last time I had a day off school due to illness - touch wood. Another Scots saying - "A creakin' gate aye hings the langest" - not that I'm creaking yet, except when I go logging with Al.

As usual here, whenever I meet someone for the first time, I am regarded as an interesting sort of specimen and at lunchtime the sub pumps me for information on Scotland, in particular the Wars of Independence. I'm surprised he's ever heard of them. All everyone here seems to know about Scotland is it produces tartan and whisky and they have no conception of how it relates to England or indeed the United Kingdom as a whole. Some don't even know where it is exactly. No wonder I am regarded as a fount of knowledge, not to say a bit of a curiosity.

As ever I am happy to play the part of resident expert and fortunately I have just finished reading Nigel Tranter's *Robert the Bruce Trilogy* and am well versed in the finer details of the wars, not having had time to forget them yet. And if Blake's temporary replacement assumes I am a walking encyclopaedia on Scotland in general and on this matter in particular, I see no need to disillusion him.

This illuminating lecture takes place in my room because it is the biggest and we're supervising half a dozen of the eighth-grade girls practicing their moves. With their red rah-rah skirts, pompoms, forked tail and little cap with horns, they are the cheerleaders for the Emerson Red Devils basketball team. Meanwhile, down in what was the dining room, after the tables have been cleared away (easy to do as they are on wheels and in an ingenious system, hinged in the middle with little round seats attached), Steve and Blake are supervising the boys in a game, probably picking the team. Normally after I have helped push the tables out into the hall I sit on the bleachers watching the kids run around while Steve and Blake referee.

I suppose this means for once I am earning my free lunch by this less-than-onerous task, not that I am paying much attention actually, being more concerned with delivering my lecture on Scottish history.

* * *

The phone goes. For once it is not Al, just when I have a cast-iron excuse not to go round for a drink. We are going to Dave and Gloria's to see the slides of their trip to Scotland. It's Gloria to advise us that the Guthries won't be coming. They moved from Scotland a few years ago. Mr is a minister and his son, David, is our paperboy. It astounded me that he had no trace of a Scottish accent, that he could lose it so completely in such a short period of time. Apparently Mrs Guthrie has been indisposed, has recovered now but has to catch up with her studies. So she says.

My friend, Fran from the bank, and from Elgin, had also called off. But I knew that already, before Gloria. I had called in to see her, even although I was no longer a patron of her bank to ask if she were looking forward to the slides. I don't know what her excuse was but this is what she told me: "God, no! Who wants to see a lot of boring old slides of other people's holidays?"

It's probably a sentiment shared by a lot of people but I was a bit shocked at the vehemence with which she uttered it. In her defence, she had never met the Andrews. She had only been invited because of her Scottish roots and it was only thanks to me Gloria had heard of her, so why should she be interested in their holiday photographs? It's not even as if there will be any of her home town.

It is snowing slightly as we leave Lincoln and we find that Dave and Gloria have drafted in a friend called Glenda who has no Scottish blood in her veins but who has a Mallen streak, unless of course, it was lovingly crafted by her hairdresser. She makes a big fuss of Hélène. George is already fast asleep in his sleeping suit on Dave and Gloria's big, wide bed. It was past his bedtime, even before we set out. Normally Hélène would be abed by this time too but she is enlivened by these unusual events and the attention from Glenda. At eleven she's still awake and starting to girn with tiredness. We start making moves to go, then a couple of minutes later, there she is out for the count on the floor, just like Al did recently, only she's not snoring.

Young David provides the commentary to the slides, some of London but mainly of Edinburgh and Banff. To accompany them there is cheese and wine, Dave Senior's of course, only I am wiser now that I know of their potency and stick with the delicious blueberry as I also know it's not a good idea to mix his brews. Besides, I have plenty huckleberry at home.

This morning Tony Zweig had presented me with another half-gallon of his huckleberry, no doubt a result of my having praised his first batch to the skies. And his was not the only tribute either, for Brad Hughes presented me with a couple of antelope steaks along with a couple of bottles of his homebrewed beer. This is another cultural shock for me, for whilst primary school teachers in Scotland are in grave danger of suffering death by chocolate at Christmas and the end of the school year, I have yet to hear of secondary school pupils showering gifts upon their teachers. Unless of course, there is a conspiracy of silence for the sake of my paranoia.

Brad's mother is one of the dinner ladies who doles out my free meal as well as those of the students, who of course have to pay, though I presume some don't. I know now to wait in line as they say here, not to use teacher privilege to jump to the head of the queue, not since Matt had taken me aside and shown me the error of my ways - that we are all equal here even although I am master in the classroom, or try to be.

"Did you get the beer OK?" she asked, dropping her voice so only I could hear as she dumped my Sloppy Joe onto my plate. She makes it sound shady, like some sort of illegal deal. Which, in Matt's eyes, is not so far short of the truth.

He's very religious with a zealot's burning hatred of alcohol in any shape or form. At the fish-fry he had held at his house before the start of the school year, someone, wittingly, or unwittingly, I'm not quite sure, had taken along some cans of beer and he wasn't best pleased, to put it mildly, so if he ever got wind there was alcohol in the school and worse than that, it was made by a fourteen year-old, I can imagine death by strangulation as his Adam's apple choked him to death, or death by apoplexy as he burst a blood vessel. And of course it wouldn't have done much to raise me in his esteem either - yet another example of how I was corrupting young minds.

"Yes, thank you. Safe and sound. Mum's the word!" I replied softly, tipping her a wink.

I don't know if they use that expression in the United States but Brad's mom certainly understood the first part at least for I could her face visibly relax as if a storm cloud had passed harmlessly overhead without shedding its load. Had Brad been caught in possession, her job might well have been on the line.

In view of the risks and possible consequences involved, it's very touching that the boys should fête me in this way especially when you bear in mind I'm making them work harder than they have ever worked in their lives before. It's good to see that they don't think I'm all bad, perhaps even appreciate the exoticism of having a Scotsman for a teacher.

It is 1 am when we leave Dave and Gloria's. Who would have dreamt that we would have stayed so long and that looking at other people's slides could be so captivating, and the conversation that could ensue! Fran doesn't know what she missed. As for me, I am glad that I went easy on the wine. There has been more snow and it's snowing heavily now though there's not quite so much of it in town.

It's only a brief parting. We're going to see our hosts again tomorrow, or I should say later today for we are to be their guests at the Scottish Heritage Society's St Andrew's Day dinner. November 30th is the Saint's day and tomorrow is only the 18th but it's got to be held then because the fourth Thursday of November (usually the last) is Thanksgiving Day and you can't meddle with an American institution as great as that, no matter how great a saint you may be.

Chapter Thirty

*In which we experience some Norwegian culture, I view
a corpse, attend the St Andrew's Day dinner and have a
far from restful Sunday.*

This morning Iona has a bake sale at Supersave on
Brooks in aid of her Sweet Adelines singing group. I
am pressed into service as there had been a further
fall of snow during the night and she doesn't want to drive.
It's the first time I have met the ladies and I had envisaged a
bevy of glamorous young women (like Iona). But that's where
I was wrong - they come in all shapes, sizes and ages.

They are a friendly bunch and I am soon engaged in
conversation with some of them about all matters Scottish.
There is a free Dr Pepper or Coke just for showing up and
they have a donut [sic] machine and we get one of those free
too, just freshly made. There is nothing like a donut still warm
from the frying. I am very glad I went to the sale and of
course I am looking forward very much to their concert when
it comes.

The Scots are by no means the only ones proud of their
heritage and thanks to an advert in the *Missoulian,* after
lunch we set off to attend another sale this time given by the
Sons of Norway at the Nordic Pines Lodge, just out of Lolo. I
have a soft spot for Norway: the scenery, Grieg and Ibsen, in
that order, all appeal to me. Furthermore, we from the North-
East of Scotland have a close affinity with the country, being
neighbours across the sea. As a matter of fact, Grieg's great-
grandfather, Alexander Greig [sic], originally came from

Aberdeenshire, and those living in the Shetlands, the most northerly islands of the UK are actually nearer Oslo than London.

In fact, such is the extent of my appreciation of Norway, I think if I weren't Scots, I'd like to have been a Norwegian, given the choice. I also like the idea of being part of a small nation. As I have discovered, it bestows upon you a certain rarity value and with it a certain kudos.

No greater love hath a person for a country than he attempts to learn the language. I have been learning Norwegian and been lauded by the teacher for my accent. It was dead easy: all I had to do was speak with the intonation of my native dialect, the Doric, with its elongated back vowels. Incidentally, in the course of my studies, I was tickled pink to learn what the Norwegian word for what is generically known as a "Hoover" is. But before I tell you what it is, I need to explain that the Scots word for what lies thick in Marnie's basement, or Mrs Bates' residence if you prefer, what the rest of the world calls "dust" ⁄ is "stoor". You also need to remember that a vacuum cleaner works by sucking up the dust. Thus, in Norwegian, we arrive at "støvsuger", pronounced "stoorsooker". Isn't that a much more descriptive and colourful word than "Hoover"! It's what we call it in our house now anyway.

The sale turns out to be of Christmas decorations and we are much taken with some fir cones which have been dusted with "snow". Cheap, simple and very effective. We buy a few of those and notice that everyone seems to be ordering something called *lefse*. I may have learned some words and phrases in my Norwegian class but my vocabulary didn't extend to what that is, but when in Norway, so to speak...

"*Hvordan stor det til?*" I ask the lady taking the order, showing off. It's not often I get the chance to speak Norwegian these days.

"*Bare bra, takk,*" she replies with a smile. The fact that she's smiling should tell you it's not what it looks like. My question had not been: "Are you wearing a bra or are those sumptuous curves under your jumper naked as nature intended?" - it was merely the salutation, "How are you?" As far as her response is concerned, "bare" is pronounced with two syllables: a long "a" while the "e" is pronounced with an upward inflection. "*Bra*" is like our Scots "braw" which means "fine" as in the phrase made famous by Sir Harry Lauder - "it's a braw, bricht, moonlicht nicht the nicht" while "*Takk*" of course, just means "thanks".

And thankfully for me at least, that is the end of our conversation in Norwegian, for the next thing the lady says is not, "Where did you learn to speak Norwegian?" as I was half expecting but, "How many *lefse* would you like?"

"Er, em…" I don't like to admit I don't know what I've been queuing up for and thus destroy the illusion of my apparent proficiency in the language. "I'll have twenty," I say with a decisive tone, plucking the number out of the air.

Was that a look of surprise that flitted across her face before she wrote down my name and phone number? Reading it upside down, it's only as she puts the 20 in the column that I can make out that the most other people have ordered is five. But it's too late now.

"I'll give you a call when they are ready," she says with a sort of bemused smile, leaving me wondering just what kind of Norwegian delicacy it is I've ordered. I had better like them whatever they are.

The minute we get back the phone rings. I know for certain who that will be anyway.

"Hey, Dave, you gotta come over here an' see this deer that I shot," Al booms.

Oh, God no! There's nothing I'd like to see less. How can I tell my macho friend that I'd far rather it was still cavorting around the forest? I'll never become a real Montana man even if I stay here fifty years, that's for sure. I could never shoot an animal and I hate fishing but I admit I don't mind murdering mosquitoes. And of course I am a hypocrite too. Am I not going to be eating another antelope steak soon and what is an antelope if it's not some sort of deer? It's just I'd prefer not to think about, far less see, the gory details.

It's with a heavy heart therefore that I go over to view the kill. It's in the back of BIG AL with an ugly bullet hole in its neck with a massive bloodstain where its life's blood had run out - but that's not the worst. One side is rubbed raw. That's where it had been dragged out of the forest and along a track, by a pair of horses. At least it was dead by that time. I hoped it didn't take long to die as that wound looks much more than a pain in the neck.

Al's hunting partner is there too and Al takes a great deal of pride in introducing me as the world's leading expert in whisky, as he always does. For his part, the friend, whose name is Don, shows a great deal of interest in Scotland and as ever, I am happy to reprise my role as ambassador and the fount of knowledge on all things Scottish, not just on my national drink.

It seems I am also an ex-officio employee of the Scottish Tourist Board as Don says it sounds really "neat" and he'd like to pay a visit next summer. Naturally I have omitted to mention that scourge of the tourist industry in Scotland, the midge, which they call "no-see-ums" here. They're impossible to kill as they are so small. At least mosquitoes have the benefit of being big enough to squash.

Naturally this conversation takes place at the bar in the kitchen. This time it's vodka that's being lavishly sloshed into our glasses. I'm grateful for that as it means I don't have to try and reinvent my celebrated performance on whisky-tasting which gave Al his ill-founded opinion of me as an expert on such matters.

After only two glasses I manage to make my excuses, jokingly saying Iona will kill me if I don't get back soon. To my surprise Al doth not protest as much as usual. Maybe he wants to get started on a hatchet job of his own.

"Don't forget to remind Rob he's babysitting for us tonight. We're going to the St Andrew's Day dinner."

It's only for George as Hélène is going to be overnighting in Lolo at Sandi's, with Amy. Whilst it is good that Hélène should have someone her own age to play with, we are a tad apprehensive about how she'll manage should she miss her "mommy" during the night as they will not be able to contact us. She has never been separated from us all night before. It might have been better, for the first time, if we were standing by to take her back home if necessary…

* * *

I'm wearing my kilt, dressed to kill, ready to go, when Dave and Gloria arrive to pick us up. Iona has bought some tartan to wear as a sash over her dress. We may be ready but we can't go yet as Rob has not turned up. Despite the snow and my bare knees, I decide it would be just as quick and probably more effective to go over to his house than summon him by phone. It transpires that Al had forgotten to remind him and Rob had forgotten all about it too, so it's just as well he didn't have a heavy date on.

As well as Dave and Gloria's two boys, we are accompanied by a lady of a certain age who goes to their church. She's a spinster who has missed out on marriage by having to look after her aged father, now 92, and who has not died yet through a whole succession of winters. He originally hails from Carron, Scotland, incredibly only about five miles away from where we live. I can tell she did not miss marriage through choice, is more of a married woman manqué, as the first thing she says to me is, "What you got under your kilt there Dave, eh?" followed by a raucous cackling laugh.

"Nothing is worn under the kilt," I respond in the same witty manner. "Everything is in perfect working order."

She likes that a lot. It must mean she's never heard the old chestnut before.

Our destination is Andre's Frontier Lounge, which I happen to know, is a swanky sort of a joint, the sort of place whose threshold I would normally never dream of stepping over. I order a steak Neptune which I've never heard of before and which turns out to be a steak with a massive skewered prawn stuck on the top. I might have guessed there was something fishy about it.

A piper is in attendance. Used in battle to rally the troops, the skirl of the pipes is also intended to put the fear of the devil into the enemy. I don't know what effect it has on the company here in this low-ceilinged room but if their ears are anything like mine, they must be dirling. The pipes are best heard in the open air and preferably from a glen away.

And just when I thought it could not get any worse, horror of horrors, it does. After deaving us with a few tunes in which it's impossible to make any conversation, the piper stops and asks me through the microphone if there is any particular tune I'd like to hear. Why pick on me? How embarrassing! Not so much that I should be chosen out of everyone here for this special privilege but embarrassing simply because I can't think of a single one, so unknowledgeable am I about Scottish music. I could have asked for *The Northern Lights of Old Aberdeen,* but is that a piping tune? Or *The Skye Boat Song,* which I rather like, but is it a tune that you can play on the pipes, even if it might be murdered in the process? I just daren't run the risk of making an enormous fool of myself in front of everyone by requesting either of them in case they are not. So what happened to the expert on all matters Scottish that I was so proudly congratulating myself on being?

"Oh! Oh! Er, erm, just anything you would like to play yourself... One of your favourites would be just fine with me. Thanks."

I hope I got away with it, especially those not close enough to see my blushes. You always think of the best answers in tranquillity after the panic has gone and what I should have said was ‑ no, not *Silence is Golden* ‑ that would have been extremely rude and undiplomatic but, "I'll let my wife answer that question" which, on reflection, might not have been such a smart answer after all if she couldn't think of one either and when she got me home, gave me a few words of advice about never humiliating her in public like that again.

Dave tells me this honour has been accorded because we are special guests. The Scottish Heritage Society has only been in existence for three years and the word has apparently spread that we are gracing it with our presence ‑ the first native Scots ever to have attended a St Andrew's Day Dinner here in Missoula, Montana. Isn't that an incredible thing!

After the meal young David gets up and says a few words before proposing a toast to "St Andrew - the greatest Scotsmen who ever lived". I catch Iona's eye as we stand to raise our glasses to the saint, newly elevated to the ranks of one of the most inventive and greatest nations in the history of the planet. Somehow we manage to swallow the toast without spluttering or choking and thus giving the game away.

I thought everyone knew, as I learned by rote in Sunday school: "Simon, called Peter, and Andrew his brother" - by profession a fisherman on the Sea of Galilee and promoted by Jesus to be a "fisher of men". And if he ever set foot on the shores of what is now Scotland, I'd be mightily surprised. Travel wasn't so easy in those days. I wonder how many other people here assume the same thing as young David - that Andrew must have been a Scot, just because we adopted him as our patron saint. It wouldn't surprise me if they did.

After that I am called upon, unexpectedly, to say a few words. Diplomatically I do not set them right about St Andrew but eulogise on how wonderful it is to see so many people here and how delighted I am to see their interest in their Scottish heritage. I know it's not a very good speech apart from having the virtue of brevity. I could have turned it into a party piece if only Dave had warned me. Iona is always telling me I like the sound of my own voice and this would have been a perfect opportunity to let more people hear it instead of my usual captive audience of students. I could have told some jokes, like the one about nothing being worn under the kilt since it was so well received earlier and probably the first time the majority of people here had been exposed to it also.

After the meal, the dancing, as I feared might happen, but fortunately, there are so many people who wish to engage me in conversation with questions about Scotland, that I am kept too busy jawing to engage in the jiggin' - and I make sure I am.

Dave very generously picks up the tab for all of us. He says no thanks are necessary; it is his honour and the Society's to be graced with such distinguished company as ours. I've never felt so exalted since we were the guests of the British Embassy in Washington D.C.

Giant snowflakes are tumbling from the skies, a moment white then gone forever as the windscreen wipers sweep them aside. But on the ground, they lie deep and crisp and even.

* * *

"C'mon, kids, let's go outside and build a snowman."

It's Sunday morning. Hélène is safely restored to us and both she and Sandi assure us she had a whale of a time. Iona is at church and I am looking after the kids as usual. It's no hardship for me to miss church. Going to church was another of the things I was made to do as a boy and it put me off for life. Moral: parents should think carefully before making their kids do what they think is best for them.

I get them all suited up in their warmest gear and out we go to the back garden where the virgin snow is two feet deep or more, in other words, nearly up to George's waist.

"Let's build a snowman!"

But then I get a big surprise. Instead of forming a clump like it does in Scotland, this snow just tumbles from my gloves like confetti. It is so dry, it just won't pack, what I believe skiers call "powder snow" and very popular with them which is why, during the winter, Montana is a very popular destination for skiers and why there are several slopes hereabouts. And another thing, since the air is so dry too, it's not nearly as cold outside as it looks or the thermometer tells you.

This truth is borne home to me as I begin digging a path out the front door to where it meets the path that runs parallel to the street. This path I must keep clear by city by-law. If I don't and should anyone slip and fall and, God forbid, break a bone, then I could be sued. There's nothing like digging to keep yourself out of trouble.

It's warm work and I'm soon stripped down to my T-shirt, despite the thermometer registering 8° F - that's minus 13 C. And when I've finished doing that, I create a path out the back door to the back gate as that is the way I take the bike out to go to school.

The hunt for the shovel in Mrs Bates' demesne brought to light an axe, a much heavier sort of implement than I have been using so far (and far better removed out of her sight), so by way of a bit of light relief, after the path is dug, I set about the splitting of some logs, for the burning of, not that I need any fire to keep me warm at present, thank you very much.

I hope it's not going to be a bad winter…

Chapter Thirty-one

In which I see how snow is cleared Missoula-style, there is a crisis at school and monsters rear their ugly heads.

"Well, good mornin', Mr. A! Did you walk across the bridge?"

As usual, Steve is burning with energy and ready to face the day while, as usual, I had had to drag myself out of bed and am ready for a lie down, worn out by this morning's earlier start and exertion due to the snow.

I dare not meet his eyes and like George Washington, I cannot tell a lie either.

It was hard work cycling through the snow. The hard-packed, where the cars have been, is much easier. I chose the path of least resistance and I would bet my last dollar that most other people would have done the same. Anyway, I don't have the puff for the untrodden powdery stuff and that's what I tell Blake and Steve.

Blake has a habit of swinging his right fist into the palm of his left, making it swing like a pendulum. All of a sudden the pendulum stops, while, for his part, Steve's eyes are out on stalks above the bristling moustache. Both shake their heads in wonderment and disbelief that anyone could be so stupid to disregard their sage advices, like Tam O' Shanter did his wife Kate's.

"Boy, you carry on doin' that an' you're a dead man, laddie!" says Steve.

"He's right," says Blake and without any shadow of a doubt, I know he's being deadly serious for once.

I *was* full of good intentions but everyone knows what the road to hell is paved with. Only my road will be paved with hard-packed snow if I am struck by a two-ton truck. And I have no illusions that's where I'll end up since I am by no means as saintly as Andrew.

A huge bank of snow had been piled along the centre of the bridge, effectively cutting the width of the road in half. I am not the complete idiot that Blake and Steve take me for however. A quick look over my shoulder told me the nearest vehicle was some way behind me. I reckoned if I put my head down and pedalled like all hell let loose, I might make it across before it caught up with me. I didn't but it didn't hit me either.

Some instinct tells me not to mention that plan or to point out that I'm just as likely to be mown down by a two-ton truck while pushing the bike as riding it - indeed, I would be over the bridge and out of danger much, much sooner if I stayed in the saddle. But I think they would just tell me not to be so stupid and I should push it through the knee-deep snow on what they call the "sidewalk". No well-worn track there: very few people here walk any further than necessary from where they have parked their car. Having said that, you see scores of people jogging. But not in the snow of course.

As soon as I go into my room I am greeted by an icy blast. The custodian has left one of the windows open, overnight, by the looks of it, for snow has blown in and formed a drift at the back of the room. The thermometer says it's 40 F and all the kids complain it's too cold to hold a pencil or do any work at all as they can't think of anything except how freezing it is. I get the same complaint from each class. But then of course, they are dressed in jeans and T-shirts just as they were in the summer, making no allowance at all for the wintry conditions. They are hothouse plants, used to a room temperature of twice what it is now. No wonder they find it such a monumental effort to do any work, most of them collapsed over their desks with their heads pillowed on their non-writing arm. I have long since given up the battle of telling them to sit up straight.

At break time I am lucky to see a demonstration of snow-clearing Missoula style. It's a sight I'll never see in Scotland. For one thing our snow is too wet and secondly our streets are not nearly wide enough. Here, the snow is blown into a truck running alongside the blower, like a combine harvester on the prairies and when it's full, it dumps the snow along the middle of the road. So that's how that bank of snow on the bridge got there!

I wish I had brought my camera, not just to record that and the snowdrift in my room, but also at lunchtime, Matt gussied up in a white apron and white forage cap as he served ice cream in the dining hall. This shows he's a man of the people, not too proud to serve those beneath him, which is everybody as he is the principal. I can't help feel however, he loses more respect than he gains, since he looks not in the least like a professional but the very image of an Italian ice cream vendor with his little cart, selling his wares at a street corner.

For my part, I serve two of my students with Iona's shortbread as a quid pro quo for the wine, beer and antelope steaks.

* * *

I hope Steve and Blake are proud of me. I didn't just walk over the bridge this morning but walked the whole way to school also. I reckon I would have had to push the bike most of the way, never mind just over the bridge. Walking takes a lot less effort though it does mean it takes a greater-than-ever effort to haul myself out of bed so much earlier. Today I have my camera, but typically, the gods have arranged it so the snow blower does not show up and Matt is soberly attired in his green suit behind his desk like a real principal.

In order not to waste the extra energy expended by the carrying of the camera, I ask Steve and Blake to stage the roughing up of a couple of boys which they do from time to time, whenever the mood takes them. When I saw this display for the first time, I couldn't believe my eyes and no-one back home would believe it either unless I have photographic evidence. They call it "fun". If I tried the same thing with any of my pupils, apart from my ending up second best in this unprovoked encounter, they would call it "assault" and they would be right.

"C'mere, Tony," says Blake and suspecting nothing, Tony (of the huckleberry wine) does as bidden and the next minute Blake has him in a grip and the minute after that, he is writhing about on the floor, begging for mercy as Blake kneels beside him tickling him to death. Meanwhile, Steve has seized another victim and has pinned him down, kneeling on his biceps, his bum an inch above his face, all the better to tickle him about the waist.

Being tickled is a form of torture. It's a wonder the Spanish Inquisition never adopted it. Or maybe they stopped it when they saw the victims were laughing, thinking they were having too much of a good time. Red-faced with exertion, tucking their shirts into their trousers, the students go to their class and after this entertainment, lessons can begin. I wonder what Matt would have made of it if he had happened to come along just then. And if Blake and Steve had explained they were beating up the kids so I could photograph it for the folks back home, I could imagine him having another apoplectic fit and demanding the film be destroyed. Meanwhile his opinion of me would plunge to new depths.

I hope the photos turn out all right. If not, I'm going to have to ask them to stage it again.

* * *

After school Art gives me a much appreciated lift to Sam's and but for this it's possible I would have missed the scandal that is rocking the lower school. Not a whisper of it had reached me in the exalted heights of the top floor. Whether it reached the ears of Steve, Blake and Nat I couldn't say. If it did, they did not mention it in front of me. Perhaps it smacked too much of washing dirty linen in front of a foreigner. Art and Sam on the middle floor have no such inhibitions however.

We are sitting drinking beer in the basement before a roaring log fire in the stove Sam had built himself in a metalwork class. It is one of life's great pleasures to sit by a fire, "bleezin' finely, wi reamin' swats that drank divinely" as Tam O' Shanter would testify, especially if the craic is good, which it is.

It seems that Molly Sanderson, a Title 1 probationary teacher, is being transferred to another school. Title 1 is designed to support kids from poorer backgrounds and who also tend to be less academic, what we call "remedial". She is a good friend of Kathy Kuhn's, George's teacher. In fact, I would call her a "very good friend indeed" as, like Tweedledum and Tweedledee, you never see them apart. According to Art, after her divorce, Matt gave her a hard time though what that had to do with anything, he doesn't say and I don't like to ask.

Being a support teacher meant Molly worked in conjunction with the other teachers and two had filed complaints against her, saying they didn't like the way she was teaching their kids. One was Ms Monk, the one who patrolled the corridors when Matt was at a meeting of principals in Great Falls and who thus had delayed our Canada adventure. The other was Martha Mason, the 3rd Grade teacher who had asked me if we had Coca-Cola in Scotland.

Apparently Ms Monk has the other teachers down in the bowels of the school in the most absolute state of fear and terror and obviously has the ear of Matt. No matter what Molly did, Ms Monk found something to complain about and Matt was out to get her fired.

"Can he do that?" I ask, aghast.

"Sure," says Art. "It would have to involve the superintendent an' the school board, but if he's out to get you he's got some clout as he is considered a big wheel amongst the other principals."

"Is he really?" I ask surprised.

He always struck me as being a bit shy and diffident, scared to make a decision in case it brought about a hostile and angry response, forcing him into having to defend it which I could see him doing with a great deal of bluster and fluster. I can't really see him being *primus inter pares* but what I *could* see was that forced to take sides between Molly and Ms Monk, he would be far more scared of her than Molly, just like he was more scared of the parents who complained about me than me - especially if they happened to have some influence on the school board, as indeed one of them had.

Anyway, Molly is off to pastures new which I imagine will be a great relief to her; Misses Monk and Mason will be glad to see the back of her and Matt will be thankful not to have his ear bent any more. So everyone is happy. Molly is going to be replaced by an aide, so I suppose if there are any losers in this affair, it will be the kids who have lost a qualified teacher, though I suppose their loss is the other school's gain.

That subject exhausted, I tell Art and Sam about Blake and Steve tickling the kids.

"You know what I'd like to do?" I ask, ploughing on without waiting for an answer. "I'd really like to visit some other schools, for comparison's sake, to broaden the exchange experience." What I really want to find out is if the curriculum is as undemanding as in Emerson; if the kids are as lazy and if the teachers treat them with the same informality as Blake and Steve, though actually I think I already know the answer to that one.

"Forget it, David," says Sam, shaking his dead. "Matt will never agree to it. He'd be scared you'd tell tales outta school."

"Such as?"

"Like how he never supported you against Mrs De Bone an' sent Ray Taylor's mom out to get you in the park instead of defusin' her. He's a dildo."

"I'll drink to that," says Art, taking a swig from his Budweiser.

At the risk of sounding too saintly I wouldn't have mentioned those incidents to any school I visited as it's not likely that the subject would have come up but on the other hand, I might have mentioned, as the subject of my family would have been pretty likely to have done, that he was instrumental in getting George into Kathy's class. I'll always be grateful to him for that and in my eyes at least, he is not all bad.

However, in the interest of education and in the spirit of the exchange, I feel it is incumbent upon me to look further into the matter of seeing another school even if it does put me on a collision course with Matt...

* * *

It's a double celebration. First of all it is Molly's leaving do and Iona has been busy baking shortbread again as a leaving present. Secondly, it is Thanksgiving Day tomorrow and there is no school, or on Monday either. Nice work if you can get it. We've only been back a week from the trip to Canada and what is Thanksgiving but a practice for Christmas which will be coming up in four weeks' time? Who would be a turkey in the USA, with that double whammy? It's bad enough being one in the UK, not to mention lots of other countries where this latter-day feast of Saturnalia is celebrated.

The plan is to meet at The Depot for Happy Hour but when Sam, Art and I get there, we find we are too early, so we go to The Silver Dollar to while away the time as it *is* Happy Hour there. And there's another great thing about this wonderful institution: the management of these establishments can't tell the time. It normally lasts for twice as long as the hour and different bars have different Happy Hours, so with a bit of planning, you can drink for hours for half the price, to say nothing of gorging on tasty snacks for free. What a country!

The Silver Dollar is a rough sort of joint, the sort of place that my colleagues and I in Scotland frequent in our infrequent nights out and after a couple of beers we move upmarket to The Depot where we are joined by Molly, Kathy and Sally, a mutual friend of theirs. Because we are six, a pitcher of beer is ordered. Along with the Happy Hour aforesaid and free food accompaniment, it's another great American idea that I had first come across in Washington DC during our week's-long orientation courses. Saves a lot of endless trips to the bar and waiting to be served.

The conversation naturally turns to Matt about whom less than complimentary things are said. You would hardly call it a meeting of his fan club, or Ms Monks' either, for that matter. I just sit and listen since I have nothing to contribute. Later on we are joined by Mike, Molly's supervisor, thanks to whose intervention she was given a transfer instead of being fired. He brings a friend, Pete, who works in the admin building.

"Do *you* believe, Dave?" Pete asks.

It's not what you might think. Pete is not a proselytising evangelist and I've met a few of them in my time, I can assure you. We had got round to talking about the "Lock" Ness Monster as he calls it.

"Loch," I corrected him, as if clearing my throat, to emphasise the point. If we had been in the Silver Dollar it might have been seen as preparatory to making a deposit in a spittoon, had it extended to such refinements.

"Lock?" he thought he was repeating what I had said.

"No, *loch*. Not "lock". *Loch* Ness."

"Lock Ness?"

Good grief! What's the use? He can't help it. The English, our southern neighbours, can't pronounce it properly either. It's one of the tests if you want to tell a true Scotsman from a Sassenach. I bet our patron saint couldn't have done it either. But hang on a minute, maybe he could. Almost certainly he spoke Aramaic, a language spoken around the Sea of Galilee where, as you know, he was a fisherman, and for all I know, it might have so many deeply brought-up-from-the-depth-of-the-lungs "ch" sounds it should have been obligatory to carry a spittoon on your person, like the lady in the nursery rhyme who had music wherever she went on account of the bells on her toes.

"Well, Pete," I tell him, "a lot of people do and a lot of people don't."

He may not be a religious zealot, but Pete has the look of a believer about him and I have a feeling if I tell him what I really believe, namely that the monster is a lot of hooey, he will take that as coming from the mouth of God, since lack of knowledge about piping music apart, I am the resident expert on Scotland, certainly in present company, and it will ruin his day. And yet I cannot tell a lie, as you know, and so I don't tell him the most conclusive and damning proof of all, namely that even, by some miracle, had some dinosaurs survived the asteroid holocaust, there is no way anything could have survived the last ice age, the time when the glaciers were actually carving out Nessie's home as a matter of fact. Instead this is what I tell him.

"Did you know, Pete, that Loch Ness is the biggest loch in the UK in terms of volume and is so long and deep that all the rivers and lakes of England and Wales (that's what they are called down there) could be poured into it with room to spare?"

I can see he's impressed. "What's more," I add, "the water is so murky, it *could* be home to some prehistoric creature such as a plesiosaur. It's got a long neck like Nessie is said to have."

I stop to let Pete drink that in. "Of course there would have to be more than one," I continue. "They would *have* to be breeding after all this time, since the extinction of the dinosaurs, I mean. As well as the long neck, Nessie is supposed to have humps but actually they might be young ones, not Nessie herself. Or it might be some sort of giant serpent. Who knows?"

Pete seems to be pondering the possibilities. The glint in his eye inclines me to believe he is buoyed up by the thought that not only might there be one monster in there but a whole family of the blighters.

"We've got our own monster here you know, Bigfoot or Sasquatch. You heard of that?"

Indeed I have, a monster ape supposed to inhabit the forests of Montana, Idaho, Washington and Oregon, even forests as far south as Northern California. I have seen how vast just one forest in Montana is, having been lost with Iona and the kids in it and I was never more scared in my life. I had visions of dying there and our bodies never being found, having been devoured by bears or mountain lions, though the lunatic fringe might prefer to believe we had been abducted by aliens. All the searchers would have found, near the Skalkaho Pass in the Bitterroot National Forest, would have been the abandoned Big Blue Mean Machine, silent testimony that we had once been there.

"Do *you* believe in Bigfoot?" I respond. One good question deserves another.

"Sure! They've found footprints an' he's even been caught on film."

Yes, I knew that too and I also know that most people regard them with scepticism but Pete goes on to cite further sightings as evidence and I listen gravely and don't mention the word "hoax" even once.

After a while the group gravitates nearer the fire. As I said earlier, there is nothing like drinking beer in front of a roaring fire, and by chance I fall into conversation with a young lady called Jerry who happens to be a teacher of Social Studies at Hellgate Elementary which is up by the airport somewhere. I tell her of my desire to see another school and she says she'll ask if the Language Arts teacher would be interested in swapping with me for a day.

But there's a snag. Apart from any objection that Matt may have, it's not in our district and that may provide him with sufficient wriggle room to veto it. But I mustn't get too far ahead of myself - first I have to wait for the phone call.

Chapter Thirty-two

*In which we experience the great American institution
of Thanksgiving Day.*

American readers of course, need no history lessons from me as to how the tradition of Thanksgiving Day came about in the United States, though readers in the UK might only have a hazy notion that it has something to do with the *Mayflower* and Pilgrims and Indians. For those who don't know the details let me (briefly) flesh out the bones.

A hard winter they had of it, the Pilgrims, that first autumn and winter of 1620-21, many of them dying of disease. On the other hand they had an enormous stroke of good fortune. In the sort of coincidence which, if you read it in a novel, you would dismiss as too fantastical, they met an Indian, or should I say, "Native American" called Tisquantum (Squanto for short), who could speak English and who acted as an interpreter for the Pilgrims and the local tribes. What were the chances of that!

A member of the Pawtuxtet tribe, Squanto had been abducted by that early explorer and colonist, John Smith (whom many people might possibly know better as the lover of Pocahontas), and sold into slavery. Somehow he managed to escape and get himself back to his native shores ⸗ no mean feat, almost the equivalent, in those days, of getting back from the moon. He showed the Pilgrims how to plant corn (maize) and squash (marrow) and where best to fish and which plants were poisonous. In the November of 1621, the Pilgrims invited the Wampanoag tribe to share with them the fruits of their first successful harvest, which was a very nice quid pro quo indeed. But unfortunately as more and more white settlers arrived with their insatiable desire for land, relations became less friendly.

I don't have to tell anyone how it ended.

That was the start of Thanksgiving in the American tradition but of course, in Christian Europe, people had been giving thanks to God for a successful harvest for centuries, as had the pagan worshippers long before them. However, to the best of my knowledge, it's only the Americans who make such a big song and dance about it with the possible exception of their cousins on the other side of the 49th parallel who hold a similar celebration in October, more sensibly closer to harvest and further away from Christmas. Incidentally, in the US, Thanksgiving Day tended, like Easter, to be a bit of a moveable feast being held on different dates in different states, but on Boxing Day 1941, Congress fixed the date as the fourth Thursday in November (as I mentioned earlier, you may remember).

But before we set off to experience this extravaganza at John and Carolyn's, there is much clearing of snow from the paths to be done, and no sooner have I done that when Terri and Al drop by to wish us the compliments of the season. They know we've been invited elsewhere and I wouldn't mind betting my last cent they're disappointed we are not going to be spending it with them. I would also stake my life that Iona is immensely glad we are not. It's sure to be pandemonium with God knows how many people and kids running around long after we would prefer ours to be in bed. It will be much more relaxed at John and Carolyn's. I'm not sure how much there will be to drink but half as much as Al plies me with will be more than a sufficiency and twice as good as far as Iona is concerned.

Naturally I offer Al a beer the second he steps over the threshold. It's the etiquette, like offering visitors a cup of tea back home. He would expect no less and probably hopes for more, like a few drams of whisky, though it is a bit early in the day for me to start on the hard stuff, though the beer is welcome after the exertion of shovelling all that snow.

It's a funny thing, but over here Al is a different person altogether. He picks George up and swings him about by his arms to his giggling delight. Normally, in his own pad, Al never pays him any attention at all. I suppose there are other things to occupy his attention.

"You gotta come over an' have a Thanksgiving drink, Dave," says Al as they leave. They haven't stayed long.

I thought that's what we had been doing but Al means a proper drink and he is not an easy person to say no to. But first I need to have a shower and don my kilt as it is such a special occasion. This takes a bit of time, during which, if the sun is not yet over the yardarm exactly, it has crept considerably nearer it. Iona gives me one of her Gorgon looks as I leave.

"You haven't got long."

"I know." I also know if I leave it much longer the phone will ring and it will be Al: "Hey, Dave, where ya' bin, for Chris' sake?"

I can't keep up with him, the speed with which he pours out his three-finger measures and the commensurate speed with which he dispatches them, but it's impossible to take my leave without my first refill. As a result, it is a mellow sort of fellow who arrives at the Snivelys' house to find others are expected but we are the first.

Next to arrive are Russ and Linda. He's a dentist, like John, and also new to Missoula. She comes from Chicago and is only here to see how she likes it. I wouldn't have thought that would have posed much of a dilemma, having to make a choice between the Windy City and the Garden City.

I'm not a great fan of big cities it has to be said: all those crowds and all that pollution hardly compensated for by the theatres, cinemas and art galleries of which I was never a great patron, even before the kids came along. But perhaps Linda is, in which case she may be pleasantly surprised to discover Missoula is very far from being a cultural desert. Being a city lover, it's unlikely she's much of an outdoor type. But you never know, the fresh mountain air filling her lungs might turn her into a convert. Indeed, it's for the great outdoors and the sporting life that many non-natives of Montana told me was the reason they moved here, albeit that by "sporting", the majority mean hunting and fishing. As you know neither hold the least attraction for me. All the same I'd far rather live in Missoula than Chicago.

Iona gives voice to that very thought.

"Have you ever been to Chicago?" responds Linda icily.

"Well, no," Iona is forced to admit, blushing furiously.

I am very glad indeed that it wasn't me who said it. For her part, Linda deems it unnecessary to say anything further, such as extolling the virtues of the city, which is a pity as it would have given Iona a chance to say how misguided she had been and she could now see what a wonderful place it was. Instead there is an awkward silence in which I imagine Iona feels about two inches tall.

The other couple are Dave and Janine who are both very musical and come with their instruments, prepared to entertain us. He has an acoustic guitar while she has a dulcimer, of all things. I've never come across such a thing before, at least face to face, the closest being the "damsel with a dulcimer" in Coleridge's visionary poem or fragment rather, *Kubla Khan*. Perhaps it's because of that association with the poem, but the word "dulcimer" conjures up for me an ethereal, other-worldly sort of image, the sort of instrument that the Fairy Queen's attendants might play to her as she brushes her long, golden hair. But it's only me being a romantic: a dulcimer is actually a sort of portable piano, the strings over the sounding box being hit by a hammer instead of being plucked like a zither to which it bears a resemblance.

We are down in the basement and what a difference to the one in the house from *Psycho* that Mrs Bates inhabits! Here three walls are panelled with wood while the fourth has a stone fireplace. There is a sofa and armchairs and a big desk and shelves and shelves of books. And if you don't feel like reading, there's a TV you could watch, in colour.

It's a whole other nether world, a cosy world far removed from the world above where a storm might huff and puff and do its worst but unless you happened to glance at the scarcely noticeable two little windows near the ceiling (but at ground level outside), you wouldn't have the faintest idea of the conditions outside. If you were chionophobic, like Iona, you could easily hibernate down here until the snows had gone.

It's time for the meal, upstairs, in the dining room. There is turkey of course, just as there was at the very first Thanksgiving. We know this because the governor of the colony, William Bradford, sent out a fowling party and since wild turkey (from whom our domesticated bird is descended) was plentiful, it is almost certain that they laid their lives down for the banquet along with other birds such as geese and ducks. One thing they also had which we are not having today, was venison ⁄ because it is also documented that the Wampanoag contributed five deer. And so it came about that the first Thanksgiving was also the first potluck.

Along with the turkey we have celery, sage and onion stuffing and cranberry sauce and potatoes ⁄ so far so good (and it is good) just like our own Christmas dinner, only the potatoes are not roasted but mashed and there is nothing I like better than a roast potato. There is also another type of potato, the sweet potato or yam, which I had heard of but never seen before, let alone tasted. They were coated in brown sugar and baked in the oven.

This is turning into a day of discoveries ⁄ a dulcimer and now this. Time will tell what I make of the dulcimer but I must admit I don't care for the yam very much ⁄ too sweet by half for me as I find this mixture of the sweet and the savoury rather a strange combination. Never more bizarre when, at school, to my amazement and disbelief, I saw Steve cut a slice of tinned peach in half with his fork (from a pocket on the tray, like a soldier's mess tray) then scoop up a forkful of Sloppy Joe and put them both in his mouth *together.* I thought this such a remarkable sight that I couldn't wait to get back and say to Iona, "You'll never guess what I saw today!" And even stranger to relate, he wasn't the only one, just the first ⁄ they all did it, Steve, Nat and Blake!

For sweet, what I called once upon a boyhood, "pudding", there is pumpkin pie with whipped cream, another great American institution which I'd tasted for the first time at Hallowe'en and I confess I didn't rate very highly. I apologetically refuse both on the grounds of being replete. It's the absolute truth and I'm not just saying that because I am not a sweet person.

And if I had been worried about not being wined in the style to which I am accustomed by Al, I needn't have been. There was wine with the meal, even if John politely waited until we had drained our glasses before filling them up again, unlike Al who is forever topping you up, like the bottomless cup of coffee they have here. Maybe that's where Al got the idea, come to think of it, but I doubt it. I think he thought of it all by himself.

Before the meal there was an aperitif to get those of us who needed it in a merry mood. It's hot cider with a dash of whisky or whiskey: from my land or the one to the north of here, take your pick. I didn't see the cider before it was heated and therefore have no idea what alcohol percentage it has but I've never seen a cider yet that was not stronger than your average beer, and as long as it was not brought to the boil which would have resulted in the angels getting a share through evaporation, that would pack a punch in itself, never mind the punch it becomes after the whisky or whiskey is added.

I may not have seen the cider but I can see the choices of whisk(e)y on offer. Had it been a malt, I would never have put that in the cider as that would have been sacrilege, but since it's only a blend, that's what I choose, the Scotch. Iona, of course, not being a whisky person, the very smell of it enough to make her boak, elects to have neat cider. That doesn't surprise me in the least but I am shocked to see that everyone else chooses the Canadian whiskey. But on reflection I am mollified by the thought that they might regard even a blended whisky as too sacred for the sacrifice of being polluted by another product.

I make it sound as if there were no children there, but of course, there are ⁃ ours. John and Carolyn haven't any and can't, but are looking into adoption. It's nice of us to let them practice on George and Hélène as they have much to learn when it comes to the matter of kids. It's something you learn on the job, but it's good to have a demonstration of what they are letting themselves in for. They have a very nice house. Unusually for Missoula it has a brick façade and they are justifiably proud of it but once the kids arrive, they will have no hope of keeping it in the pristine shape to which it is accustomed.

If Iona felt uncomfortable at the Chicago solecism, we both feel embarrassed at the sight of Carolyn clearing up the crumbs and other detritus that the kids drop on the floor. And here's another thing they need to learn - it's just impossible to keep a just-turned three-year old sitting quiet at the table whilst the adults quaff wine and bore on about things miles over their heads, so we allow Hélène to get down from the table.

Enjoying her new freedom, Hélène sets off to explore her new environment and strays into the adjacent kitchen, which typical of American homes, does not have a door to separate it from the dining room. The moment she crosses the border, Hélène must have been amazed to find herself suddenly swept up and plonked on Carolyn's knee.

"Listen, honey, I'd prefer you not to go in the kitchen, OK?"

How much of that Hélène understands I don't know, but Iona and I do and from that moment on we live on our nerves, on the qui vive for anything that the kids might do which might cause offence to our hosts. It gets worse when we move back to the basement where we are entertained by singing to the tune of the dulcimer and the guitar.

It makes no difference to George of course, who can't hear a thing, but it's not the sort of music that is ever going to make Number One on a three-year-old's hit parade. She just won't sit quietly and listen appreciatively but will wriggle on Iona's lap and to keep her from girning and struggling, Iona has to let her go. In the course of her travels which we follow anxiously with our eyes (and which I am sure Carolyn follows even more keenly), Hélène happens to stand on a book of music which the musicians have discarded. Well, if you will leave books lying about on the floor, what else do you expect when a three-year-old is tottering about?

"Don't stand on the book, darling," Iona says, picking her up.

"Can I walk this way, Mummy?" Hélène asks a little later.

That's because we have both been saying, "Don't do this" and "Don't do that" so often and getting up to stop her touching something or other, that the wee soul doesn't know what she *is* allowed to do. It began well enough with Hélène and I playing *Mousetrap* (which Carolyn had produced) but she had long since lost interest in that as well as the toys we had brought to keep both George and her entertained. And of course trying to read one of their books to them is impossible because of the concert.

At last it is the kids' bedtime which probably comes as great a relief to Carolyn as it does to us. I won't be around to see it when they get their kids (if they do) but I hope she remembers this Thanksgiving Day when hers are the age ours are now. Unless of course, after this display, they change their minds.

In our mind, both kids were actually very well behaved, considering. Ironically, had we gone to Al and

Terri's, Hélène would have been able to play with Amy, wandered at will and nobody would have bothered what she was up to as long as she didn't fall into the fire. She would have had a much better time and Iona, especially, would have done too, not having to live on her nerves all the time, keeping an eye on Hélène. Or maybe it would have been other nerves that were tested, watching Al pour drinks into me every five minutes.

Sometimes the gods arrange it so you just can't win. They tend to like to have the last laugh.

Chapter Thirty-three

In which we take our driving tests and entertain the
faculty - with disastrous results.

I spend the morning boning up on the Montana Highway
Code and when I think I know it backwards, I drive the
Big Blue Mean Machine up to the County Court House
and park on the street right outside the entrance. I have come
to sit my driving test. No appointment necessary: just turn up.
Simple as that. Before the hour is out I hope to be the proud
possessor of a Montana Driving Licence which will make it a
whole lot easier when we buy something at the supermarket.

When I sat my test in Scotland more than a decade ago,
I had to apply for it when I *thought* I could pass it as it took
weeks and weeks before you were given an appointment.
When I finally got a date, the earliest appointment was in a
town where I had never driven before. I could have, had I
been prepared to wait longer, got the small town of Keith
where I could just about have gone round the route blindfold.
But I was impatient to get my licence, borrow my father's car
and go trapping for girls, as living out in the boondocks as I
was, I was severely restricted in this hormone-induced
activity. It was my undoing. Uniquely in Banffshire, Buckie
has a dual carriageway, something I was unfamiliar with as a
driver (though I should have been more familiar with it from
my study of the Highway Code) and when the tester asked
me to turn right, I did not get into the right lane quickly
enough and failed. I also failed to get another test until I had

left home. I passed that time, but now I did not have access to a car, according to the gods' immortal plan.

In the Court House I begin by filling in a form and then am taken to a machine for an eye test, just like at the opticians. You get the answer straight away. Pass. Next two sheets of paper on which are printed ten questions. Multiple choice with five possible answers. The first sheet is on road signs. Easy-peasy. They are universal. 100%.

The second sheet is on Rules of the Road with trickier questions such as: *What is the distance you have to stop from a railroad crossing?* and *How far have you to be behind a car at night before you have to dip you lights?* and *Whenever you see a school sign, when should you slow down?* The answer to that, as I correctly guessed, is whenever you see it, even if it is out of school hours and holidays. Better to err on the side of caution when sitting the test, even if, in practice, you use your common sense, especially when you can see Al and his colleagues are not lurking about.

I hand my answers to my tester, a stout phlegmatic hombre. I get them all right except for one - something to do with procedures at a railroad crossing. I am surprised that I didn't get that right because after years of driving in France I know that *Un train peut en cacher un autre*. I have never seen such long trains in my life before as here - freight trains, a mile long or maybe two. I'm not very good at judging distances. We have repeatedly tried to count the wagons but lost count somewhere in the forties. Difficult to do as they were either coming towards us or we were overtaking them. Should we have been unlucky enough to have arrived at a crossing and parked the correct distance from the tracks (don't ask me - I've already forgotten) the precise moment the locomotives lumbered by - they usually have at least two - by the time the last wagon had passed, I would have had time to read a novella or Iona could have tried on a new dress, had we been near the shops.

Fortunately, you don't have to get a perfect score. I don't know how impressed my examiner is behind his sphinx-like mask, but my powers of intuitive guesswork certainly impress me.

"OK. Take me to your vehicle." My eyesight is evidently good enough to pass the driving test but had my hearing been less than perfect I might have mistaken his flat and emotionless voice for an alien command to be taken to my leader. I am through to the next round, the practical.

"This it?" asks the tester, giving a nod in the direction of the Big Blue Mean Machine. And he is human after all, for the mask has slipped and there is no mistaking the look and tone of suppressed disbelief.

"Yep." I try to sound supremely confident and not at all ashamed of the brute. If it were sitting the test instead of me I think it would have been fail on first sight. Regaining his mask-like composure, the human robot climbs in beside me.

"You had better start, you bastard," I threaten the BBMM internally as I slot the key into the ignition.

"Pull out," instructs the tester and I move smoothly into the traffic. It's a bit difficult not to when you are driving an automatic.

"Take a right." I do and we've hardly gone any distance before I have to stop at the next junction. "Take a right," reiterates the emotionless voice again.

It was a bit further to the next intersection but not much. "Take a right." Having done that, I smoothly pull up at the next junction. "Take a right." (Has his needle stuck?) A few yards later I'm ordered to pull in. We are back to where we started. "Park up," the robot commands, then adds brusquely, "Follow me." He sounds just like Mrs De Bone did before she ordered me down to see Matt, charged with corrupting the minds of the young and impressionable. He is already clambering out as I slot the shift stick (see how my American has come on, never mind my driving) into the slot marked "P".

Can that really be it? No emergency stop, no reversing, no parallel parking? The latter was worrying me as this thing is as long as a train. I've never had to do it, fortunately, but I bet I couldn't. In my second test in the big city of Dundee, which, at 180,000 souls, is sixty times bigger than Banffshire's largest metropolis, I had to reverse up a hill parallel with the pavement. In all the lessons I had had before the test, I never managed to do it, not once. But on the day of the test, to my enormous relief, a car was parked at the corner which meant I had to do the manoeuvre at another street which happened to be on the level. I executed it perfectly. Mostly I find the gods are agin' me, but they were looking after me that day, I will give them that.

But what had I done so utterly badly this time that my examiner had to curtail the test so speedily? And that's something I definitely hadn't done ⁃ speeded. If I had committed some traffic violation that was so horrendous that I needed to be brought back to base so peremptorily, he hadn't shown the least sign of it but it's impossible to tell with him. Like a lamb, but hopefully not to the slaughter, I follow him into the building to find out what my fate might be.

"Take a seat." His tone, as impassive as ever, at least does not sound hostile.

Wordlessly, he scribbles something on a sheet of paper, signs it, pushes it towards me, indicating I should sign it too.

In the brief time while he was doing that and reading it upside down, I thought I was able to make out: "Permit to Drive in the State of Montana".

So that really was it! I had passed! Not only passed but if measured in percentage terms, I bet I would have got something like 99.9%. What a skoosh! It takes a Scotsman to show these Missoulians how to drive! Next a mugshot and my signature and moments later I have my Montana Driving Licence, the size of a credit card. At that precise moment it is my proudest and most useful possession and it will be a great souvenir when we leave.

And then, in my elation at the ease of it all, a sobering thought. In this state, if fifteen year-olds take what's known as "Driver's Ed" at high school (and wouldn't you just love to take a course like that instead of English Lit or even American Lit?) you can get a driving licence, as long as you pass the test of course. Is that the same test as I just sat? I was eighteen when I passed my test and drove as if the devil was on my tail afterwards as I thought I was the best driver in Scotland, and immortal besides. And if that's what I thought at that mature age, fifteen-year-olds here must think they are the best in the solar system. Still, if it comes down to a choice between the Driver's Ed class or "The American Way of Death" (yes there really is such a course) I can see lots of youngsters having a great deal of trouble deciding which to choose. There may not be as many immortal fifteen year-olds driving the streets of Missoula as I may think - I don't think!

Now it's Iona's turn.

I tell her the questions and as many of the answers as I can remember but they're not so stupid in the driving licence department as I had thought. They have a different set of questions for her. One of hers was: *In what year was the driving test introduced to the State of Montana?* She got that one wrong and yet they let her pass. Imagine allowing someone loose on the roads who doesn't know something as basic as that! I bet any fifteen-year old knows the answer to that, as long as they been paying attention in the Driver's Ed class.

Maybe that's why she got a harder practical. She was made to go anticlockwise round the block, across the stream of traffic, and for the *coup de grâce*, when she got back to the Court House, she wasn't allowed to just pull up like I did but had to parallel park. Maybe I was just lucky there were no other cars nearby, or maybe, as a woman, she had to show she could handle the big blue beast just as well as any fifteen-year-old.

* * *

After having been invited countless times to other people's houses, it is time for us to repay the compliment and on Saturday evening we have invited the whole faculty for a meal and to see the slides of the backpacking trip to Idaho. "Faculty" sounds very grand, as if we four were academics at the university in our lofty ivory tower rather than merely on the top floor of Emerson: it's just the American way of talking things up.

At 11 pm on Friday evening the phone rings. It's Blake to say he and Diane will be able to come tomorrow. It's late to make a non-essential phone call, even in Scotland. In Montana terms, it is very, very late. Terri had told us she would think carefully about making a phone call after 9 pm, so when it rang, we both leapt to the conclusion it must be bad news from Scotland.

The next morning I am dispatched to the Inland Market for ingredients. It's going to be a Scottish evening, naturally. Forfar bridies for the main course - "ground meat" mixed with diced carrot, potatoes, onions and seasoning - all parcelled up in croissant-shaped shortcrust pastry. We have the same sort of thing in Banffshire where I come from, but with flaky pastry and shaped like a D. It is much nicer. But I would say that, wouldn't I? We call them "braddies", but the recipe book only has the Forfar version, so that's what the guests are going to be treated to.

I'm not familiar with the layout of the Inland Market and it takes me an age to find the shortening, not having a clue what such a thing looks like for a start, apart from the inkling that it's probably very small, which makes it even harder to find. The Dairy Whip cream and vanilla were easier, especially the former. The reason for this Great Supermarket Treasure Hunt is because we are going to be having scones with vanilla-flavoured cream and raspberry or strawberry jam as dessert. That's about as good as it gets: Scottish food does not rank high amongst the world's greatest cuisines, especially when you remember that the humble haggis, which is offal, is our most famous dish.

Not long after I return with the goods, Sam arrives, just calling in, apropos of nothing. I'm pleased about that as it's one thing to be invited, but it's another thing entirely just to turn up unannounced. I'm flattered it must be a sign he regards me as worth spending time with. I have a good supply of beer laid in for the faculty, so no problems in that department. Meanwhile, Iona is slaving over a hot stove preparing the feast for our invited guests - perhaps it's the sight of her doing that very thing that prompts Sam's next remark.

"You know, David," he drawls, "I'm kinda worried about my wood stove."

Yes, I remember it well. He built it himself and not so long ago, we sat drinking beer in front of it. Not quite the same thing as an open fire, but it's a very pleasant experience to bask in the warmth of the flickering flames and quaff your beers.

"Why, what's the matter with it?"

"Well, you know, it gets kinda hot," he says, giving a little chuckle followed by a slug of his beer.

That's typical Sam. He's so laid-back but not afraid to stand up to Matt either. I imagine if there is anyone Matt would like to see off the payroll next, it would be him. But if there is one thing I think he should definitely not be laid-back about, it's that stove in the basement of his wooden house...

* * *

Nat and Mae are the first to arrive and it's clear from the look on her face that she would rather be somewhere else.

"She ain't feelin' too good," Nat comes out with right away.

I'm glad about that; not that she's ill of course, but glad that's the reason. In fact it's to her credit that looking like death warmed up, and I imagine feeling that that state of affairs might be preferable to how she is currently feeling, she has nevertheless made the supreme effort to come here and not cause us any possible slight by not turning up.

Blake and Diane are next to arrive. We drink beer and engage in banter, waiting for Steve and Jackie to turn up. They are late. That's unusual for these parts. It's especially surprising as we have asked them to come at 7.30, an hour later than the time we are normally invited when we go to their place. We had made it later to let us get the kids off to bed, albeit a bit earlier than normal, so we could give our undivided attention to our guests.

At last they arrive, Steve apologetic because he had been out hunting. (There's a surprise!) A little later, Iona, who has been busy in the kitchen, announces that the food is ready and we can move through to the dining room. No one moves. Instead there's an embarrassed silence.

"You never told us we were invited for a meal, you dumbass," Blake says, fixing me with his gimlet, ice-blue eyes. "We've already eaten."

"He's right! So have we," chimes in Steve the Stooge, as predictable as ever. "Boy, you sure messed up good this time," he adds, his eyes shining with excitement at this unexpected turn of events.

"I'm sorry," Mae pipes up. "But I don't feel like eating anything."

It's just about the first words she has uttered. There are not enough chairs for us all, so she is sitting on the floor in a foetal position with her back to the wall next to where the kitchen door would be if there had been one. That's another mistake I've made. I should have released her from her duty, given her permission to go home and get straight to bed. Iona might have done so if she hadn't been so busy in the kitchen, putting the final touches of the meal together, and if I hadn't been so busy listening to Steve and Blake's double act. Another reason to add to Mae's misery no doubt. There's nothing worse than people being bright and cheery when you just want to be left alone to die.

Nat says nothing at all so I don't know if he has eaten or is just too polite not to say he has. It's to Iona's credit she doesn't give me a bigger dressing down than I deserve but it could be she's saving that until they leave. Not so long from now.

"Well, I thought you would have known you were invited for a meal," I protest in self-defence, "after all the meals you have given us!"

Unfortunately I can't bring out my biggest gun, namely that I would hardly have invited them round for drinks since they hardly drink anything at all. (Al just wouldn't waste his time having friends like them.) But from their end of the telescope, the comparatively late hour at which they'd been invited must have told them that they would have been expected to have eaten by then, especially since I hadn't mentioned anything about food. Had I seen them all yesterday as I normally would have, our intentions regarding the evening might well have come to light, but I hadn't, so we are in the embarrassing situation where we are now.

Iona persuades them to try to eat a little and out of politeness and deference to the effort they can see she has made, they troop through to the dining room where morsels of the bridie are served up to everyone, except Mae.

"It's a kind of pastry," I feel it behoves me to explain, "from a small town in Scotland, called Forfar." They are so lucky to have landed up getting me as an exchange teacher, I smugly congratulate myself, enriching their lives with all this exotic Scottish culture.

"It looks like a Butte pasty," observes Jackie unenthusiastically at the object on her plate and with all the insouciant innocence of a child.

"Butte pastry?" I repeat, astonished, translating the second word back into Scots. "What's that?"

Blake lets go his fork (Americans hardly ever use the knife accompaniment except to chop food up before the forking), slaps both palms on the table and throws his head back in a loud guffaw. Steve's rip-roaring laugh is ready chorus. What could be so funny about that?

"Well, Dave," says Blake when he has regained his composure and the laughter around the table has subsided, "you know those stickers that strippers have over their nipples? Some of them have tassels an' they can make them go round in different directions. That's what a pasty is."

That's the sort of question I just can't give the right answer to. I'm condemned out of my own mouth if I admit to having seen such a thing, or confirmed as the innocent and/or idiot they already think I am if I haven't. Honest to God, I never knew there were such things. In my innocence, I thought they waggled their attributes about bare, as nature intended. The best I can do is to retain my composure by looking utterly blank, which provokes a renewed round of laughter. At least I am giving the faculty a good time even if it is not in the way I intended.

Pointing to the food on his plate, Steve elucidates, "See, that here is a pasty, what you said was "pasty". Now do you get it?"

Iona and I can both hear the difference. Jackie had said "pahstay", I said "paystray" and apparently they had not picked up the "r" which is surprising as the Scots are supposed to be renowned for the rolling of them.

It reminds me of Ira Gershwin's song *Let's Call the Whole Thing Off* from the 1937 movie *Shall We Dance* in which Fred Astaire and Ginger Rogers dispute the pronunciation of words which look the same but are pronounced differently. And that was never truer in the case of Jackie and me, coming from either (or eether) side of the Atlantic, as we do.

But since she had brought it up, I want to know what a Butte pasty is, though of course I have a pretty good idea by looking at what's on the plate before me.

"It's what the miners used to take down the mines with them," explains Steve. "It's a complete meal an' you don't need a plate or cutlery. An' dependin' on when your wife made it, it might even still be hot when you had it for your lunch."

It's certainly a more hearty meal for pick-wielding workers than sandwiches and the Butte pasty was almost certainly not invented there but an import from wherever the miners in Butte came from, probably Ireland, as another thing Butte is famous for is its large Irish population. And now I come to think of it, now my mind has been set on that track, I remember there is such a thing as a Cornish pasty and there used to be a great deal of tin mines in Cornwall.

So much for my Scottish delicacy.

I pity the poor bachelors who had to make their own pasties as well as having to dig for a living, like moles, in the bowels of the earth. I bet that as well as the pasties, there were a good number of paystays [sic] about too, miners being miners and men being men, married or not, in need of some rest and relaxation when they surfaced from a long slog pick, pick, picking away at the seam.

But we can now move on to what *is* undoubtedly, a Scottish delicacy. The bridie may have been a disappointment, regarded I wouldn't be surprised, as a poor man's meal and even a bit insulting to give to guests. But not to worry, the best is yet to come, the *pièce de résistance*. Whilst our main courses are hardly *haut cuisine*, when it comes to homebaking,

Scotland is second to none with its shortbread, pancakes and scones.

Leaving our guests to talk amongst themselves (and probably just as well that we can't hear them), Iona goes to the kitchen to fetch a pile of scones whilst I bring forth the vanilla-flavoured cream and the jams.

"These are scones," I explain. "We quite often have them with what's called 'high tea' - sandwiches and various savoury things like vol-au-vents and sausage rolls."

"They look like biscuits," says Jackie with the same outspoken frankness as before.

"Biscuits?"

"We have them with gravy."

"Gravy!"

"Yes, when we have a roast dinner, we serve these warm, along with the gravy."

Well we didn't have them at Thanksgiving with the roast turkey so maybe it's a family thing but I am devastated to find out that what I was sure was a Scottish treat isn't a stranger here either! But what a strange way to treat a scone! And what a strange thing to call it too! And how strange they must think the Scots are to spread butter and jam on them and even a dollop of cream if you are that way inclined, which I am not. But they would, the Americans, wouldn't they - serve something sweet along with the savoury!

These would have been warm too once, but have cooled down since they were made. Our guests are persuaded to try this strange Scottish delicacy eaten with butter and jam and cream if desired, and out of politeness I'm sure, they do, apart from Mae. No-one is tempted to have a second one. But then I have to remember they have all eaten before, apart from Mae who has a get-out-of-jail card and who doesn't have to sample anything.

The whole evening has been a bit of a disaster. We had done our best, but as Burns so wisely put it two hundred years ago: "the best-laid plans o' mice an' men gang aft agley". When the gods have it in for you, there's not a lot you can do about it. We are merely their playthings.

Chapter Thirty-four

*In which I step into a crisis and some interesting
revelations are made.*

It would be nice I think, just as Sam had arrived
unannounced yesterday, if I at least paid an uncalled for
visit to the Hertz house for once instead of Al always
bellowing down the phone for me to come over and have a
drink. It's my turn for time off as I've been looking after the
kids all morning whilst Iona has been at church, the First
Presbyterian Church, where Dave and Gloria are members. It
was a special service for St Andrew's Day and the Bible was
piped in! Gloria had been up till 4.15 in the morning finishing
off a kilt that she had made for Dave. Imagine that! I mean
making a kilt in the first place and staying up to that time in
the morning!

I had imagined I would be warmly welcomed with my
bag of scones (even if they called them biscuits) at this
unexpected visit but instead I find myself walking straight
into a family crisis. I had long since got my feet under the
table and could dispense with ringing the bell and waiting for
admittance.

I find Al reading the riot act to two of his sons, Little
Al and Don, the next brother in the hierarchy, and my
sudden appearance does nothing to interrupt his rant. In fact
I'm not sure if he has even taken in the fact that I am there
even although he could not have failed to see me. As for me, I
am rooted to the spot, frozen into shocked immobility at the
scene unfolding before my very eyes. As far as the "boys" are

concerned (they must both be in their early twenties), I saw their eyes flick over me with complete indifference so it's not like I'm eavesdropping at all.

There is a new bridge being built in Missoula, out to the west. Well, built actually, but not yet open to traffic and Little Al and Don have boldly crossed where none have crossed before apart from contractors' vehicles presumably. But that wasn't what Al was getting aerated about. When they were picked up by the cops, they had searched them and found marijuana in their possession. Since they were Al's pals, or colleagues at least, they had turned a blind eye to that, but had escorted them back here to face the wrath of the patriarch, just a few minutes ago apparently.

"Jesus Chris'. You gotta lay off that stuff!" Al is shouting. "Do you realise what you get if you're caught doin' that shit?"

No answer. But far from hanging their heads in shame, the guilty pair don't look in the least contrite. I'd go so far as to say there is even a degree of arrogance about their body language which says Al may rant and rave as much as he likes but it won't make any difference as far as they are concerned: he's just an old fuddy-duddy an' he don't know where the scene is, man.

"Six months in the Pen! An' that's where you would ha' bin if it wasn't for me. You gotta lay offa that shit from now on. You hear me?"

They can't help but hear, as Al is more bellowing than speaking, but it looks like water off a duck's back to me. They don't say anything like, "Really sorry for embarrassing you in this way, dad" and "We're really grateful to you, dad, for gettin' us off this rap" and "We've learned our lesson, dad an' we'll never touch the wacky baccy ever again". In fact they say nothing at all. It's what my mother used to call "dumb insolence" and hit me with the bamboo cane for my cheek. But these two are well beyond correction of that sort; maybe beyond correction of any kind.

Something of this unrepentant attitude must have permeated through to Al, for he is off again. We've heard it all before: how stupid they are and reminding them that if it hadn't been for the happy circumstance of him being a lieutenant of police, they'd be facing jail sentences at this moment and they had better get their act together because if they didn't, sure as hell, they wouldn't get off with it again. They're on their final warning.

"Jesus Chris', the dumb bastards," Al says to me after they had been dismissed, shaking his head in wonderment and disbelief that he could have fathered such a pair or retards. "What they wanna do that sort of shit for?"

He takes a gallon of Bacardi out of the fridge and without a by-your-leave, pours me one of his little measures and tops it up with Coke. Plainly Al needs a drink after this stressful start to the afternoon.

"I just don't get it," he muses, shaking his head and apparently talking to himself rather than to me. "What they wanna get involved in that shit for, for Chris' sake?"

We're on our second Bacardi when Terri comes back with the unpasteurised milk from The Dairy, where we also get our milk. Hard luck, M. Pasteur, there you were knocking your pan in for I don't know how many weeks or years even, to the process that bears your name and which keeps us safe from nasty bacteria, but as far as we are concerned you were just wasting your time. To tell you the truth I don't know why we, and especially the kids, are drinking raw milk except habit is a hard thing to break and we inherited it from Marnie and Terri. They seem to have survived all right anyway.

Naturally Al has to tell Terri of these latest developments which sets him off on another rant. Really, it's enough to drive you to drink, because he pours her a glass, drains his and refreshes mine. None of his anger or energy seems to have been dissipated in this reprise of their idiot sons' misdemeanours.

For her part, Terri listens to this devastating turn of events with her habitual sang-froid, as if to say, "Well, they're adults you know; what can you do?" You can practically see her shrugging her shoulders at this particular genie having been let out of the bottle, along with I wouldn't care to hazard a guess at how many more million kids the length and breadth of the land, doing what the younger generation has always done and always will do - rebel.

For all Al's ranting and raving, I would say he has achieved nothing. He might just as well have been talking to George.

I change the subject by presenting Terri with the bag of scones.

"Gee, thanks for the biscuits," she enthuses after having a peek inside. At least that is what is conveyed by her tone of voice but I bet she is wondering why anyone would give anyone a whole batch of cold biscuits which could well be stale by the time she got round to cooking another turkey dinner. Well actually just a few days away as Christmas is coming fast.

"Well, actually they are scones. You have them with butter and jam."

"My, how neat!"

Whether she ever will try one, I don't know but I have the feeling that she thinks it's a very odd thing indeed to do and it would be better as food for the birds by then than served as an accompaniment to the bird on the Christmas table.

"Say, why don't you all come over later for dinner? We've got masses of cold turkey."

Which, I imagine, is not a state of affairs that Little Al and Don will be aspiring to any time soon.

* * *

When we arrive, not a long time later, we find a couple of other guests already ensconced behind the bar in the kitchen. One of them I have already met before, Chris Mendez, Al's Mexican friend whom Al describes as a "hair bender" and who "fixes the hair of all the rich dames in town an' not just the hair on their head either!" There's obviously money in the hair bending business - Chris is so dripping with gold if I hadn't known better, I would have thought that he was a jeweller who was so dedicated to his work that he had to take it home with him. He is also accompanied by a new girlfriend, Rosie, who is divorced (of course) as is he. That is the American way of marriage, I have discovered.

We must have arrived not too long after they did, because Al is reprising his rant to Chris and Rosie about his sons' latest escapades. Chris seems to find the tale amusing but Rosie does not.

"I wish you'd shown the same consideration to my boys," she says without rancour.

Al blinks in bewilderment. The moustache twitches in consternation.

"I found them with the shit, called the cops an' you attended," Rosie reminds him.

"Oh yeah?" says Al.

But Al has obviously no recollection of the incident. How could he be expected to remember it out of so many? But what would have been less considerate than the right-royal bollocking he had given Little Al and Don? Arrested them? Does that mean that they are in the Pen as we speak, or are out again, on parole, or freed for good? Presumably Rosie knew what the penalty was when she took that brave decision to shop her kids. Maybe she hoped this would be the scare they needed to make them break the habit but it had backfired. They had ended up on a charge, just as the law decreed, and she ended up divorced because her husband hadn't gone along with her decision.

But maybe she merely means Al had ripped through them like a chainsaw. What Rosie had just heard was nothing like the actual scene I'd been witness to. Al has calmed down a bit by now and I'm inclined to think this is what must really have happened in the case of her sons. If everyone caught smoking dope in Montana was given six months in the Pen, it would be bursting at the seams with a queue right round the block waiting to be admitted.

Sam had told me that Al had a reputation in the town as a "good cop", an accolade he would not have earned if he had been throwing every dope-smoking youth (or adult) into the Pen at every available opportunity. It might also explain why Little Al and Don looked so unimpressed with Al's rant. If word had got around that the law was more observed in the breach than the observance, that the worst that could happen was a bollocking from the cops - unless one of them happened to be your father of course.

"We met another time after that," Rosie continues, volunteering nothing further on the matter of her sons and the marijuana, much to my disappointment. On the other hand, this sounds potentially more interesting.

"Oh yeah?"

"When you arrested me," she hints, displaying the same lack of resentment as before.

"Oh yeah?" Al reiterates blankly. Like my driving tester of yesterday, his needle seems to have stuck in the groove.

"For bein' a hooker," Chris interjects and throws his head back in laughter at his own wit and at which Al joins in readily but the most I can manage is a wan smile as I'm still in shock. I'm not accustomed, in my social circle, to meeting people who have been arrested, far less from mentioning it in front of someone she's only met five minutes before. Not to mention the other matter of having two sons in the Pen, possibly, thanks to Al.

That's Americans for you, so much less reserved than we Scots. Nothing hidden. There's a kind of refreshing honesty about that I suppose. But what did she really get arrested for? That's what I would really, really like to know.

At this point, with immaculate bad timing, Hélène, on walkabout, appears in the kitchen and Rosie, who I am sure was just about to refresh Al's memory about the occasion, is distracted.

"Well, hello, sweetie! You're a wee cutie aren't you? What's your name?"

"Aine," says Hélène and Rosie continues to make a big fuss of her. The moment has passed. I can't see me coming out later, as cold as scones (or biscuits), with: "So, Rosie, as you were about to say two hours ago ‑ why did Al arrest you?"

All I know is it wouldn't have been for being a hooker but it does leave me reflecting on life's curious twists and turns. When Al arrested her, neither of them could ever have imagined, years later, that here they would be, in his house, having a few drinky-poos together. But then, possibly they don't know, as I do, that we are merely marionettes and up there, beyond the clouds, the gods are pulling our strings and what we mere mortals think is thunder is actually them having a right-good belly laugh at our discomfitures.

Al sets about making what we call "chips" and Americans call "French fries" to go with the turkey sandwiches but then the second crisis of the day occurs. There is not enough oil and even worse, something I never thought I'd ever see in the Hertz household - he has also run out of beer despite my contribution and no doubt Chris and Rosie's too. That tells you how much we must have got through since Iona has not been of any help, nursing a white wine. Next to whisky, she thinks beer is the most repulsive drink known to man. No wonder Al shakes his head in wonderment and disbelief that I married such a broad. Ever since I met Al, I am beginning to wonder myself.

But not to worry, we have both oil and more beer that the faculty could drink and it is the matter of a moment to fetch them both and a bib for George while I'm at it.

It's back to school tomorrow and an early start will be required after four days of comparatively long lies. There's nothing like an extended weekend to make you more reluctant than ever to prise yourself out of your cosy bed and trudge through the snow on a cold and frosty morning. I'm grateful to Al for recent events to keep my mind off it, as he has done before. There's never a dull moment at the Hertz house. I doubt if any of my faculty have ever been arrested or even smoked dope.

But you never can tell. Considering all the whacky things that Steve and his pals got up to in Dillon, it would be truly amazing if they didn't do a little wacky baccy too.

Chapter Thirty-five

In which pigeonholes play a prominent part, I make a confession, and my name gets around.

There are some unintended benefits when you walk to school. I pick up a book which someone had dropped, and further on, an envelope, which, not surprisingly, bears a stamp. Such things are not to be sneezed at if you are a voracious reader like me and a philatelist, or at least a stamp collector, as I also am. Despite them lying on top of the snow they have not come to any harm, it being crisp and no new stuff having fallen.

But every silver lining has a cloud and the book is a Western by Louis L'Amour. A likely name I must say, though I would have thought, better suited to romantic fiction and "Louise" would have been better still. With a name like that you can just see the books flying off the shelves. I've never read a Western as the genre does not appeal to me but if there is ever a time to start, there is no time like the present, whilst I am here, living where these tales of derring-do took place.

Tamed down a tad it may be but I have seen plenty of its legacy all around me from architecture to "cowboy hats" and not least the love affair with guns. Old habits die hard but if there is one habit more likely to do you more harm than marijuana, it is the gun. They don't walk down the street with them strapped to their sides any more but every house is an arsenal.

As for the stamp, I have it already but that doesn't matter too much as back in my school in Scotland I run a stamp club and it may be a new one to the kids.

The first thing I do on arriving at school, I expect we all do, is go straight to my pigeonhole situated outside Matt's office on the middle floor. If his door is closed it means someone is in trouble; if he's not there he will be in the building somewhere, but usually he is sitting behind his desk doing whatever principals do. Today he's somewhere in the building. And there is something in my pigeonhole, just as there usually is.

Before we broke up for Thanksgiving, I had put my latest project in Matt's pigeonhole, a unit based on humorous stories and poems which I'd compiled with the help of Millie Ferguson, the school librarian. Although it went against the grain not a little, I thought it better to let him see my lesson plans and get them ratified. Thus, the next time I suffered the slings and arrows from outraged parents complaining about how I was corrupting young minds, I could deflect them straight to Matt.

He is probably the first person to arrive in the building and now I have an inkling of what he must do in the mornings before we lesser mortals arrive, for on my document, attached by a paperclip, is a scrap of paper on which is written: "Terrible! See me!"

Unbelievable! What on earth could he have found to object to this time? Clenching my fist around the document and gritting my teeth, I stomp up to my room. Blake and Steve are standing outside their rooms as usual waiting for the students to arrive.

"Would you just look at this!" I explode. "Look at Matt's latest! He says my lesson plans are "terrible". What could he possibly find to object to in this?"

"Dunno, Dave. I'd have to read it first," Blake says, taking the paper which I have been waving around, fanning the flames of my anger.

"Think it might be this poem he doesn't like," he says eventually, rubbing his chin thoughtfully. "Here, what do you think, Steve?"

I wait in suspense as Steve gives it his serious consideration. "Think you might be right, Blake. *Faithless Nelly Gray.* Sounds like she's a hooker or somethin'."

"Oh, for God's sake!" I exclaim in exasperation. "Has he not read it? Can't he see that the poem is all about puns? Is the man totally devoid of humour?"

"Have *you* got a sense of humour, Dave?" Blake asks, looking the most serious I have seen him since I made an appointment behind Matt's back to meet the Director of Curriculum after the De Bone debacle.

"Yes, I should hope so," I respond hesitantly, wondering why he is asking *me* when he should really be directing that question to Matt. I bet he just read the title and leapt to the same conclusion as Steve. And being a fundamentalist Christian that probably stoked his disapproval even more.

"In that case," says Blake, removing a piece of paper from the breast pocket of his short-sleeved shirt, "I hope you'll find this funny."

I take it from him and puzzled and intrigued, unfold the single scrap of paper. On it is written the single word: "Terrific!"

Steve is already bent over double with laughter while Blake lets out a huge guffaw as soon as he sees the expression on my face. And I have to laugh myself at the sight of them laughing their guts out, though I think it's more to do with relief than that. What would have happened if Matt had been in his office when I picked up the paper and I'd gone straight in to see him? And I probably would have done precisely that as I'm a great believer in avoiding stress and worry by facing the music as soon as possible, even if the early morning is not the best time for me to defend my corner with the brain still in first gear. But I imagine that scenario would just have added to their hilarity even more, Matt having been sucked in to the "joke" too.

Actually I reckon I was pretty lucky to get off with a minor prank like that. Blake had once put a cow's vagina in Steve's pigeonhole and he, recognizing it for what it was, merely thought, "Oh, Blake up to his tricks as usual!" and without giving it a further glance, tossed it at random into Mary Mason's pigeonhole. Blake had been hanging about, waiting for a reaction, and he had told her it was a beaver pelt. Uttering a little squeal of delight, she bore it off triumphantly to show it to her class of little kids.

And another time, Blake had put the guts of a cow in a girl's desk (as you do when you are looking for something to do with them). You should have heard her scream and watch her leap a foot in the air!

But of course there is a long time still to go. God knows what other practical jokes they might still play on me before the year is out. I'm going to be on my guard more than ever.

* * *

That wasn't the only thing in my pigeonhole: there was a fat envelope containing a pile of letters from my pupils in Scotland and a covering note from Marnie, telling me how "nice" the kids were and how amazed she is at how hardworking they are. I can certainly see why she thinks that. And she'll be working hard herself with all that marking she is unaccustomed to.

My students are excited when I tell them the letters have arrived but first I tell them I'll have to allocate them as best as I see fit. I'd suggested this possible spin-off of our exchange to Marnie when we were in DC long before I had any idea of what reluctant writers my students would turn out to be. Hopefully they might be more motivated to write to their assigned pen pal but I don't expect it to last long after the initial enthusiasm wears off.

Meanwhile George's holiday was unexpectedly extended. After behaving impeccably for so long, The Big Blue Mean Machine refused to start again this morning and when Iona wiggled the wires as she had been shown by the AAA man, she was alarmed to see flames suddenly leap up but fortunately die down just as quickly as they had appeared. He merely laughed and said he wasn't surprised, the state the wires were in. She didn't see what he did but he did something, it only took a moment, and that was it fixed - until the next time. But by then it was too late for George to go to school, the lucky devil.

One of my students, Perry, has an even more alarming tale to tell about a fire.

"Our house was burned down on Wednesday," he tells me in a matter-of-fact sort of way.

"Burned down! Oh, my goodness! What happened?"

"It was the wood stove. It burned a hole at the back and then the house just caught fire."

"But you all got out in time? Nobody was hurt, I hope."

"No, we're all OK."

"Thank goodness for that! And was the house completely destroyed?"

"Yep."

He doesn't look perturbed in the least about these calamitous events, at how close a brush with death he might have had and at the personal possessions he and his family must certainly have lost. He's naturally phlegmatic; that he has come up to my desk to confide this information, evidence that deep down under that passive exterior, it has dawned on him that having your house burnt to the ground is an extraordinary event.

"And where are you living now?"

"In a motel."

"Something to tell your pen pal about, eh?"

"Yep."

I hope they were insured. Must remember to communicate this cautionary tale to Sam as soon as possible, if it has not already percolated to the floor below. Wood-burning stoves haven't yet evolved to being able to distinguish the difference between the wood that is fed into them and the wood that surrounds them - they have an insatiable appetite for wood and a house made of that combustible material has plenty of that. And the villain of the piece will be the only thing left standing when all around them is burned to ashes.

Perry's not the only person who's had an eventful break. It's amazing what can happen in the matter of a few days. Before we get down to educating young minds, or in my case corrupting them, Matt calls a conference of the upper floor teachers. What can it mean? It sounds serious. We meet in my room, but any room would have done as there are only five of us.

Matt is plainly finding it difficult to spit out whatever he has come to tell us. His Adam's apple is bouncing up and down as he swallows hard and his face is distinctly red which has nothing to do with his collar being too tight but everything to do with embarrassment. What can it be that is making him so hot above the collar? My conscience is clear. Have I not written a "terrific" lot of lesson plans and not had time to put a foot wrong since?

"Well, you see, ahrrum, the thing is that er, ahrrum one of our students, ahrrum, Christina Blankenship, was molested by a neighbour yesterday." Matt has been able to spit it out at last, but then he is all confusion again, "So, er, ahrrum, just to let you know, ahrrum, if you see her acting kinda strange... An' I don't need to tell you ahrrum, this is strictly confidential."

We understand perfectly and Matt is released from the purgatory a principal sometimes has to endure - the imparting of embarrassingly bad news to colleagues.

* * *

Another day and another fat envelope in my pigeonhole. On the outside is written: "Food for Stamps Program. David Addison. Emerson School". The sender is someone called Nancy Adams whom I don't know from Eve, so how does she know me? She has provided her phone number. Food for Stamps Program? It sounds like a worthy cause but what's that all about? And how come it ended up in my pigeonhole?

If I were a cat, I could die of curiosity but I'm not, so I don't think I am in any imminent danger but I am intrigued. Courtesy alone requires I ring the number to proffer thanks and hope it will resolve the mystery, and like Sherlock Holmes, I have found a clue. The envelope bears the words "The Missoula Bank of Montana". My new bank in fact.

"Hello, this is David Addison, from Emerson School. I just wanted to thank you for the stamps."

"David who?" Who is this person with the funny accent? After I have explained, Nancy says she had given the stamps to someone, she didn't know his name, who said he knew someone who knew what to do with them. The mystery deepens. Who is this mysterious person; how did he hear about me and how on earth did he know about my Stamps for Abbotsgrange Middle School Program?

At lunchtime I go to see my friend, Fran from Elgin, at the First Bank of Missoula - the one I had recently left. She isn't there but her lovely friend Barbara is and I tell her about the Case of the Mysterious Stamps in the Pigeonhole. She says they also save the stamps that come into the bank, gives me what they've already collected in their box, and says she'll keep them for me in future. In my turn, I'll send them to my colleague, Maureen, who helps me run the stamp club and if there are any surplus to requirement, which I imagine there will be since there are so many duplicates, I will ask her to pass them on to Oxfam. Thus, via Missoula, Montana and Grangemouth, Scotland, they will end up in Africa feeding the hungry. So it is a "Food For Stamps Program" after all.

Just before the end of classes, big white feathers tumble from the sky again and my heart sinks. Normally, at home, this would be a cause for celebration, but not here. In Scotland there is always a chance you might be snowed in and not be able to get to school, or the kids being sent home early, or the ultimate holy grail of school being closed altogether. But there is no point in praying for a massive dump of snow here, for apart from Iona being terrified to drive in it and my having to keep the path clear (no mean task as Marnie's frontage is yards long), any school days lost to snow have to be made up and the summer holidays cannot begin until they are. You can imagine the level of concentration the kids would bring to the classroom on those sun-splitting-the-sky days!

I happen to reach the school exit just as Harry is leaving. He teaches "shop", or woodwork as we call it, to young adults with special needs down in the bowels of the basement. Now, at ground level, he sees a Scotsman in special need of a lift.

"Thanks very much, that's very kind of you, just as long as it's not taking you out of your way."

"Forget it. Now tell me, whereabouts is your house?"

I express my dismay at the sight of this new snowfall and tell Harry I was hoping to cycle to school tomorrow but it doesn't look likely now as the sky looks leaden and laden with an inexhaustible supply of downy feathers.

"I was in Oregon for Thanksgiving," Harry continues, "an' we got snowed in. I just got back today."

This does not bode well for our proposed trip to Canada for Christmas. But worse is to come.

"I asked for the days to be taken as personal leave days, but they wouldn't go for it. I've gotta pay the substitute myself."

I express my sympathy. In the light of this I'm going to have to carefully reconsider our plans to go to Canada for Christmas. It's one thing to take a chance on the passes being clear and in all likelihood having to fit chains (which I am not in the least confident I'll be able to do), not to mention another "little" worry ⁃ relying on the Big Blue Mean Machine not to let us down. But now here's another thing to factor into the equation ⁃ can I literally afford to take the risk of being holed up somewhere for God knows how long? I think I already know what Iona will say when I tell her Harry's story.

When I get back, Iona has something to tell me ⁃ the results of George's visit to the university this afternoon. He had another hearing test and another mould made. It's important that it fits tightly or else the hearing aid won't work properly and because he is growing, the mould has to keep on being remade. Mike is still looking into the possibility of us renting a phonic ear.

I've said it before and I'll say it again: we could never have landed in a better place as far as George is concerned. The service really is second to none.

* * *

One service I really miss is the BBC World Service.

I have a confession to make. I am a bit of an insomniac. I go to bed tired and wake up tired, often more tired than when I went to bed, thus the reason for my reluctance to get up in the mornings is now revealed. I am not really just the lazy pig you may have thought. At home I like to spend the sleepless hours listening to the World Service, a mixture of plays, current affairs and news. But here I can't.

Apart from the endless nights, I also feel I am not keeping up to date with events in the wider world as much as I would like. The *Missoulian* is good for local news but sadly lacking in depth when it comes to world affairs. There has been a lot recently in the media about the horrendous events in Jonestown, Guyana, where the mad and exceedingly bad Reverend Jim Jones of the Peoples [sic] Temple persuaded his flock of 909 people, including 304 children, to commit suicide by drinking poison. They were the first to die, having it fed to them first by their brainwashed parents. God preserve us from religious zealots!

I don't know where God was in those dreadful days in Guyana (and in the past, lots of other places of mass extermination) but believers may think they see the hand of God in my being assigned to Emerson and all the help George has received. I'm sure God had nothing to do with it; I would have been more impressed if He had fixed it for George not to be deaf in the first place.

Funnily enough, help for my insomnia problem arrives this morning out of the blue as I make my way to school. I have just struggled through the snow to the other side of the bridge when a truck stops and the driver motions me to get in. I am not in the habit of accepting lifts from strange men and besides, the worst and greatest part of my journey is over - yet there is something vaguely familiar about his face, so I throw caution to the icy wind and clamber into the shelter of the cab.

Once inside I am able to place the face - it belongs to the owner of Wood's Second-Hand Store where I had bought the chains for the trip to Canada. I know it won't take long before we get to my destination and knowing he has everything short of an anchor in his wonderful emporium, after the thanks, I waste no time in telling him of my sleep and radio deprivation because if anyone has the answer to my problem, he's the man.

"No worries, Dave. Come on round to the store. I got some radios you can try out. If they don't work fo' ya, just bring 'em back."

I can hardly believe my ears. Isn't that amazing! In fact it's almost as amazing as the six impossible things that the White Queen could believe in before breakfast. I still haven't quite got over the fact that he recognised me, considering he had only met me once before and then only briefly. But what gets me more than anything is he remembers my name! And imagine him trusting me enough to borrow a radio or radios and bring them back if I couldn't get the World Service on them!

Just another instance of the kindness of people in Missoula which had impressed me so much when we first arrived and evidently is showing no signs of diminishing. It's not just George, by any means, who landed lucky when we ended up here. I can scarcely believe my Donald Duck.

Incredible as it may seem, yet another amazing thing is in store for me (no pun intended) when after grateful thanks to Mr Wood (I don't even know *his* first name), I go to my pigeonhole which has been producing some unexpected items recently but today contains something even more astounding. It's a phone message from Rachel Watson, a teacher at Hawthorne, asking me to phone her at home, number supplied, with a view to swapping classes for an afternoon.

The call would have been fielded by Judy, Matt's secretary. There will be nothing going on in the school she doesn't know about. Apart from the letters she sends out in Matt's name, she would at least see who has the door closed behind them in the inner sanctum, even if she can't hear what goes on - and it wouldn't surprise me if she could, especially if it got a bit heated in there. I'm sure she would keep her mouth shut if she did but is it part of her duties to whisper into Matt's shell-like any possible rebellion she is aware of in the ranks, such as a Scotsman planning to visit another school, telling God knows what tales?

I look at it, doubting the evidence of my eyes. Can it really be a serious offer or is it just another of Blake's practical jokes? He knows I would like to broaden the school experience, even if he doesn't know part of the reason is because of him. I don't know who this Rachel is but it's not so surprising she, at least, would have heard of me. I expect most people in the district are aware there is an infiltrator in their midst.

I don't mention this to Blake or Steve as they are masters of the poker face and acting the innocent. If it *is* another of their tricks, that would just heighten the anticipation of the fun they'd get tomorrow when they asked how it had gone with Rachel. I reckon I have nothing to lose by saying nothing at all to them and giving her a call.

"Rachel? This is David Addison here."

"Oh, hi, David. Thank you for getting back to me. What do you say to swapping classes with me?"

"That would be wonderful. Yes, I'd love to do that. When have you in mind?"

"Leave it to me. I'll discuss it with my principal and then I'll get back to you."

"But what about Matt?"

"My principal will speak with him."

"That would be brilliant!"

So there you go, my desire to see another school sorted, as easy as that! Assuming that Matt would be opposed to the idea, which in fairness to him, he might not be, it looks as if he has been outflanked and outmanoeuvred. *A fait accompli.*

Nothing to do with me, I'm just a pawn in the process, merely responding to an invitation, part and parcel of my ambassadorial duties.

It's not quite the like-for-like I would have chosen however. Rachel may be in the same school district, but teaches a combination of 6th, 7th and 8th graders. 6th graders are a bit young for me but I'm sure I'll cope. Nothing to worry about. After all, if I can handle hormonal 8th graders, surely I can cope with the younger, littler kids whose horns haven't come out yet.

All Rachel wants me to do is tell her students about Scotland; as for her, she will teach a poem to my classes so I don't need to leave any lesson plans. I think I know who is getting the better deal. Poetry is one of the hardest things to sell to young teenagers and little do my poor students know they are in for a double whammy because when I get back from this jaunt, I'm going to be hitting them with *Faithless Nelly Gray*.

"That sounds really great, Rachel. I'm really looking forward to this."

"My pleasure. It will be a great experience for the kids to have a Scotsman talk to them."

"I hope so."

Chapter Thirty-six

In which we are invited to another faculty dinner where
I hear a cautionary tale.

It's not quite a week since our disastrous dinner, a Friday evening, and we and the rest of the faculty are invited to Steve and Jackie's for spaghetti and meatballs. This frequent socialising amongst one's colleagues comes as a bit of a (pleasant) surprise for me. In Scotland, as far as I know, at least in my experience, you tend to distance yourself from your colleagues at weekends. You will be seeing them again all too soon and you don't want to be reminded of work any sooner than necessary.

But it could be I'm not getting a typical picture (as mine back home might not be either) and it's just another instance of my good fortune in having been posted to Emerson and what I'm experiencing is due to the special relationship between Steve and Blake, their shared love of hunting and sport in all its various forms and not least, their shared sense of humour. I couldn't imagine either of them having the same relationship with Nat for instance - he's a nice bloke, a very nice bloke indeed, but he's as straight as a poker compared to those two and as far as I know, the only thing he shoots is squirrels. Which is a bit of a shame as they are so cute.

Rob can't babysit but Debbie can, so there's no problem there, but there is with the kids. For once they won't settle, understandable in George's case as he is teething. When Debbie arrives I am upstairs trying to get Hélène to lie down and go to sleep. She may not be able to tell the time yet but her biological clock tells her that this is way before normal bedtime, and she's quite right, about two hours earlier. No wonder she is refusing to settle.

As for George, as I am rubbing Bonjela on his toothless gums, he clamps down on my finger with such force I scream in agony and after somehow managing to extract it, I dance about like a Native American at a powwow, blowing on my finger and shaking my hand, which provides him with a great deal of amusement - so much so that for the moment at least, the pain of the incipient tooth or teeth was forgotten. If you are prepared to put up with the pain you could save yourself a fortune on Bonjela.

Heading to Steve's, armed with a six-pack of beer, we leave Debbie to cope as best she can, promising to phone in a little while and if the kids still haven't settled, we will come back and relieve her. When we call a while later Debbie reports all is quiet and we can enjoy the craic.

Like Al's famous spaghetti dinners, there are masses of meatballs, enough to feed an army and although there is wine, there are not lashings of it and my glass is allowed to remain empty a long time before Steve notices it is empty. That's because I seem to be quaffing it must faster than anyone else. I call it "the Al effect". I wasn't like that before I came here.

It's impossible for teachers to be together for long before the conversation inevitably turns to shoptalk which I imagine leaves the wives less than enthralled. Actually I am the one to blame, telling them about my yet-to-be-confirmed visit to Hawthorne but omitting to mention that it had ever crossed my mind that I had suspected Steve and Blake of a hoax. Not that they would have been offended. Quite the opposite in fact - more likely they would have been flattered I thought them capable of dreaming up such a scheme.

Steve offers to drive me past Hawthorne tomorrow so I can see where it is. It is very kind of him and I know it will be Hawthorne and not some other school altogether as it will surely have its name written up somewhere, though a trifle worryingly, Emerson doesn't. But he wouldn't pull a stunt like that, would he? Maybe I'm getting too suspicious in my old age.

I also bring up the subject of Christina, the girl Matt had asked us to keep an eye on because she had been molested.

"I've not noticed any difference in her, have you?" I ask the others.

They haven't.

"You know that very same day I had a pizza party for the girls' basketball team," Blake confides, "an' she acted like nothin' had happened."

That's dedication. Dedication on Blake's part, firstly to coach the girls in his free time, but especially generous to take them all for pizza afterwards. Unless, of course, he gets paid extra, which Steve does, for coaching the football team. And dedication on the part of Christina, prepared to put the trauma of the assault behind her and go to the practice (and for pizza).

It's curious, I reflect, that in this state where everyone seems so mad keen on sport they leave the running of the teams to the goodwill of the class teachers. I wouldn't be surprised when it comes to a job interview, regardless of what your subject is, if getting the job might very much depend on what sports you are prepared to offer after school.

But Blake and Steve are so utterly dedicated to sport that these extra-curricular activities represent not the slightest imposition on them. In fact, the reason Blake didn't know whether he would be able to make it to our disaster last week (not that he or us knew it was going to be one of course) was because he had other priorities: pitching balls to his sons who are in a baseball team and who had a game coming the next day.

His dedication means he takes them to play all over the state and Montana is the fourth largest (you can fit the entire UK into Montana and still have room to spare) which means driving vast distances and staying overnight in their camper van to save hotel bills. I hope to God my kids don't become addicted to sport of any kind. I have little fear of that. Iona is even less sporty than me, which is saying a lot, and hopefully the genes will out and any sporty ones they may have inherited from further back will lie dormant. But you know what teenagers are like; they'll do anything just to annoy you.

Now Blake is boasting about how well one of his sons performed in the baseball game aforesaid by giving us a riveting blow-by-blow account. When he is finished, Nat picks up the baton and tells us about his girls who are hotshot basketball players and who, like Blake, he ferries all over the state to games. Steve and Jackie haven't any kids yet, having been married only three years, and ours are mercifully too young for their lack of sporting ability yet to have manifested itself, so we can't contribute to this fascinating conversation. I hope for their sakes when they come along, Steve's kids show some sort of aptitude for sport otherwise he, for one, is going to be one deeply disappointed parent.

Apart from the kids and their sporting activities, there's always the latest thing they have killed to talk about, and fishing (same thing), as well the latest Grizzly game and when all those topics are exhausted, they can always turn to discussing professional sport which, far from being the pinnacle, they seem to regard as the least interesting. Their love of sport comes from the grass roots.

Steve, who is a New York Yankees fan (I'd never have guessed from the baseball hat which he is wearing at the moment), takes us down to his basement to show us his collection of marketing merchandise - pennants, posters, shirts and caps which he has proudly displayed on the walls. Why he should support a team at the other end of the continent I haven't the remotest idea unless they happen to be a team in the habit of winning and he can identify with that image of success. It's a phenomenon not unknown in Scotland where a good many Scots who have no connection with Glasgow, support one of the two main city teams, Rangers and Celtic, unfortunately usually split along sectarian lines, where the first is Protestant and the second Catholic and never the twain shall meet.

Baseball may be Steve's first love but he also likes football and the Washington Redskins, who are based in Washington DC, are represented on the wall too. In the unlikely event that I ever become converted to American football, that's probably the team I would support too because of their logo. On what could be a round shield, or targe, if it were in Scotland, encircled by a band of gold, the silhouette of a noble brave with a couple of eagle feathers in his hair faces to the right. Attached to this band, on the left, and much larger than the circle itself, are two more feathers whose tips look as if they have been dipped in gold. I don't know how good the team is but the logo is very fine indeed.

It's a real man's den with a desk and TV and armchairs and a sofa and it seems the natural thing to do to stay down there and talk men's talk while the women blether about whatever women blether about - probably their husbands. It also means that Blake can uninhibitedly let off a resounding fart.

In some middle-eastern countries it is considered polite to burp after a meal as a compliment to your host and what is a fart but a burp from your botty? I don't know who did the cooking, Steve or Jackie, but I would also like to think it's also a bit of a compliment to all of us down here that he favours us with this uninhibited voluntary trumpet blast and had the ladies been present, the compliment might have been much more muted or deadly silent even.

With Blake you can never be sure, for as well as being a practical joker, he also has a lavatorial sense of humour. When he knows he can do a really smelly one he deliberately calls a kid up to his desk on the spurious pretext of explaining something or other, then lets it sneak out and the poor student has to stand breathing in the noxious gases whilst Blake slyly watches their discomfiture as they pretend they can't smell a thing even although they are turning blue for want of fresh air.

On the desk is a photograph of Steve in his smokejumpers' outfit. I knew he had once been one of these courageous band of men who are parachuted in to fight forest fires. They could start anywhere and spread everywhere, miles and miles from any road or any track even, so dropping them in with their equipment is the only way to tackle them. I was amazed to hear that the training lasted only four weeks. It is very rigorous and they have to be at the peak of physical fitness. Apart from their survival possibly depending on it, they have to dig a ditch a foot-and-a-half wide and the same down, and the quicker the better, to try and contain the fire. They also spent half days in the classroom learning such things as map reading, first aid and fire management.

I was also amazed to hear they only had seven practice jumps with the target area becoming smaller and smaller each time. The sixth was into the forest and the last was when they had to backpack everything out: their 'chute, tools, sleeping bag, food and water, because the only way for the jumpers to get out again is to hump it all to the nearest road, wherever that may be.

I take my hat off to them, I really do. Having a fear of heights, the last thing I could do is jump out of a plane and certainly not with the knowledge that I was leaping into what could potentially be the everlasting bonfire as well. But I would never have passed the physical anyway. I am a ten-stone weakling, so no need to worry, I'd never get through the training.

Next to the smokejumper's photo is one of Steve and his bride, on their wedding day. He doesn't look the happiest of chappies, I have to say, and do say, since I know him well enough now to be able to take this liberty.

"Ah, well, Dave, there's a tale behind that. I nearly never got married at all!"

"Really? What happened?" Had he taken cold feet the night before? If the photo was anything to go by, he looks more like a man on his way to the condemned cell, not one looking forward to a night of connubial bliss. Or I might have got that wrong. It might have been taken as he was coming out of the cell on his way to the hangman's noose as is the preferred method of state execution in Montana.

"It was my smokejumpin' mates' fault. The wedding was on Saturday an' I had my bachelor party on the Friday night."

So he begins but doesn't really need to say anymore as I can already see where this is leading. I know of someone whose friends got the groom so drunk on his stag night he passed out. Hilariously, they had the brilliant idea of hiring a taxi, going to the station and pouring him into the first train they found standing there. By the time the groom revived sufficiently to realise he was on a train travelling he knew not where, there was nothing he could do about it until it stopped at the next station ‑ by which time there wasn't enough time to get back for the wedding.

Reader, unfortunately I do not know the outcome of this unfortunate tale. Happy or unhappy, choose your own ending. I don't believe in fairy tales but maybe you do. But let's not dwell on that tale which some may regard as apocryphal but which I swear to you is absolutely true. Let us return to Steve's story.

"We began by goin' to a local bar an' havin' a few beers but then got on the ladder to tequila an' Lemon Hart (a brand of dark rum). I was outta it by then an' I only remember parts o' the rest until I woke up on the front lawn, in the foetal position spillin' my guts out."

I make suitable noises of abject sympathy, wondering how your "friends" could be so unsympathetic, remembering that the groom had to be at the church on time, like Mr Doolittle in the musical. I assume that is the end of the tale. No wonder he looks so bad in the photo. But Steve's tale is not over yet. That was just the beginning.

"From there it is a blank until about noon on the day of the weddin' when I woke up with the dry heaves. I continued that way until 6 pm when the wedding was. But sometime afore this, an' remember I was outta it, my smokejumper friends put me in the tub (bath), stripped me naked an' rolled me in coffee grounds, crackers an' molasses."

"Oh, my God!" I can hardly believe what he's telling me, yet I don't doubt it for a moment and can hardly wait for him to continue the story, for I know, despite these bad omens, it is going to end happily and there is nothing I like so much as a happy ending.

"A bit later they realised I was in such bad shape they began feelin' sorry for me, gave me a bath an' checked my pulse every so often to see if I was still alive. They were worried I had alcohol poisoning."

No greater love hath a bridegroom's friends than seeing he was no longer in danger of dying, they tucked him up into bed expecting to see him the following morn, alive and well and ready to be mystically transformed from the state of bachelor into married man.

Sometime later, Jackie arrived (does she not know that the bride and groom should not see each other before the ceremony?). Perhaps she did not expect to find him there at all and like in a horror movie (cue suspenseful music), the first thing she saw were dark stains on the wall and carpet. Following the trail, she found the husband-about-to-be lying dead in bed, or so she at first thought. She set about reviving him and made him a cup of coffee. Little did she know what she did, for it started off the dry heaves again.

Understandably she was pretty angry, not least because she had spent a lot of time getting the marital home into a spick-and-span condition and there he had gone and mussed it all up by rolling down the stairs covered in ground-up coffee beans, just for a bit of a laugh, as you do, on your last night of bachelorhood because it's your last night of freedom and you know you'll never get another chance to indulge in such a lark.

He made it to the ceremony, just, but that's the reason why he hardly drinks any alcohol to this day and can't bear the smell of coffee. It's also why I am given my intact six-pack of beer to take back with me.

"What did you lot talk about?" I ask Iona when we are in the car. Boy, have I a story to tell her!

"We talked about our husbands."

"Oh yeah? Such as?"

"When you were most drunk."

"Oh! Really?" I'm disappointed. I wanted to tell her. "And what did you tell them about me?"

"About the time when you were so drunk on sherry you proposed to me of course."

Of course. The effects of too much alcohol can have very serious consequences indeed and might last for years and years. Maybe even a lifetime. I've already served seven years in the institution called marriage.

Reader, you have been warned.

Chapter Thirty-seven

*In which I make an exhibition of myself and attend an
exhibition on Christmas decorations.*

The phone rings. For once it is not Al commanding me
to go over for a drink, but Terri asking if Hélène
would like to come over and play with Amy. Iona is
at the sales, or should I say the introductory offers in the Mall
(thank you *Missoulian*), the newest thing in town and about
which everyone is raving, apparently. It's always coming up in
conversation: "Have you been to the Mall yet?"

Personally, I couldn't care less. This is what I like: a
lazy day reading, in this instance, Sherlock Holmes, in my
dressing gown. It helps me feel the part. In response to the
call, despite it being a small distance, I put Hélène into her
outdoor clothes and watch her all the way from our front
door to Terri's. I know she won't have any problem getting in
because their door is not so much wide open but lying flat on
the porch with Al bending over it doing something to it.

When Iona gets back to our temporary home, the
Holmes story is finished and I am dressed. It would have made
her furious if I hadn't been. No sooner has the Plymouth been
parked outside when the phone rings again. We are invited
over for coffee. Naturally Al was not the one who issued the
invitation with a beverage like that on offer. He is still
working on the door. He's sanded it down and is now gluing a
veneer on it, or trying to. It's not going well and he's shouting
things like "this Goddamned door" and at people who get in

his "Goddamned way" with their "Goddamned stupid helpful remarks".

That's exactly like me. I am not a practical person. A minor task, which in theory seems quite simple, invariably turns out to be a major operation, fraught with difficulties. When I attempt to repair something or give it some much-needed maintenance, there is always a rusted-on nut or some other problem and I fall at the first hurdle. I curse and swear at these practical jokes the gods play on me though naturally I tend not to invoke the Christian deity as much as Al does since I know He is not at all to blame, but *them*. Instead I turn to my university education and borrow from the Anglo-Saxon to vent my frustration and anger.

In the afternoon, Steve takes me on a drive to show me where Hawthorne is. It turns out to be somewhere near where Al's dear old dad lives. And it *is* Hawthorne, most definitely, because I can read the writing on the wall. I never seriously thought Steve would pull a fast one like that on me. Whatever day is decided upon, I will need to have the car. I also hope I remember how to get there and that it also happens to be one of the Big Blue Mean Machine's working days and not one on which it chooses to go on strike.

That done, we are now on our way to the extremely plush Court House - deep-pile carpets in the lobby with classy Ionic pillars. Nothing to do with the law, or driving tests, but appropriately named because it has a whole lot of courts - badminton courts, squash courts, basketball courts. You get the idea. No carpets there, obviously.

I have been here before. This is where I was introduced to the wonderful Jacuzzi to ease away the pain of a pulled muscle. It made me feel quite the latter-day Roman and I am looking forward to immersing my body in those soothing warm bubbles again. But that's not the reason why we are here, for me to indulge in some historical fantasy. Last night it had been arranged we would all meet to have a game of handball. I'd never heard of it before, but I've made the intellectual leap and expect it to involve hitting a ball with your hand.

And indeed that's what it is, a sort of poor man's squash for those who can't afford the racket. I've never played squash but I know it's fast and furious and people with heart problems are told to avoid it. And exercise addicts tell you exercise is good for you! I expect I will be hopeless at it but this looks like another of those new experiences I promised myself I would try at least once - as long as it was not paragliding.

But the minute I see Nat and Blake in action through the clear glass wall in which the door is set, I realise this might be one of those experiences which I might have been better to avoid. There are other ways to die playing this game apart from suffering a heart attack - like sustaining a broken skull. They are flinging themselves about like mad, knocking the hell out of the little black ball with the palm of their hand and dodging and ducking out of the way as it rebounds from the wall with the speed of a bullet and a sound like thunder. All around the walls are black marks where the ball has left evidence of this explosive impact. Imagine getting that in the face!

Blake and Nat seem to have given some slight consideration to that eventuality. Although they don't have helmets or face grids like their football players do, they both have kneepads and elbow pads. Blake goes a bit further and is wearing goggles and over his T-shirt, a long belt like a truss for a hernia, the very condition it is probably designed to prevent. It looks a deadly serious business but now I realise I shouldn't have been in the least surprised to find them kitted up like that, for I know sport for them is much more than a game.

Steve and I go and change and then it's our turn. Blake, sweating profusely, hands me his glove. Like golfers, you only have one. When I put it on, it's warm and wet (yeuch!) and a bit big for me, but bigger is better as it means I have a better chance of making some sort of contact with the ball, for it's a very small ball indeed that I am holding in my palm. I try to squeeze it but I might as well have tried to squeeze a stone. Blake doesn't offer me his other equipment and I think I know why - he knows I'll not be flinging myself about or stretching to reach the impossible ball while Steve, he assumes, will be merciful and give me a gentle baptism so there will be no need for the goggles to protect my eyes from being knocked to the back of my brain.

Nat's girls have come along to watch and they never knew the fun they were going to have as they watch me swing my arm and miss the ball time and time again as it whizzes past me like a bullet. From their perspective, it must have been like the Jacques Tati film I saw years ago, called *Jour de Fête* in which there was a scene, I think it may have been the opening one, which was absolutely hilarious.

The postman, seen from a distance, was wobbling on his bike as he waved his arm, at first in quite a casual way, but increasingly frantically until he fell off his bike. He proceeded to pick himself up, his arms windmilling about madly. What could the reason for this hilarious and eccentric behaviour possibly be? The camera zoomed in, sound was added and the explanation became clear: he was under attack from a bee intent on stinging him.

Thus my performance with the ball must have appeared to the girls and although I was too busy trying to hit it or avoid it hitting me to notice their reactions at the time, when I stopped, I could see they had been laughing so hard their faces were wet with tears. And I wouldn't mind betting that Nat and Blake had been wetting themselves too.

But occasionally I do manage to hit it and that evokes a different memory. In Scotland we have a form of corporal punishment known as the belt, sometimes called the "tawse" but not in my part of the country - normally two fingers of thick, hard leather, though softer, three-pronged versions are available, and administered to the palm of the hand of a miscreant pupil by the teacher. It's like the sting of a thousand of M. Tati's bees - and that's just what hitting this ball is like, if you make proper contact with it. (And to think they call this "fun"!)

It's no fun at all for Steve having to play with an incompetent idiot like me so I call a rapid halt to this making an exhibition of myself (and the girls' entertainment) by having some fun myself - sitting in the Jacuzzi. So warm and relaxing, and just by way of a change, I go into the sauna and the steam room and sweat as much as the others without having to move a muscle. I'm all for the easy life and this seems to me the easiest way to lose weight I know of, not that I need to lose much I would say.

But all good things must come to an end and it's snowing heavily again as Steve deposits me back at the empty house. We have been invited to an exhibition on how to make Christmas decorations at Dave and Gloria's church and which is to be followed by a potluck dinner. I am not looking forward to it one bit.

Making Christmas decorations sounds like women's work to me and one of those experiences I would care to avoid. The potluck may be all right, another chance to meet other people outwith the teaching fraternity, but I'm not altogether sure that a congregation of churchy people will be the biggest bundle of laughs in the world. Besides, before that happens, there is all the decorating demonstrations to be endured, then the making of them.

That is why I asked Steve to drop me and my wet towel and trunks at the house: it would use up a bit of time before I walked to the church. I leave them at the back door. They'll not come to any harm there; they're already soaking wet. Despite these precautions and having to trudge through the snow where people have not cleared the paths from the front of their houses like good citizens, I arrive in bags and bags of time before the potluck - just my luck.

As I expected, there are hardly any men there. I'm sure that my craftwork would be just as bad as my handball and I manage to avoid making anything by being constantly on the move and chatting inconsequently to those who are making things. Another chance to escape comes when Iona asks me to go to the car and get the trifle which is our contribution to the dinner. That takes a lot of time, or rather I make sure that it does.

It's all rather boring, just as I feared, except for one moment, not long after I arrived when I asked with a joviality I didn't feel, "So what's going on at this table, eh?"

"Use your eyesight," snaps one bespectacled old woman, nodding at the completed decorations on the table.

I'm shocked, I really am. Apart from the parents I've managed to offend, not to mention their darling offspring, I've met nothing but kindness, friendliness and extraordinary generosity from the people of Missoula. This is the last place I ever expected to meet this unmerited unfriendly response ⁃ in a bunch of supposedly Christian people whose leader taught them to love one another.

But strangely it's the Goddamning Al who provides the most likely explanation for this unexpected treatment. Whatever the cantankerous one is making (and it's a bit hard to tell) it is evidently not going well. I know how that feels and I forgive her, for she knows not what she does.

All the same, I take her advice after that and merely observe. Even three⁃year old Hélène is in on the act, threading red plastic beads on a dark green pipe cleaner, shaping it into a wreath and finishing it off with a piece of red ribbon so we can hang it on our tree ⁃ when we get it. It won't be long now. We are in December now and one thing looks certain: it's going to be a white Christmas, which with us, it sometimes is and sometimes isn't.

Iona is attempting, nay succeeding, as she is quite crafty (in more ways than one) in creating something a bit more ambitious. Take an old⁃fashioned clothes peg, the one with a split down the middle, glue a black pompom on the round top, paint (with a very steady hand and a very thin brush) a couple of dots with a line underneath it to make a face, then paint the next part red, to where the split begins, to make a tunic, and when that's dry, in the middle, make three gold dots evenly spaced out. While the top part is drying you can paint the bottom part black, to make the trousers and the shoes, and when *that* is dry, with your oh, so steady hand, a red stripe down the left leg.

And so what does that give you? If you haven't worked it out already, it's a soldier, fresh from his campaign in *The Nutcracker.* And what does he get for his pains?

Garrotted by a ribbon (red or green) his body, as stiff as a clothes peg, hung up to dangle on a prickly tree.

They are a friendly bunch, apart from that one. But are they perhaps just a little too friendly, just too, too civil and just too, too polite, a veneer, like Al's door, that masks the real personalities beneath? No-one is letting their hair down at the moment but maybe it's because of where they are and away from the church premises, they could turn out to be a right bunch of ravers who could drink Al under the table even if they couldn't outblaspheme him.

All there is to drink is Kool-Aid which is a shame really as such fine food deserves a better accompaniment than a sweet, fruit-flavoured drink. There are pies and quiches and salads and a whole variety of cold meats and pickles, not to mention the sweets of course, but as you know, I am not a sweet person. I have two helpings of the savoury dishes and that speaks for itself.

And of course you can't have a gathering of churchy folk without getting off with a jolly good helping of religious stuff. We begin by watching a short film on "Warm Fuzzies". A Warm Fuzzy is a furry creature with a face but without a body and whenever someone gives you one it makes you feel very happy. It also makes you feel very warm and tingly and good inside when you give someone else a Warm Fuzzy. And since there seems to be an unlimited supply of these creatures, what a wonderful world it would be, wouldn't it, if we gave each other Warm Fuzzies all the time?

I disagree. Thank God that the frustrated spinster (she wasn't wearing a ring) who had told me to use my eyes, and others like her, are fighting back or otherwise the entire planet would be drowning in a sea of furry, disembodied faces. Life would be just too, too twee and dull.

There is carol singing during which I remain silent because as well as not being a sweet person, nor a sporty person, nor a very useful-with-my-hands sort of a person - I am also not a very musical person, can't sing a note in tune. When the talents were being given out, I was still in bed and the early birds had eaten them all up. I suppose I may have some others somewhere which I hope will come to light from under a bushel some day. Maybe after I am dead, like a lot of writers.

It's very good indeed to hear the carols because they really do make it feel like Christmas is in the air. Here though, although the words are the same, they sing them to a different tune.

Just what you might expect in the land where the Warm Fuzzies live.

Chapter Thirty-eight

*In which I experience some Mexican culture
and get into trouble.*

It's back to church in the morning for Iona, as it's a
Sunday, and back to clearing the paths of snow for me,
like Sisyphus rolling that pesky boulder up the hill.
Unfortunately when I dig down to the bottom layer I find it
packed and frozen rock hard and a pick rather than a shovel is
needed. Down in Mrs Bates' basement, I search for such an
implement without success but I do uncover a sledge. Great! I
can take the kids sledging.

I put George into his snowsuit and Hélène into her
duffle coat and hood and plonk them onto the sledge. It's like
walking through treacle. With their combined weight on it,
the sledge sinks into the snow and the only bit where the
going is easy is where it has been cleared down to the icy base.
All my back-breaking efforts have succeeded in doing is to
increase the chances of someone breaking a leg and suing me.

Pulling the kids round the block has been exhausting
and sweaty work. I need a shower and a lie down. Fat chance!
The phone rings. I know who it will be.

"Hey, Dave, you gotta come on over here. Chris is here
an' he wants to show you somethin'."

Chris. Chris Mendez, Al's Mexican friend. I knew he
was there because I had noticed his big flashy Buick parked
outside and I also noticed that the door was *in situ* too, which
is just as well. Without it, the house would be as frosty as the
look Iona gives me as I set out to answer the summons.

"Don't forget that John and Carolyn are coming for tea. Don't be late and don't come back in a state." That's three things I have to try and remember which is a lot for my little brain, but like Queen Victoria, I will try to be good.

"You made a good job of the door, Al," I tell him as soon as I walk in, as usual, without knocking. There is a massive fire burning in the grate of the lounge as there always is and Al is in the kitchen where he usually is when there are guests in the house as that is where the bar is.

Al brushes the compliment aside as if it had not been such a dearly-wrought achievement.

"Chris wants to introduce you to some Mexican culture, Dave."

"Sure," says Chris, grinning. "I'm gonna show you how we wetbacks drink beer." Wetbacks, so-called because of swimming across the Rio Grande to get to the land of milk and honey.

I notice they are both drinking beer out of glasses, which is unusual. But that can't be the Mexican way. There must be more to it than that. Al gets a glass for me and a can of Budweiser out of the fridge. Why, that's not even Mexican beer! What he does next surprises me. He adds a couple of pinches of salt then squeezes in some juice from a battered lime which was lying on the bar.

"What you think of that, Dave?" Chris asks while Al looks on as eagerly as he did the time I gave my celebrated whisky-tasting performance.

I'm dreading this. What if I don't like it and my face involuntarily betrays any white lie I was already preparing in my mind. You can't insult a man's culture especially when he is so proud of it he wants you to experience it too. I take a cautious sip, then another, then a proper swallow. I can't say I notice much difference so it's not too bad, but why would you bother?

"Well, eh, erm, it tastes just fine!" I give my verdict and just in case there should be any doubt, I take another hefty swig, like you do when taking nasty medicine to get it over with. "Yes, that's very good," I pronounce definitively. "It gives it a certain *je ne sais quoi.*"

Chris probably can speak Spanish like a native but I would be surprised if he'd been exposed to the French expression before - or Al. They murder the French language over here. Not long after we arrived, I happened to see a football game on Al's big colour TV featuring a team called "Notre Dame". To my horror, they pronounced it "Noder Dame," with a long "a" like the dame in a pantomime.

"Hey, Dave, you ever tasted tequila?" Chris asks as if the idea had just occurred to him.

As if I would! Why would anyone who comes from the land of the most famous spirit in the world ever want to abandon it in favour of Mexican firewater distilled from the juice of a cactus? But I merely reply in the negative and that also turns out to be another correct answer.

"We gotta introduce Dave to tequila, Al, don't we?"

"Goddamn right, Chris. Only I ain't got none at the moment."

"No problem. Let's hop over to my place."

Oh, my God, if Iona could see me now, she would kill me! I was only meant to be going over to Al's for a few minutes and now I'm heading off to Chris's pad in his posh Buick.

On the way he points out a couple of houses he owns and which he lets out. There's even more money in the hair bending business than I had realised. He probably left school without a qualification to his name and is as rich as Croesus, whereas look at me - four years at university and as poor as a church mouse. But then, being a person in want of a talent, if I'd gone into the hairbending business I probably would have bent the hair all the wrong way and the wrong hair too.

I'm not surprised to find his hacienda is a very swanky sort of place in a decidedly Mexican or Spanish style. Inside, there are little cacti on the windowsills with their bigger, weirder, wonderfully spiky brothers forming a feature in each room. Impressive. But what impresses me much more than that are the oil paintings, all quintessentially Mexican: desert landscapes, houses, village scenes and a bullfight.

If I hadn't liked them I wouldn't have said anything but it's easy to praise them because of the consummate skill with which they have been executed. I may not care especially for the subject matter, the last in particular, but I can see why Chris likes them.

"They were done by my nephew," Chris says in a casual sort of way but I know, once again, I have said the right thing. I can't seem to put a foot wrong as far as praising Mexican culture is concerned but I still have the tequila test to undergo.

He shows me some photos of his recent trip to Mexico and tells me that's where he met Rosie. Then he shows me photos of an ancient couple.

"That's my mom and dad. They are still alive. He's 96 and she's 89. They've been married for seventy years."

"Wow! That's amazing. Maybe it's the tequila!"

That is a very funny thing to say apparently as Chris and Al throw their heads back in laughter. Like Steve and Blake they are a bit of a double act in that respect, laughing uproariously at each other's jokes, only this time it's me who is the joker and it makes me feel as if I've been accepted as part of the group, the third musketeer so to speak.

Chris goes to the fridge and yanks out a bottle of tequila and I dare say I would have had a tequila lesson then and there but unfortunately the cupboard is bare as far as limes are concerned so we will need to stop at the Grizzly Grocery near Al's on the way back as they are a vital ingredient, apparently, just as they were with the beer. What did they do in the past when limes were not in season?

This detour means that we approach Lincoln from the wrong direction in order to park the big Buick behind Al's T-bird but Chris has a novel method of turning the car round. Where I would have executed a demure two-point turn (no need for a third on these wide streets) or just a U-turn if there were no parked cars about, Chris pulls on the handbrake and suddenly the car spins through 180 degrees and there we are facing the direction we've just come from, neat as you like. Of course it helps that the road is slippery and one of your passengers is a cop with good connections, should you be spotted by a patrol car. I just hope Iona was not watching this circus act, or if she was, she did not realise I was in the car.

So let the lesson begin.

"See this, Dave," says Chris holding up the bottle. "See that worm?"

Sure enough at the bottom of the bottle there is a little, white, shrivelled-up worm.

"It's put in live," Chris continues. "The only worm to die with a smile on its face! The fact that the worm is at the bottom tells you it's a good tequila."

I nod sagely though I am sceptical. Surely it's just a matter of gravity, pure and simple and every worm must sink to the bottom eventually?

"We got as many different brands of tequila, Dave, as you've got brands of whisky," Chris continues.

Oh, well, maybe there is something in it after all, but surely there must be more to it than that? What about those inferior brands where the worm is floating in suspension like a soul in limbo and not resting in peace at the bottom? Does it mean its ghost is haunting the earth?

As if reading my thoughts, Chris continues his exposition.

"You want the worm to be at the bottom, Dave, 'cos that way the game can go on longer, see? You share a bottle with your pals an' it's considered very lucky to be the guy who gets to swallow the worm."

Aaargh! I suppose it's a variant of what the early bird catches but I would consider myself very unlucky indeed to end up devouring the maggot, for that's exactly what it looks like to me. I notice with relief that the bottle is more than half full and there is little chance of that unless ⁄ an ice-cold hand suddenly clutches at my heart ⁄ the plan is that we three *compadres* should begin the game right now. Whether or not I got the worm, it would be beyond bad luck for me if Iona ever found out that all this while I had been over here indulging in drinking games instead of waiting to receive my guests. But there's every possibility it's not something I would be able to hide, especially if I came rolling back as drunk as a Mexican bandit.

"It makes you virile," Al interjects with a hearty laugh to which Chris responds in like fashion and I join in weakly, not wanting to seem less manly and be left out.

"What you do, see," Chris goes on, "is you throw ten bucks or twenty bucks in a hat an' the person who gets the worm, gets the money. That's why it's lucky."

Worse and worse! I don't have any money with me but that wouldn't matter - one of them would certainly lend it to me and it would almost certainly be twenty bucks as ten would be too paltry a sum to be interesting for Chris. It might even be fifty dollars. Oh my God! How am I going to get out of this one without besmirching the honour of my country in this three-nation drinking game? And it's just about to begin because Al has placed three shot glasses with a purposeful bang on the bar and filled them up to the brim. Meanwhile, Chris has cut three limes in half.

"Right, this is the routine. First you put some salt on your hand, like so." Chris demonstrates by placing a peck on his clenched fist in the space between the bottom of his thumb and the first knuckle of his forefinger. "An' then you lick it, so... an' then you drink your shot in one go" - he's as good as his word - "an' then you suck on the lime like this... An' that's all there is to it, Dave. Now it's your turn."

Al has not stood on ceremony during this demonstration and it *is* my turn and what's more, if I hadn't known better, I might have thought it was pure water the way they had tossed it back without their eyes watering, let alone coughing and spluttering. Right, for the honour of Scotland, here goes.

Somehow I manage to keep my left fist steady and not show the fear I feel inside as I place the salt on the spot and lick it. God, that is nasty! It's almost with eagerness I reach for my glass and emulating my friends, down it in one. I gasp as the fiery water hits the back of my throat and burns a trail of fire down my gullet. I know my eyes are watering and popping as I suck on the lime to tame the fire but I think I've carried it off not too badly, considering.

"What d'ya think of that, Dave?" Chris laughs. Al is laughing too of course. Which is when I realise I haven't managed to carry it off as well as I had thought.

"Well, er, erm. It certainly was an interesting experience. I never knew about this custom before. Thanks for showing me this little bit of Mexican culture."

Does that sound too faint an endorsement and the first attempt to wriggle out of this game that I fear I may be sucked into (like a poor, helpless lime)? I vowed I would try most things that came my way on this exchange, within reason, but is it reasonable to try something twice when you don't care if you never do it again?

"Ready for another?" Chris asks redundantly as Al has already filled up the three glasses, as is his wont, and he won't take no for an answer, apart from Iona. She knows how to say no to him and he just shakes his head in sad bewilderment at how I could ever have married a broad like that who doesn't drink diddly squat.

"Well, I'll just have one more, for the road. You see, we've got friends coming round for dinner and Iona will kill me if I don't get back in time."

We raise our glasses to each other, we three bosom boozing *compadres* and down the hatch it burns. But how many can I get away with before I manage to get away and what sort of state will I be in by that time?

The phone rings. Is it divine intervention? Al picks up and I can hear Iona's voice shrilling down the line. Surprised at the volume, Al holds the instrument away from his ear and I can hear every word, clear as a glass of tequila.

"Tell David he's got to get over here right now! John and Carolyn have arrived. And I mean right this minute!"

There's a pause to make the point, "And tell him he's in big trouble! And I mean Big Trouble!" Then the line goes dead.

Out of the frying pan into the fire. It *was* divine intervention after all ‹ the gods save and the gods condemn and in the meantime they all have a jolly good laugh at our discomfiture.

I'm glad Iona relayed the message rather than spoke to me personally. Al is dumbstruck except to say, "Gee! That's some broad! You got time for one more, man."

He has always been very liberal with other people's alcohol, like mine for instance. With head held high but getting lower as I get nearer the house from *Psycho*, I bow out from the drinking game and go to meet my other friends ‹ and my fate.

Chapter Thirty-nine

*In which I am put under scrutiny, go to Hawthorne and
acquire a possible answer to my insomnia.*

It is a truth universally acknowledged that Monday
mornings are the pits. Wet Monday mornings are even
worse. There has been a rise in the temperature, snow has
turned to rain and the snow on the ground has turned to
slush. Walking through snow can be quite pleasant; sloshing
through slush is decidedly not. And to cap it all, as if things
could not possibly be even worse, they are. Matt is coming to
observe one of my lessons. This unwelcome news was brought
to me on Friday afternoon, just in time to spoil my weekend.

"Say, Dave, er... ahrrum, when would be a convenient
time for me to come and er, observe one of your lessons?"

I looked at him, dumbfounded. Did I hear him
correctly?

"Observe one of my lessons?" I repeated when I
recovered the power of speech. I haven't had that done to me
since I was a student. I hated it then and I hate the idea of it
now. For one thing I can't be natural under such conditions
and for another, I find it a mite insulting. I've been teaching
for seven years and I'm in a promoted post too. I thought
those days were long gone and good riddance to them too.

"Well, you see, Dave, I've got to evaluate every teacher
in the school."

"Really? Oh, well then, whenever you like. How about
Monday?"

"That's just fine, Dave." Was that a look of surprise on his face at my readiness to accede? "Any particular class you'd like me to visit?"

None of them. But what I actually say is, "How about my homeroom class?"

"That would be just great, Dave. I'll look forward to that." He gulps in that embarrassed sort of way he has, as if swallowing a stone, gives a slight smile, a slight inclination of the head and off he goes. Out of the blue, in an instant, he has brought a big, black cloud into my life.

If 'tis to be done, 'twere well it were done quickly and not have it hanging over me the whole day. We all begin the day with our homeroom class. But is this observation really necessary in my case? After all, I'll be gone in a little over six months and what's Matt going to do if he thinks it's the worst lesson in the world? Tell Marnie all is forgiven, to get her skates on and get back here as quickly as possible? It's nothing I should worry about really, but all the same I resent being subjected to this humiliation, my authority diminished in the eyes of my students as if I were some sort of rookie teacher.

At dinner that night, at Steve's, I had brought the matter up and was told that every "tenured teacher" has to undergo this ordeal every three years. I tell them about our system where we have an army of inspectors who give you fair warning they are coming, admittedly, but which only serves to put you into a heightened state of fear and alarm as you set about trying to rectify what you think they'll find fault with, and they will, because they have to justify their own existence. They stay for a whole week looking into absolutely everything, even interviewing pupils and asking them questions about you as well as watching you teach of course.

One thing I know they'd find fault with me is the way I have my classroom set out. I don't put my pupils in groups according to the current thinking, but have them in serried rows facing the blackboard. During my training we were told that was an evil that needed to be eradicated. One of these days the inspectors will catch me out. But until that sad day when I hear of their impending visit and I hastily mend my ways (only to be caught out when my pupils are cross-examined), I will carry on in my own sweet old way. And should their visit happen whilst I am over here, all Marnie needs to do is shrug her shoulders, show them the syllabus and say, "I'm only doing what it says here" and it is I who will have to face the music when I get back.

But probably it won't happen to Marnie. She's only there for a year and under our system it's theoretically possible to go through your entire career without being confronted by the education Gestapo, especially if you become a moving target, moving from school to school after its inspection as they won't be back for a minimum of five years. That's the theory but impossible to achieve in practice. I'll get my comeuppance one of these days, that's for sure, but in the meantime give me the way they do it here any day: one lesson every three years in front of your principal. What a dawdle!

The fact that it's such a matter of little import here cheers me up quite a bit but it still sticks in my craw. I have a feeling it's just Matt being nosy, an excuse to see me perform, like a circus animal. Very well then, since he thought my unit on humour was so "terrific", let it be *Faithless Nelly Gray* and a lesson on puns, just as I intended anyway. I'm not going to put on a special show for his benefit.

And so on Monday morning, Matt takes a seat at the back and listens diligently. He certainly doesn't yawn, he's far too polite and professional for that, but I can tell from the expression on his face and his body language that he's far from enthralled. After thirty minutes, he gets up and with a nod to me, his face like a poker player's, he takes his leave. He can do that; he's the boss. The kids have to endure another twenty minutes of pun and punishment before they are allowed to be free.

So that was it. How did I do? Was it so bad he couldn't bear any more? Will there be a re-trial, another trial by ordeal? Surely you can't be condemned on the basis of one lesson? Or was it merely a case of Matt being merciful? Was he merely paying lip service to the system and had done his duty? Will he ever let me know the result?

* * *

It is later than usual that I get up and dress this frosty morning. During the night temperatures had dropped below zero and now the roads are slick with ice. I have the car - Iona would never have used it in these conditions anyway, and it was a luxury to lie abed for those precious extra minutes, knowing I don't have that long walk ahead of me. Today's the day I am giving my talk at Hawthorne, in honour of which I don the kilt. But that is in the afternoon; this morning it's business as usual at Emerson.

My appearance there attired in such strange garb gives rise to a great deal of odd looks, tittering from some students and outright unconcealed laughter from others. I'm sure they still think of my kilt as a skirt and the Scots as a nation of transvestites, despite my having set them right about that, or so I had thought, in the talks I gave during my first week of classes.

"What's that?" says one, pointing to my sporran, more in a tone of disgust than a desire to know, as if I had slung something dead and furry, like a rat, round my waist.

"That's the scalp of one of my students." I reply, deadpan, just like Blake would. (And yours could be next, if you make any more remarks like that.)

The staff shows a more mature response however and I am requested to pay a celebrity visit to the kindergarten. Those kids look and see and gaze in awe but if they feel any desire to laugh or snigger, they manage to suppress it beautifully. It's more a case of being lost for words. They rarely see a woman wearing a skirt; a man wearing one is beyond belief.

Pointing to my sporran, I ask them, "You see this? Has anyone any idea what this is used for?" No-one has, or can even hazard a guess. "That's where I keep my money ∕ if ever I have any, as my wife keeps it all!" Some instinct told me not to crack the scalp joke with the little ones. No laughter at this either. "The kilt has no pockets, see?" and I do a little twirl. Now that *does* look like a dame showing off her new dress.

I had been looking forward to the Hawthorne visit, doing my ambassadorial stuff, but now, in the light of the reception from my students, the very same age as the ones I am about to be addressing, doubt and anxiety begin to melt my confidence much as the snow disappeared yesterday.

And so it is a nervous kilted figure who, after a very hasty lunch, climbs into the Big Blue Mean Machine. Perhaps if it doesn't start, my visit will have to be postponed and I can appear in my safe and sober suit at a later date... But reliably, when for once, you wouldn't mind if it didn't start, the engine bursts into life at the first time of asking and I point the vast blue bonnet in the direction of Hawthorne, not far from here actually. Definitely not enough time to go back and change and get to Hawthorne on time.

At reception I ask for Mrs Watson and a passing kid is detailed to escort me to the teachers' room. This he does without laughing, which is a relief, but without saying a word or even expressing the least sign of curiosity either which is just as discomfiting in a different way. I follow my guide with increasing misapprehension until at last we reach our destination.

The door is closed and without knocking and before I realise what he is about to do, before I can stop him or say anything, my anonymous guide flings it open and departs, leaving me framed in the doorway. As heads swivel towards me I get the feeling as if I had been suddenly caught doing something in private, something so utterly shameful that you would rather die than have anyone know you indulged in such a habit.

I hope those who had been so rudely interrupted in whatever innocent pastime they had been engaged in don't assume it was me who had opened the door in such a peremptory fashion. But who else could it have been, apart from this strange apparition that they now behold? That's just what a weirdo transvestite like him probably would do.

"Er... em... sorry... it wasn't me. It was er..." I make a helpless gesture in the direction the invisible guide had taken and my words tail off as I realise what an idiot I must sound. "I'm looking for Rachel Watson."

I'm too confused and embarrassed to note how many there are in the room exactly but something like a dozen women and only one man. I do notice that. There are a lot

356

more men than women in Emerson in the upper and middle schools particularly. Well that's something different for a start, but then not everyone is necessarily here, Rachel for one.

"She's in her room, down the hall. I'll take you," volunteers one lady. "You'll be Dave, right?"

"Yes, that's right."

"Follow me, please. So what do you think of Montana and Missoula?"

"I think they're both absolutely wonderful," I tell her without a word of a lie. "I'm having a great time. (But not necessarily at this precise moment.)"

"That's wonderful," and that's all we have time for as we have arrived at Rachel's room.

"Hi, Dave, it's great to meet you," she says, smiling, extending a hand. "I'm glad you decided to dress up for the occasion. The kids'll just love it!"

"Oh, well, er, I hope so... Have you got the projector set up?"

Almost as soon as I have said it, I realise that's probably the sixth stupidest thing I've said today and it's only early afternoon. If only I had paused to have a proper look before I panicked. The casual sweep my eyes had made of the room registered it was much smaller than mine and there was no carpet on the floor. There seemed to be more desks but they were of the same type, the ones I was familiar with from Snoopy cartoons. Whoever designed them must be laughing all the way to the bank.

"There it is," she says, turning slightly to her right to indicate it with her outspread palm, like presenting the star of a show to the audience. "Everything is ready for you. Oh, and by the way, my principal and the librarian are hoping to come along too. I wish I could stay. I'm really sorry to be missing your talk."

"That's fine. No problem."

Two observations from two principals in one day! There is a time and a tide in the affairs of men...But I'm not worried about this one in the least. In fact it might even be helpful, for what I *am* worried about is the way the kids are going to behave. If my nonchalant guide is typical, it doesn't look as if they might be the best brought-up pupils in Missoula.

"Oh, and erm, the 6th graders are nice kids but the 7th and 8th are a bit noisy."

It's as if she has been reading my mind. My heart sinks. For "noisy" read "disruptive". She didn't mention this before and I think I can now see another possible reason behind the invitation. From her point of view, an afternoon away from the blighters is better than no time away from them at all. Well, I wanted to see another school and my wish has been granted. You should never look forward to anything too much. I know how the gods work.

"Good luck," says Rachel, "sorry I can't stay to introduce you but I am sure you'll be perfectly fine. I expect the principal will be here shortly anyway and you've got the nice 6th graders to start off with."

"That's fine! And best of luck to you!" and with that I am left alone to face the unknown. The waiting is the worst. I check the projector. It's working. That's a relief.

In they troop, the chattering sixth graders, the "nice" ones. I am going to be getting the classes in chronological order which means I'll be finishing off with the eighth graders. As soon as they see me, there is a sudden hush, but it's only a momentary lull before they start again, no doubt passing remarks about the "skirt". To my dismay, amongst them I recognise my guide. Are they all going to be as lacking in respect as he was? And if these are the "nice" ones, what are the seventh and eighth grades going to be like? I am aware of my heart suddenly beating faster and my mouth becoming dry.

"All right, settle down," I tell them when there is no sign of them doing so any time soon. "My name is Mr Addison and I'm here to tell you some things about Scotland and show you some pictures."

A renewed buzz of chatter. I wait for it to subside and for them to divest themselves of their baseball hats, those who have them on. I am less optimistic that they will empty their mouths of the chewing gum. If there's one thing I can't bear, it's chewing gum and the ceaseless masticating of the mandibles. I have weaned my students off the habit, in my classes at least. Likewise, the wearing of the baseball caps in class.

But the chatter shows no sign of subsiding. "Right! That's enough! Quiet!" I bark.

That does the trick. They look at me in surprise and before they have time to recover, I plough on. "Now, I'm going to take you on a trip to Scotland and we're going to do things the way they do them there. I don't know if Mrs Watson lets you wear you caps in class or chew gum, but in Scotland we don't, so get them off and empty your mouths now!"

The last word and syllable has been uttered with a hard edge like I mean business and woe betide anyone who disobeys. To add emphasis to the instruction, I cross my arms and glare at them. It's moment of truth. What if they refuse? What if even one does? That's all it would take. What would I do then? I am mad to have embarked on this strategy, I tell myself in the endless moment while I wait to see what their response is going to be. I am only going to be with them for less than an hour. I could have tolerated the gum-chewing for that long couldn't I? Well maybe I couldn't, but it would have been better than the escalating row I might just have created for myself or the humiliating climb down I'm going to have to make instead.

I breathe again as I see the caps are doffed and some gum is deposited in the bin even if I know it won't be everyone who has made the sacrifice and some will have it secreted under their tongue or somewhere else in their mouths and will have a surreptitious chew when they think I'm not looking. If I do catch someone I'll pretend I haven't noticed.

"That's better. Now first of all, what I'm wearing is not a skirt. It's called a 'kilt'..." and I am off.

The slides and talk didn't last all that long and I was relying on questions to fill out the remainder of the time but they either couldn't think of any or weren't interested enough to find out more. One cheeky beggar did have the nerve to ask what I wore under my skirt. But was it impertinence or just an innocent desire to know?

"It's not a skirt. It's a kilt." Ye gods! How many more times will I have to say it and will I ever get the message through? "You *may* not realise it," I say, directing a meaningful look at he who posed the question, "but that is a very rude question. You wouldn't ask your mother what she was wearing under her dress, would you?"

As soon as I've said it, I realise I should have said "a woman" or "lady" or "girl". What if his mother had recently gone to heaven and this mention of her provoked an outburst and a flood of tears? In any case, I should have said "mom". And when did he last see a woman or a girl in a dress for that matter? Maybe, in his young life, he never has. I think the only pair of women's legs I have seen since I came to Missoula are Iona's and I haven't seen them so frequently once the snows came. It crosses my mind to wonder if there are women's legs fetishists all over the United States, as I bet Montana is not the only state where they are covered up, like women's faces in certain Arab countries.

But it's all right. My interlocutor accepts this non-answer without further comment. Whether he was chastened or not or merely satisfied with the answer, it's impossible to tell. His face might just as well have been concealed behind a yashmak for all I could tell.

And just for the record, though I normally am a true Scotsman, today I am not. I am taking no chances. If they thought at Emerson I was corrupting the minds of the young with my writing tasks, what they would say if I fell on the ice and gave the students a demonstration on what is truly worn under the kilt doesn't bear thinking about.

The lack of questions forces me to think on my feet and come up with other things to say about Scotland. The natives are getting restless and I am required to reprise my Mr Strict act. It will be a relief to see them go but that is tinged with apprehension at the imminent appearance of the "noisy" ones. Actually, in the event, there was no shortage of questions from the older kids, a sure sign that they were much more receptive and better-behaved, contrary to what Rachel had told me to expect.

At college we were told as long as our lessons were interesting, we would have no discipline problems. Phooey! There *may* be a scintilla of truth in it but I think Abe was nearer the mark in his celebrated remark if you substitute "please" for "fool" in "you cannot fool all the people all the time". Had a member of the education police been present at this lesson he would have told me I had pitched it too high, there weren't enough visual aids or enough variety and that is why it was getting a bit difficult to control them at the end. So you see, their bad behaviour was not their fault but mine. That's the way they think. On the other hand, I am sure I would have got brownie points for the way I got them to take their hats off and emptying their mouths (at least some of them). Credit where credit is due.

The librarian did make an appearance but I only saw the principal, Jim Dent, after it was all over. I thought it only polite and politic to thank him for the opportunity to have come and talked to the kids.

"Not a bit of it, Dave. The thanks are all ours. I'm sorry I couldn't make it. Something cropped up. Maybe we'll have you back and I'll catch up with you then."

"That would be great," I reply, hoping it would only be to the older kids and wondering what I would say to them if I *were* invited back. I couldn't do the same thing again.

* * *

On the way back, having the car, I decide to swing in past the second-hand store and visit my friend Mr Wood.

"Hi, Dave!" he greets me like a long-lost brother. "Come to look for a short-wave radio? Nice outfit by the way!'

"What? Oh, yes!" I had forgotten. "Yes I have actually, but you don't have a cent for the parking meter do you...? Thanks. Back in a tick."

You get twelve minutes for a cent - the best bargain in town. And twelve minutes will be more time than I need to choose a radio.

Mr Wood shows me four. I pick the cheapest at $22.50. There's no point in going further up-market if it serves my purpose. It even comes with an earpiece so I can listen to it in bed without disturbing Iona.

"I'll take this one please."

"Sure, Dave. That'll be $22.50 please."

Eh? That brings me up short. I thought the idea was I would bring it back if I couldn't get the World Service on it and buy it if I could. Now, in a blinding flash I realise he is not so generous and trusting as I had supposed - or so stupid. But I don't want *him* to realise the enormous depth of *my* stupidity.

"Well, you see, erm, the thing is I forgot to put my wallet in my sporran this morning." It's nothing less than the truth and it's a pretty safe bet that someone who needs a cent to feed the parking meter doesn't have a single dollar on his person either. "I really just came by to look and see what you've got. I'll come back tomorrow."

"No worries, Dave. Here, take it. If it works for you, just bring the money next time you're passing."

So it turns out I wasn't so stupid after all - he *is* as trusting and friendly as I had supposed.

It could only happen in Missoula, Montana. As I've said before and I say it again now: what a place!

Chapter Forty

In which I receive the report on my lesson, have a scary experience in the Big Blue Mean Machine and we make another attempt to entertain my colleagues.

"Dave, a moment, please." It's Matt speaking from behind his desk. He has seen me at my pigeonhole. "Close the door please. Take a seat."

Oh, God what I have done now? A closed door always means trouble. Who's been complaining about me now?

"It's about your lesson, the one I saw on Monday."

Oh, God yes. I'd almost forgotten about it. He hands me a type-written sheet, a headed form really. So now Judy, his secretary, knows what kind of teacher I am too.

"Just read it and if you agree with it, sign at the bottom to show you've seen it."

I skim read it, looking for the bad bits but none seem to leap out at me. All I can find are things like it was "a pleasant experience", "a no-nonsense attitude" and "a touch of humour". I could take issue with that last point - the whole damned thing was about humour but that would be churlish and I sign readily before he has time to change his mind.

"Thanks, Matt. That's very kind of you."

"Heard you got on great at Hawthorne yesterday."

Had he phoned and asked or had Jim Dent been on the blower already to trumpet my success?

"Yes, it seemed to pass off all right."

"You know, Dave, I'm thinking we should make more use of you. I think it would be a plan if you went and talked to the lower grades in the school too."

"Sure, I'd be very happy to do that, Matt," I lie. I know my forte is with the older kids.

"And I was also thinking that you could go to Clemens. I'll fix that up, but it won't be till the new year now. And another thing. How would you like to visit a meeting of the principals?

I'm sure my jaw must have been hanging open before I manage to gasp, "Hey, that would be great, Matt. I'd really like to do that!" I'm not lying this time. Imagine me present at a meeting of such exalted company! A real privilege. I bet there can't be a teacher in the district who has experienced such a thing until they become a principal themselves. What a chance to see what our lords and masters get up to! I wonder if I'll have to sign a non-disclosure notice first.

Matt gets up from behind his desk and before opening the door puts his arm around me. It's been a while since he did that.

"We're really privileged to have you here with us, Dave. It's a great honour to have you here with us."

"And it's a great honour and privilege to be here, Matt."

It's a great thing to be appreciated.

* * *

The festive season approaches. There are signs. At the staff meeting this morning our names are put in a container which Matt had sent me down to pick up from his room. That's very odd. Was that just an excuse to get rid of me, so they

366

could talk about me behind my back? But it's probably only my paranoia speaking. In any case, what have I to worry about?

The idea is that on the last week of term we put something small in the pigeonhole of the person whose name we draw out of the container. It can be something small and stupid like a teabag or a clothes peg but on the last day we give a proper present with an upper spending limit of $3. They call it "Kris Kringle" and it's up to you whether you reveal your identity at the end or not.

I can reveal that I have drawn Lesley Ibbotson with whom I have only a hazy acquaintanceship as she comes from that shadowy nether world in the bowels of the school, though I have seen her with a cigarette clamped between her fingers. I wonder who Blake has drawn. He or she might find some very unusual things in their box. In a masochistic sort of way, I hope it might be me.

Next Matt wants to know by a show of hands who would like to attend the Christmas dinner at the Elks. There is a big show of hands but I notice I am the only person from the top floor apart from Millie Ferguson, the librarian. She's Canadian, and a nicer person you'll never likely to meet in a month of Sundays. She had sought out the texts I wanted for my humour unit including the tracking down of the *Faithless Nellie Gray.*

Another sign that Christmas is on the way is some presents have arrived from Scotland and there has been a phone call to say that the *lefse* from Norway is ready to be picked up from a house in Beverley which happens to be John and Carolyn's street so I know where that is. Easy.

"You could pick them up on your way back from your class," Iona suggests. "I'm dying to find out what they are."

"Dying might be the operative word," I respond wryly. "Have you seen what the roads are like out there? It's like a skating rink."

It's my signing class this evening as usual, with Kathy, down at the university. I was intending to walk but if I'm to pick up the *lefse*, I'm going to have to drive as it would involve a detour.

"Just as you like," says the trouble and strife in a disappointed tone, so I take the car after all. It's quite a long way to walk to and back from the university anyway.

But there is a problem. In the interim, my mind has become confused regarding the number of the house. It was either 537 or 357 but if it's neither of those then it must be 753 ⁃ I think. At least they are all odd numbers so I know which side of the street it is at least, and the grid system helps as there is a sign at each intersection which helpfully tells you which block you are in. But that's just about as good as it gets.

"Damn! Damn! Damn!" Curses on the American system of numbering their houses according to the size of the "lot", what we call the "plot". I'm trying to find a number, any number, as I crawl along Beverley. Difficult to do because the houses are set so far back from the road you need the eyes of an owl, especially in this non-light, to see them. But what really is irritating is even if I do manage to find a number *and* read it, it will be of very little help in telling me how near or far I am from the house I am actually looking for. And knowing my luck, when I do find it, it will probably be the wrong one anyway and I'll have to start the process all over again.

It seems to me whoever is responsible for adopting this crazy system must have lost the plot and it would have been a whole lot better if they had. So much more logical to have numbered the houses consecutively, like us, for provided you have basic numeracy skills, which even I have, you would be able find the house you are looking for quite easily, a whole lot easier than having to estimate how many houses would fit on a lot. This quest for the *lefse* would try the patience of a saint and that is something which I do not have a lot of (if you pardon the pun). I decide to abandon it and resume the search in daylight which will be trying enough. This *lefse* had better be worth it. Especially as we seem to have ordered a mountain of it.

Troubles never come singly, so they say, and mine are not over yet. At the corner of Eddy and Arthur, as I brake to stop at the intersection, the Plymouth goes into a skid ˗ sideways. It is a terrifying moment and there is nothing I can do but try to steer away from the car in front while simultaneously trying to avoid a parked car at the side of the street. My fate is in the lap of the gods and time seems to slow down as I see the rear of the car in front loom nearer and nearer as I slide inexorably towards the inevitable collision. I close my eyes, not in prayer, but as an instinctive reaction, anticipating the impact ˗ and open them a nanosecond later when the expected bump does not happen. Mercifully, the car has pulled away and I glide to a stop into nothingness, even if, like a crab, I am parallel with the street I want to cross.

Damn this *lefse*! I was never as desperate to find out as Iona what it is, or in any danger of dying to find out, but look at the mess it nearly got me into!

* * *

It's Saturday. I spent the morning clearing the paths of snow. The thaw is over and it's back to the white, fluffy stuff cascading from the skies. That seems to be the pattern. Snow, snow, thaw, thaw, snow. It's leading us a merry dance, the weather. Now in the afternoon, Iona is at a Sweet Adeline's Christmas Sale, leaving me to look after the kids and peel a mountain of potatoes in preparation for another Scottish delicacy with which Iona is going to regale our guests this evening - stovies. Let's hope it goes better than the last time.

First to arrive is Art, followed by Millie and her husband, Lee. Next are Sam and Margaret and finally, my teacher and Richard's, Kathy, and the lately departed Molly. They are dressed identically, like twins. I expect what they are wearing goes under a different name over here but my word for it would be "dungarees" - trousers with a bib attached at the front with crossover straps at the back.

The last word in elegance it certainly is not, not what a well-dressed lady would wear unless she was going to do a bit of painting and decorating or mucking out what we call the "byre" in Scotland or "cowshed" in England. But then I wouldn't call these two "ladies" in the English sense of being cultured and refined, the sort who drink a cup of tea out of a delicate china teacup, holding the handle between thumb and forefinger with the little finger extended. No, these two in their pants with bibs are a right pair of women's libbers if ever I saw one.

Another thing they have in common is their ability to sign, which they do to each other right from the start as soon as I usher them into the family room and where they sit cross-legged in front of the fire like a couple of Santa's elves in mufti.

"I wish you two would stop doin' that," says Art, after a while. I don't suppose they are talking about us but they could be and I agree with him, though I say nothing.

I suppose collectively, with the possible exception of Lee, who doesn't know him, you could call this a gathering of the Matt Olsen Non-Fan Club and I convene it by telling them about my trip to Hawthorne and far from putting an obstacle in my path about going to other schools, Matt actually seems to be promoting the idea, even arranging for me to go to the principals' meeting.

"That's 'cos he's getting' the kudos of havin' you here, David. He wants to show you off to the other principals. You're good publicity for Emerson an' he's enjoyin' baskin' in the reflected glory."

It seems quite a different tune to the one Sam was singing before about Matt being scared of my telling tales out of school and I am beginning to wonder if he's not judging him a bit too harshly, though I keep my thoughts to myself.

Conversation is a fickle thing and like a will o' the wisp, can go anywhere the wind may take it. Our talk turns somehow to the time when I was nearly devoured by that Alsatian once upon a babyhood in Crovie, Banffshire, thence to Missoula and Matt. Apparently another of his hobbies, apart from killing animals and stuffing them, is breeding gun dogs. A variation on a theme. He once even had the distinction of owning and having bred, the champion gundog of Montana.

"Did you hear what he did to his wife's poodle, Dave?" I shake my head and Art continues. "He wanted her to get rid of it as he said it was 'feeble-minded' but she wouldn't. One day it was out in the yard an' wouldn't come in so he left it out all night. It was 20 below that night."

"Good God! Did it die?"

"No, but it wasn't in too good a shape."

I wonder how this shameful story ever got into circulation. From Matt who didn't think it was shameful at all, or his wife, or a neighbour who had heard the poor poodle howl and whine all night, begging to be let in? Whatever its source, I don't doubt the veracity of the tale, can easily see how Matt would have little time for animals if you couldn't hunt them, hunt with them, eat them, or stuff them.

The story is shocking enough but what I think almost more shocking is the way he seems to have ridden roughshod over his wife's feelings and her fondness for the pooch. There is something very much Old Testament about this attitude, where a woman's rightful role is to be subservient to the man and do his bidding. If it doesn't sit easy on my shoulders, you can see how Kathy and Molly couldn't stomach it. And here's the thing: I wouldn't mind betting that the Church of God which Matt attends, is very much steeped in Old Testament mentality because that's what these fundamentalist churches base their beliefs on. I should know. I escaped from one in my late teens.

Although I know it is never a good idea to talk about religion amongst people you don't know really well, or even some you do, I feel I am amongst kindred spirits here and I reckon I am on pretty safe grounds bringing it up.

"Did you see that article in the *Missoulian* this morning, about the Christmas stamps?" It's another sign that the festive period is drawing nigh and of course, stamps is a subject that interests me.

Some have; some haven't. For the benefit of those who haven't, I explain there is a report that three women in Kansas are complaining that the Christmas stamps are obscene because one of them depicts the naked baby Jesus. And in another piece of lunacy on a related subject, I saw on the TV news that a case has gone to the Supreme Court about the singing of carols in schools.

Schools are supposed to be secular in this country and atheist parents are complaining about the religious element in the carols. They may just have a point there, depending on the carol. I can see how the oxymoron of "virgin births" must drive committed atheists into a paroxysm of fury. Far be it from me to step into a national debate which must be costing the nation millions (the lawyers are laughing all the way to the bank) but I have a suggestion: if it's such a big deal, why don't they compromise by sticking to less contentious carols like *Good King Wenceslas*? That'll be $100,000 please.

Millie pipes up. "Our daughter in North Carolina sent us a clipping from her local paper. It seems there was this person going around dressed as a devil terrorising the neighbourhood. People actually died of fright."

"No! Really!" I interject, impressed.

"They've just arrested him. And d'you know *why* he did it?"

Well, apart from being a lunatic, none of us can think of a reason, just as Millie expected, her question being more for dramatic effect than anything else.

"He was trying to scare people into joining the church!"

Where no doubt, they would have the fear of God drilled into them. Well, there is a certain twisted logic to that, to be sure. You can't have one without t'other. According to his reasoning, where would reluctant churchgoers run to other than the church for protection from His evil adversary? Three hundred years after the Salem witch-hunts, the Devil seems to be alive and well in North Carolina at least.

But now for the feast.

It turns out to be less than a roaring success, just like the failure before. We should have known by now there is nothing new under an American sun in this land that has absorbed, like blotting paper, so many nations from all over Europe along with their cultures and cuisines. That's what I like about this country ⸱ it's wonderful diversity.

The traditional Scottish stovies, a mixture of potatoes, onions and left-over roast beef with the odd carrot or peas thrown into the mix, is known as "hash" here but a far cry from the sort of hash on Little Al and Don's menu. It's a poor man's dish, not the sort of thing that you would serve up to guests, not if you wanted to impress them and I can tell that our guests are not, even with Iona's homemade oatcakes with which they are traditionally served and which do not seem to be on sale the length and breadth of Missoula.

"You know, in Scotland, some pubs, that's 'bars' to you, serve them free. They have to close at 10 pm but if they serve food, they can stay open until 11."

Well, on reflection, that maybe wasn't the wisest thing to say. If they give them away free, it must reinforce the notion of how cheap they are to make. Iona knew not to bake biscuits but she did make pancakes and shortbread which, alas, we could see were eaten more out of politeness than with relish.

Once again, in our eagerness to give our guests a taste of Scotland, we have failed. But it's not really our fault. When it comes to haute cuisine, Scottish food just does not cut the mustard.

Chapter Forty-one

In which we embark on a sea of troubles.

It wasn't the best of Sundays. Hopefully it wasn't the stovies, but Iona was unwell during the night and was poorly for most of the day, which meant that the early shift of child-minding fell to me for a change, not to mention a lot of the rest of the day.

I dressed the kids and allowed Hélène to choose her clothes herself, which is why, when Iona came downstairs much, much later, she was treated to the vision of Hélène in living Technicolor, dressed in egg-yolk tights, a rust-red dress, a lilac cardigan and to top it all off, a turquoise cap on her head.

"Oh, for goodness sake! See what happens when I leave you in charge of the kids for just a minute!" she had said the minute she clapped eyes on her, then the next second, just had to laugh.

Once Iona took over looking after the kids, a renewed bout of path-clearing was necessary because during the night there had been a massive pillow fight in heaven again.

Happily, by the evening, she was a lot better and this morning is as right as rain, apart from having a bit of a headache and will be able to take George to school. But later during the morning, a messenger from Kathy tells me that neither her youngest student nor his mom has arrived. I send the messenger back down explaining about the headache. (Better not mention the turbulent tum in case the stovies were to blame and she had had the same problem.)

At breaktime I phone to find out how the invalid is. No answer. That's funny. If she has a headache she should be at home. Maybe she has gone to Carolyn's, the headache being so bad she needed to lie down and Carolyn is looking after the kids. Yes, I expect that's it.

Nat's room is nearest the phone at the end of the hall and sometime after my call, one of his students appears at the door to tell me I'm wanted on the phone. But how odd to be interrupted in the middle of a lesson! Who could it be? Whoever it is, it can hardly be good news. My heart is beating faster as I pick up the dangling receiver.

"Yes?"

"It's me."

Only two words but it's enough to tell me she is on the cusp of tears and as mad as a hornet from hell.

"What's the matter?"

"It's that bloody car. You've got to get rid of it!"

"Oh, my God! Have you had an accident? Are you OK? Are the kids alright?"

"No, no! It's not that." The tone is irritated, impatient, stressed. "It's that bloody car. You're going to have to get rid of it. I can't stand it any more!" She is openly sobbing now.

I don't know what to say. It's difficult to console a sobbing woman when you're miles apart. Your arms simply aren't long enough. What I do know is she's got me worked up into a state of anxiety. I can't begin to imagine what's happened but present fears are worse than horrible imaginings.

"For God's sake, tell me what's happened!"

It takes her a moment to regain control of her voice.

"It was terrible! It conked out at Beckwith and Stephens."

That's not good. It's one of the busiest junctions in Missoula. Stephens is actually a major road, Route 93. I make suitable noises of sympathy.

"Fortunately Al happened to come along -"

"Hey, how lucky was that?" I interrupt. "What happened next?" (And why is she crying?)

"He towed me round the corner and tried to start it, but it wouldn't. He recommended a garage and then left."

"Was it H.O. Bell's?"

"What the hell does it matter what bloody garage it was?" snarls the trouble and strife. "He drove off and left me stranded with two small kids."

Well actually it *does* matter because it was at H.O. Bell's that we bought the Big Blue Mean Machine and it was Al who had introduced me to the salesman who he said was a friend of his and instructed him to give me a good deal. So much for friendship. All's fair in love and war, to which you can now add car dealerships. And this little escapade is not going to endear Iona to Al any more either.

"Well, maybe he had to go to an emergency or something. Maybe there was a murder." It's not as strange as it sounds. In this friendly city, murders do happen. I suppose it's inevitable really with the whole state kitted out like an arsenal.

"Huh! I had to walk Hélène to Margaret's carrying George and then carry him all the way back here. My arms are dropping off."

"And where is the car now?" As soon as the words are out of my mouth I would like to stuff them back in and I get what such a stupid question deserves.

"Where I bloody left it, that's where! You've got to do something about that damned car. You just can't rely on it. I've had it up to about here with it."

I can imagine her making a slitting motion at her throat. It would have been mine if I had been there. It was my fault for buying the damned thing.

"Right! Right! I hear you," I say soothingly.

But what can I do? What *am* I going to do? The first thing, obviously, is to get the bane of my life back to the house from *Psycho*. Maybe it's Mrs Bates' fault. She has put a jinx on it.

Nat says Iona should tap the accelerator pedal once it gets warmed up and that should sort it. Probably the choke was stuck and it stalled because it was getting too much raw fuel. Tapping the pedal would cut the choke off. So much for technology and American cars. On my car back home, there is a choke that you pull out to start and push in when you are underway. What's wrong with that? With the Plymouth you can't tell if it's working at all or not shutting itself off when it should.

But if what Nat says is true, it could save me having to hunt for another car, though I wouldn't be sorry to see the back of the BBMM - if I could first persuade someone to part with good money for a heap of mechanical troubles.

Steve says he'll give me a lift and see if it will start, but first of all of course, we have to collect the keys from Iona who seems to have simmered down. The Big Blue Mean Machine starts first go, as good as gold, as if it knew its life depended upon doing so. But despite that, it's still not going anywhere. That's because Al had thoughtfully towed it into a snowdrift, considerately thinking of other road users by not blocking the highway - well this less-busy street at least.

But not to worry. Like every good Montanan, Steve has a towrope in the back of his truck, but pull with as much might and main as he can, the Big Blue Mean Machine refuses to budge and remains stuck fast.

"You need any help there fellas?"

The speaker is a guy in a much bigger truck who happens to be passing and who had seen our problem. A moment later the BBMM is hitched up to his truck and before we know it, is out of the drift and our benefactor has drifted out of our lives forever having done his good deed. That's Missoula for you. First your friendly neighbourhood cop gets you into a right old mess and then a friendly stranger comes along and drags you out of it.

Now all I've got to do is persuade Iona to give the mechanical brute a stay of execution for the time being at least. And if it knows what's good for it, it had better behave itself. It's on its last warning.

I have just got back and am upstairs changing out of my working clothes, that is to say my suit, when Iona calls upstairs, "There's a telegram for you!"

A telegram! The last time I had one of those was when I got married and they were all conveying messages of condolence, I mean congratulations. But this is a real telegram delivered to the door and it turns my blood to ice. It can't be good news. My first thought is my mother has died.

I hurry downstairs and sit down to read it with Iona hovering over me, ready to give me a hug and words of sympathy. I prepare myself for the worst. Obviously I'll have to fly back. But what about Iona and the kids? I would like her to come and she would see it as no less than her duty anyway but if she comes then the kids would have to come too. Apart from anything else, it's going to cost a fortune, money I simply don't have.

It *is* bad news but not the awful news I had been dreading. It's only from cousin John in Canada, making his apologies but saying it won't be possible for us to go to Vancouver for Christmas after all. Five days ago they were presented with a granddaughter, born by Caesarian section. In a change of plan they are going to Edmonton instead of the recently augmented family travelling all the way to Vancouver.

The baby is good news of course and although I am initially disappointed, it also comes as something of a relief. No more dilemma about whether to go or not if the forecast had looked bad and no more worrying about driving such a long way in snowy and icy conditions and the thing that was *really* worrying me, although I had been intending to practice before setting out - putting the chains on, assuming the passes were open in the first place - which there was every chance they might not be if a storm suddenly brewed up.

I can see Iona's expression change from worry to relief and back to worry all in an instant. She was really looking forward to spending Christmas with my relations. They had been so exceptionally welcoming I could see why, but in her disappointment, she has overlooked what a nightmare the journey might have turned out to be. I think she is now worrying about something else - where we might be invited instead. I imagine we will not be short of offers, or maybe we won't have any at all, as it is a time for families. But what's so wrong with us spending Christmas with just the four of us?

I am not worried about that but there *is* something I am worrying about and not for the first time either - money. A bank statement tells me my salary ($481) has been paid into my account. Wonders will never cease! But the bad news is that that the grant, three times as much, still hasn't arrived. The grant is meant to make up for the difference in the cost of living, only the funny thing is we've found everything so much cheaper here than in Scotland. Thanks anyway, good old Uncle Sam! I'll have to write to my bank and try to get it sorted out. It would be a very nice Christmas present indeed if I managed to get the bonus paid in by then.

Next, Iona hands me a letter from her mother, addressed to both of us. She's been over to see Marnie and is not best pleased with her for being so tardy in redirecting my mail to her address so she could post it on to me. It costs nothing to redirect mail in the UK so that's not the reason why she hadn't, just her normal laid-back attitude to everything. Enclosed was a ballot for elections to the General Teaching Council, our governing body, which should have been returned to them by October - two months ago. There was also a cheque for a gas rebate of £1.20. It's not much but better in my pocket than theirs. Now it's out of date, or will be by the time I send it to my bank.

But that's not the real problem, the real reason why I am worried. Before we left I had set up a transfer of the utilities to Marnie's name - or so I thought. The one thing I did not change was the phone because it cost £100 to do so and another £100 to change it back again. But now Fiona's mum tells us the electricity company has sent Marnie a change of occupancy form to sign, which she hasn't done, so the electricity bill is still in my name and for all I know, so is the gas bill. That means that although I am more than five thousand miles away, I'm the one legally responsible for paying the bill - which she hasn't been paying. Now she, or me rather, has had a final demand which she has also ignored.

"You've got to pay it at once!" I can just imagine my mother-in-law's cry of exasperated horror.

"Hope to God she doesn't run off at the end of the year leaving unpaid bills," says Iona.

"No, no, she won't do that," I dismiss the notion with breezy conviction. "She's just the most disorganised person on the planet. She must have driven Perry nuts. Maybe part of the reason he left her. She'll stump up soon enough - when they tell her they are going to cut her off."

In this same epistle, my mother-in-law announces her intention to come and stay with us in the summer. I don't regard that as bad news. After all, she came on our honeymoon, so why not avail herself of the opportunity to see where we have been living for a year and also meet our friends? She will fly to Vancouver, which is ideal as we will be able to meet up again with my cousins, and unfortunately, bid them goodbye too.

That is quite enough troubles for one day and the last one for us, thank God, but later, in the evening, another one does crop up. We have a visit from Carolyn who says that John's mother in New York has been given twenty-four hours to live. What a coincidence! I had feared my mother had died and now John has been told his mother is all but. Had it been the news I was dreading, it would have been a terrible shock but preferable I think to the awful inevitability John is going through at this very moment. I can imagine him jumping out of his skin each time the phone rings. Except he's not standing by it at all. Carolyn goes on to say he's already in the air on his way to his appointment with death, and in all probability, will not arrive on time.

"Was it quite sudden?"

"No. She'd not been eating for some time," Carolyn tells us. "Her doctor was no good. Didn't do anything and the family insisted she was taken to hospital. Even there they didn't try to make her eat anything or find out why she wasn't. Then she had to have an emergency operation and when they opened her up - you know what they found?"

We both shake her heads but we know it's going to be horrible.

"Gangrene! Her insides were gangrenous!"

Good God! That's even worse than I was expecting. No wonder she wasn't eating and no wonder she doesn't have long to live! I wonder if it's the start of a long legal battle for negligence.

After the funeral, their troubles may be just about to start.

Chapter Forty-two

*In which I attend a couple of meetings and expound my
views on the differences between Scottish and American
education.*

It's Tuesday morning and a substitute has been drafted in
to take care of my classes because I'm going to the
principals' meeting at the admin building with Matt. On
our way to his truck however, we encounter a former pupil.

"What you doin' here, Sally?"

"I missed my bus, Mr Olsen, so I took the Emerson bus
instead."

"You go to Sentinel don't you?"

"Yes, Mr Olsen."

"And you're figurin' on walkin' there, huh?"

"Yes, Mr Olsen."

If it had been Hellgate it would have taken her ten
minutes or so from here. I pass it every day, but Sentinel is
miles and miles away right on the other side of town.

"Hop in, Sally. I'll give you a ride."

Since it's completely in the opposite direction to where
we are going, I think it's pretty nice of Matt, a Christian
thing to do, even if, with jutting jaw, he gives her a lecture on
punctuality and tells her it's only because he likes her that he's
going out of his way to do this for her. Sally says nothing the
entire journey, not even when we arrive at Sentinel. Maybe
she didn't appreciate the lecture. Without a word, she climbs
out of the truck and slams the door behind her without a
backward glance.

Like her, I am speechless. The sheer ingratitude staggers me, it really does, though for his part, Matt doesn't seem in the least put out.

"She's a special ed kid, Dave," he says. "I wouldn't have taken her if the sidewalks hadn't been so icy."

Maybe that goes someway to explaining her behaviour but I don't think it excuses it. But it's not untypical of the sort of attitude I've seen from the young towards their teachers, regarding themselves not so much their equals, but superiors even, as if they were doing them a favour by turning up at school to let knowledge be poured into the empty vessels of their heads. And it's not just the kids who think this way. I recall a debate I had with Art some time ago in which he was at great pains to explain to me that the kids *were* our equals and we should treat them as such.

Despite this detour, we arrive in plenty of time for the meeting. In that respect at least, Matt practices what he preaches on punctuality. I find myself sitting between him and Jim Dent. There are two main items up for discussion - the need for guidance for pupils 'thru' kindergarten to 8th grade. By "guidance" they mean the job that parents used to do and should do but which seems these days to have been abrogated more and more to the teacher. The proposed program is a nationwide project and the district has the opportunity to be involved in a pilot scheme. One principal spoke out strongly against that, saying the money would be better spent elsewhere. Another countered that funding would be provided as it was a pilot scheme and it might be worth considering. It was kicked into the long grass for further discussion at a later date. Matt does not express an opinion.

The other issue is middle schools, whether to have them or not. The proposal is to create schools of about 600 pupils composed of sixth, seventh and eight graders. I was aware of this proposal as I had heard Blake and Steve airing their views about it. They are against it. Most people are resistant to change, happy to carry on in their comfort zone but their reason was because they thought the kids would not get enough sport. As ever, that is their greatest priority and my least.

One of the principals speaks up against it, not the same one as before. His point is the schools would be too big and this would lead to indiscipline. I keep my face as poker-straight as Blake's when he is telling one of his stories. What a load of tosh! But it's not my place to interfere: I am here as an observer only.

The meeting is drawing to a close. Going round the table, people are asked if they have anything to contribute. After Matt says he has nothing to add (I've not seen any evidence of him being first among equals here as Art had alleged), I expect it to be Jim Dent who will speak next, even if it's just to say "nay" but instead what I hear is a nervous little cough from Matt followed by: "Have you anything you'd like to share with us, Dave?" He, at least, clearly expects me to say something more than "no" and I bet that goes for the rest of them too. Having been given the privilege of seeing the workings of the inner sanctum, it's now time for me to sing for my supper.

"Well, first of all," I have to stop to clear my throat before I continue, "I'd like to thank you very much for the opportunity to attend this meeting. I've found it very interesting, particularly the discussion on middle schools. You see, I come from a middle school with close to 700 pupils. There are only two in the whole of Scotland as a matter of fact. It's an experiment."

That's got them. All round the table principals are pricking up their ears.

"Our system has four years, the equivalent of 5th thru 8th here. Actually I think it is a good arrangement - those ages are much more of a natural grouping than the high school which has 12 year-olds thru 18. There's a big gap in maturity between a twelve year-old and an eighteen year-old, as you know. And it works both ways. Take the younger kids out of the high school and you've got a more natural grouping of kids there too. And the same goes at the other end of the scale with the kindergarten thru fourth graders."

Some principals had spoken in favour of the system and I am aware of some nodding heads but whether that's in agreement with what I've been saying or merely signifying that they are managing to decipher my accent I can't be sure, although I have done my best to speak in American for them.

"On the matter of size, my school is considered small in Scottish terms and I'm very much in favour of small schools." More nodding of heads. "That's what I like about Emerson: because it's so small it's like a family. I bet Matt here knows each and every student in the school by sight and by name."

Matt swallows and colours, not because it is not so, but because it is indeed the case and it sounds like praise.

"And because the class sizes are so small, you are able to give the students more individual attention. You really get to know the pupils, I mean students, well. In Scotland it's common to have thirty in a class."

After the praise of their class sizes, at least as far as I know them, I diplomatically omit to mention that for me, being in Emerson is like being in a holiday camp, not only because the classes are so small, but because the students produce so little work for me to grade. And if my pupils in

Scotland could see what little my students here are expected to produce, they'd think they were in a holiday camp too. Conversely, if my Emerson students were made to do what I expect of my pupils, they would notify the Children's Protection Agency or whatever they call the Royal Scottish Society for the Protection of Cruelty to Children. In fact, apart from the offensive subject matter when I tried to introduce my *Murder Mystery Magazine,* it was the sheer amount of writing involved that had contributed in no small way to the De Bone incident.

"I don't know what the proposed class sizes would be in your middle system," I continue, "but as long as they can be kept as low as they are now, I can't see that size of the school *per se* would lead to indiscipline."

"Our students are too indisciplined already," growls the principal who had spoken against the middle schools earlier. "A bigger school would just make them worse."

"I don't follow that. Discipline begins in the classroom. As long as you have your class under control and the other teachers do too, I can't see why there should be a problem, particularly if you, as principals, back up your teachers." I would have loved to have stolen another glance at Matt to see if he had turned a deeper shade of red but I can't. That would be like pointing a finger at him and saying; "J'accuse!"

Already I feel I may have overstepped the mark: what right have I to tell a principal that he's wrong? And yet I agree entirely with him that the students could do with a much-needed stricter regime.

"Actually, I wasn't quite accurate there," I hasten to correct myself. "The discipline or indiscipline doesn't begin in the classroom at all - it begins in the *home* and that's what you were discussing at the start of the meeting. The need for a guidance programme. There wouldn't be any need for that if the parents were doing their job properly. If they don't discipline their kids, how can you expect the teacher to do it? After all, they are the ones who have much closer contact with them and more influence and if *they* don't bring them up to show deference to the teachers and do what they ask them to do without challenging them - who will?"

I never intended this to be a lecture. And surely this must sound to them like some Scottish upstart who has come along to teach their grannies how to suck eggs? And yet the faces round the table don't look hostile. I might even say the body language is saying: "Go on!" and so I do.

"Why, just this morning Matt gave a ride to a former student. And you know what? She never thanked him or even said goodbye. Now that's just plain bad manners and if the parents don't bring their kids to be polite and mannerly, where are you?

"It's the same in Scotland," I add hurriedly. "I could give you lots of examples of bad parenting where the parent rushes to judgement in support of their child against the teacher without being aware of the facts. A case of what you might call the tail wagging the dog." Actually I am thinking of the Mrs De Bone incident and the Mrs Taylor fiasco before that and I'm sure the point won't be lost on Matt who is probably beetroot red by now - at least if he has any conscience at all.

"Well, that's all I have to say really. I'm used to a much stricter regime in Scotland and we still have problems. It seems to me that's where the problems of indiscipline lie. If students know that they can undermine the teacher by calling in mom, you're lost. And when the class sees one getting off with something, the rest think: I can get off with that too.

"You know, when I was at school, as a consumer (slight ripple of laughter), if I did something wrong I would never have dreamt of telling my parents ﹣ I'd have got my ass licked. Now it's different. The genie is out of the bottle and I don't know how we'll ever get it back in.

"Well, thanks for listening and thanks once again for letting me sit in on your meeting. It's been very interesting."

To my astonishment there is a round of applause and then we break up. Jim Dent and some others don't get a chance to say anything even if it was just to say they couldn't follow that. But back in the intimacy of the truck Matt says, "That was a great speech, Dave." The Adam's apple bobs with emotion. "I want you to know how lucky we are to have you at Emerson."

"I hope I didn't go on too long." It's really just something to say to cover up my own embarrassment. I wonder how the atmosphere would have been if I hadn't had the applause. Would the oblique criticism of his failure to back me up and his kowtowing to the parents have smouldered between us all the way back to school?

"No, no, Dave, it was just fine." Gulp. "I was really proud of the way you spoke."

That is a compliment and I accept it. If he has been taking in what I was saying maybe I'll have given him something to think about too. But what would be really great or "neat" is if the district does decide to adopt a middle school system and I could think that perhaps I had played some small part in that decision. That would be a real compliment and lasting legacy! And wouldn't Blake and Steve curse me!

* * *

In the evening Sam picks me up to take me to a meeting of the school board. The main reason, apart from letting me have a taste of seeing it in action, is because Sam has applied to go on an exchange to New Zealand and the vote is going to take place this evening. He thinks it might help his cause if they were to ask me to speak and I could warble on about the benefits of an educational exchange. I don't know if I am responsible for putting the idea into his head or not, but apart from the allure of a foreign land and all the experiences arising out of that, I wouldn't mind betting that getting a break from Matt is another motivating factor, and for his part, Matt wouldn't stand in his way.

The meeting is chaired by Dan Gunn, the district Supremo, and consists of various local bigwigs and worthies who do not necessarily have any connection with education, just as the composition of our education committee is made up of butchers, bakers and candlestick makers. I am relieved to see there is no sign of my auld enemy, Mrs De Bone, chairman of the powerful appropriations committee, the one that amongst other things, decides if teachers are to get a pay rise or not. That is why Matt is so scared of her.

The meeting begins with routine business of which I understand the words but not the substance. It's interesting to see that the informality that is everywhere in the American education system persists here too in this decision-making process. Then Dan pipes up with, "Matt, why don't you introduce Dave to the board and ask him to tell us about the exchange programme?"

That's the way they do things here, couch orders as suggestions as if it was something you could take up or dismiss as you please.

Matt gets to his feet.

"Er, ahrrum, this is Dave Addison from Scotland. He's a 7th and 8th grade teacher on exchange with Marnie Charbonneau. I have to say that, er, ahrrum, ever since Dave has been with us he's been a real credit to Emerson and we're very lucky to have him with us. We're learnin' a lot from him."

Now my turn to utter fulsome praise.

"Thanks, Matt. I must say it *is* a great pleasure to be here in Missoula and Emerson. Matt has been very supportive, as have the rest of the staff. Everyone has made me feel very welcome.

"Going on exchange takes a bit of courage, leaving the security of what you know behind and heading into the unknown. But I've really landed on my feet in Emerson. My son is deaf and thanks to Matt, he's been enrolled at Emerson to learn sign language and the university is taking very good care of him too. Thanks Matt."

He is blushing to the roots of his sandy hair and glowing with embarrassment. One bit of back-scratching deserves another, after all.

"The programme I'm on is actually for education and *cultural* exchanges, so as well as my finding out about your education system, it's a privilege for me to be able to find out about life over here and in return, tell my students about Scotland. I think the exchange is just as valuable an experience for them as it is for me. Just recently I've set up a letter-writing programme between my students and my pupils in Scotland. Who knows where that may lead? Some may end up life-long friends. Who knows?

"I've also been to another school to speak to the students and I hope I'll get the chance to visit some more before I leave. And when I do go back, at the end of the exchange, I'm sure I'll look back on this year as an enriching experience and one of the best decisions I ever made in my life was to apply for the exchange. I would encourage anyone to do what I did. I just hope it turns out as well for them as it did for me."

Applause.

"Great speech, Dave," Matt leans over to murmur in my ear. "Proud of you!"

Next on the agenda, Sam's exchange application is approved, *nem. con.* Was it something I said? To my surprise, Sam won't come in for a celebratory beer when he drops me off back at the house.

"Naw, I've decided I'm gonna stop drinkin' durin' the week but I'm gonna get drunk at the Elks on Friday."

That's at the staff get-together.

"Matt will enjoy that!" I tell him.

Sam chuckles. "Thanks for your talk, David. Maybe it swung it."

"Oh, I don't know," I say modestly.

"Yeah, well maybe it didn't," he agrees, pricking the balloon of my ego, "but thanks anyway. It didn't do any harm anyways."

I wish him well but there's a long way to go yet. First of all there is a suitable match to be found and even after I was told I had been matched with Marnie, I was warned that it could still fall apart at the last moment. Thank God it didn't.

That tells you how far I have come. I can still remember, not so long ago, how I was worried I'd made a terrible decision and berated myself for not being content with my lot in Scotland. Now look at me!

Chapter Forty-three

In which I go on the Great Babysitter Hunt and we both go to the staff Christmas night out.

I t's Friday, the day of the staff night out at the Elks and I don't feel like it at all. I've had a terrible night, barely got a wink of sleep. Both kids were crying: George because of his teething and Hélène because she has taken to not eating her food and wakens up in the dead of night complaining she is hungry. As for me, I had stomach problems of my own. Must be a bug. The same Iona had. Unable to sleep, I lay in bed wondering how I would manage to get through the day, never mind the evening.

And if that weren't bad enough, I had to get up even earlier than usual because of some stupid singing practice we have to do. There is going to be a Christmas concert and the massed staff choir are going to present a parody of *The Twelve Days of Christmas* for the entertainment of the students. Since I can't sing a note, it's a waste of my precious time in bed as I intend to mime the entire thing as a service to humanity.

At some stage in the morning Matt comes to my room and asks me to step out into the hall. Oh, no! Not more praise! I can't stand it. My head will burst like a pumpkin thrown from a great height onto the sidewalk.

"Have you and Iona made up your minds what you're going to eat at the Elks tonight, Dave?" He is armed with a pencil and a copy of the menu which we had been given earlier in the week in order to make our choices.

"We'll both have the New York steaks." At $8.25 they are the most expensive items on the menu but I am saving money by not having to travel to Canada for Christmas and even better, to Scotland for a funeral. I am also banking on the grant coming one of these fine days.

Matt makes two strokes on the menu. "Er, ahrrum, the staff would like you to come along as our guests, Dave."

I am flabbergasted, I really am. "Oh, no, we couldn't possibly..."

"No, no. Dave. It's all taken care of."

How kind! But how can I possibly thank them all? There's comfort in the thought that just about everyone in the school is going and so their contribution would work out at less than a dollar each despite our extravagance. But it's the thought that counts and it's a very kind thought indeed. And then I remember how I was sent down on what I had thought at time was a rather spurious reason for the Kris Kringle voting container. That's probably when Matt had made his modest proposal to the staff.

I can feel myself taking a leaf out of Matt's book and blushing furiously. "Well, in that case, thank you very much indeed. It's very kind of everybody. Much appreciated."

"Our pleasure, Dave. Least we can do," he says, putting his arm round my shoulder. "You're a credit to the school."

So it was more praise in the end, after all. But my head is firmly screwed on.

* * *

At lunchtime I go to the bank and transfer $200 (half our American wealth) from the deposit account into what they

396

call the "checking account" - too late. When I get back from school, there is letter saying we are $38 overdrawn. And there's worse. Iona had fielded a phone call from the doctor's to say that our cheque had been returned and now she lives in dread of another phone call of a similar nature. That was for the time George was having his convulsions and now I understand why they print your phone number on the cheque. Now I need the grant money more than ever. A letter has been written and is already winging its way to Scotland.

There were no other calls of complaint about bouncing cheques but there was one from Terri to say that she'd heard my name mentioned on the radio - that I'd given a talk to the school board. No wonder their radio is so deadly boring if that is the sort of thing that is considered newsworthy. And on the subject of radio, I can get the World Service (and a lot of static) on the one I have on trial from Mr Wood. The question is if I went up-market, would I get better reception?

There was some good news too. We can burn the Yule log. Grandpa Hertz arrived with my hard-wrought-for logs at last. Poor man, he must have been bullied into it by Al, who like me, was at work, so I assume. So it was up to Iona and him to unload them and stack them by the side of the house. No mean feat for a weak old man and a little-bit-stronger-than-him young woman. To make matters worse, Grandpa had been frostbitten as a child and as cold badly affects his poor, arthritic old hands, Iona had to take him in to thaw them out in front of the fire.

I have a lie down as soon as I get back from school, fall asleep as soon as my head hits the pillow and arise feeling much more in the mood for partying. This is another kilt-wearing opportunity. Because it is the season to be merry, our regular babysitters, Rob and Debbie, can't do the needful but there's no need to worry: babysitting is an industry among high school kids at a rate agreed by the Babysitters' Union of America and I set off to pick up Kelly Jensen who is a sophomore at Sentinel. That means she's in her second year.

"She lives in Crestview. Take Pattee Creek, come off at Whitaker then right onto Westview and you'll come to Crestview," Iona tells me, reading off the directions Kelly must have given her over the phone.

Simple. I know where Pattee Ceek is. But when I get to Westview, I discover it is a steep, icy slope although it has been sanded. I start making the ascent, worrying I'm not going to make it. I do, but at the summit see no sign saying "Crestview", only "Crestline". And even more confusingly, I have a choice between E and W. That can't be right. Damn! I must have missed it. Back down the hill I go, keeping my eyes peeled for Crestview.

But now, down at the bottom again, there was no sign of it and like the Duke of York, I march my mean machine back up to the top of the hill again. So what now? East or west? I elect east, hoping Crestview is off it.

Wouldn't you know it! After what seems miles, I'm back at Westview again without any sign of the elusive address, so once more up the slippery slope I go, slowly, and like someone who has sent up a prayer, looking for a sign. I don't expect there to be one, so my only option will be to turn right onto W. Crestline. If I don't see it then, God knows what I'll do. However, before I reach the junction, a car coming towards me flashes its lights and stops, waiting for me to approach. I pull up alongside and let down my window.

"You lookin' for the Jensen house?" asks a very attractive young brunette, through her open window.

My heart leaps up. A damsel to the rescue of this benighted driver! But how did she know? I confess I am indeed looking for that very place, which is a lot better than confessing to being a kerb crawler which might be another possible reason for driving so slowly. But since not a single figure is to be seen in this snowy street scene, that eliminates that possibility. Someone driving as slowly as me must be someone in search of an address. But how did she know it was that particular one?

"Take a right when you get to the top and we're on the right."

Right. Crestline, not Crestview after all and there's a clue in the "we're". This must be Kelly's sister.

"Right, thanks," is all I have time to say before, remembering the abortive *lefse* mission, I get the chance to ask her how far along on the right it is or for a description of the house, for each and every one is different and should be easily identifiable.

As for the *lefse,* what a disappointment that turned out to be! It was nothing other than what we call a "tattie scone", a potato scone to the uninitiated, or perhaps I should say "biscuit". (To think that before I came here I thought we spoke the same language!) I confess, regardless of whatever you call them, they are not something that I am particularly fond of. And they were big! Dinner plates at least in diameter! And we have twenty of the blighters to eat our way through. Some lucky people, like them or not, are going to be presented with another Scottish delicacy, God help them!

Finding the Jensens' house was a lot easier than finding the *lefse* house, thank God. Kelly is ready and waiting and if I hadn't worked it out already, as soon as I see her, I would have guessed she was the sister of the driver. If anything, she is even more gorgeous. Forget the Elks! Well, Iona can go. I wouldn't mind staying and giving Kelly a lesson on Scottish culture if she would care to hear it.

A moment later, she gets, and I give her, a bit more exposure to Scottish culture than I had intended. As I follow her down the path, my feet suddenly give way under me and I land on my back, my kilt having flown up over my waist in the process. I give an involuntary cry of surprise at this sudden fall from grace and loss of dignity, to say nothing of a cry of pain as I land with a thump on my coccyx. Before I have recovered from the shock and had time to cover up my embarrassment, Kelly has turned round to see, with her very own eyes, what Scotsmen wear under the kilt.

Both of us still recovering from shock and later than expected due to the Great Crestview Hunt, we get to Lincoln to find that Sam and Margaret with whom we'd arranged to go to Mo Mokomo's for drinks before the Elks, are waiting for us. When we arrive at Mo's, the Fergusons are also there and so is Art, resplendent in a black poloneck which perfectly sets off his gold necklace while the sartorial effect is completed with a padded embroidered jacket.

"I'm so glad you wore your kilt, Dave," Mo coos. "What would you like to drink?"

There's only one answer I can give to that if I don't want to cause disappointment. She has Johnny Walker and I compliment her on her choice of brand. I mix it with American ginger ale so that is a neat mixing of our two cultures, even if Mo is Japanese, or at least her ancestors were.

"What will you have, Iona?" As usual, that's a bit of a problem for her, not least because she doesn't know what's on offer anyway. "Would you care for a pink squirrel?" Mo suggests, seeing her hesitation.

"Er... em. What's that?"

"It's delicious. It's a cocktail made up of Cream de Noyox, Cream de Cacko and cream," she explains, handing Iona the bottle of Squirrel for her perusal.

Iona likes the look and the sound of it, but will she enjoy the taste? I ask to see the bottle, curious about the ingredients. Crème de Cacao and Crème de Noyaux. I might have guessed! It's another case of murder. Murder of the French language. And the "noyaux" turn out to be almonds because Iona pronounces it the most delicious drink she has ever tasted as she loves the almondy taste. She'd better mind her p and q's from now on. It sounds the perfect disguise for a disgruntled husband intent on murdering his wife by adding cyanide to it, like people are always dying of in Agatha Christie books.

We are the last to arrive at the Elks though I dare say we are the merriest. The place is mobbed. We are not the only group having this pre-Christian celebration, nevertheless we manage to secure a table to ourselves. I offer to buy the group a drink but Millie, especially, won't hear of it and to my enormous relief, suggests we have a kitty.

We begin with a salad and then to my horror, a band begins to play, and no ordinary tune this but *The Bonnie, Bonnie Banks of Loch Lomond* and everyone, but everyone at the table and adjacent tables is looking at us with as much hope and expectation as a dog when it presents you with a stick to throw.

"Come on," says Iona, getting up. "It's a Gay Gordons." As we leave for the dance floor, she adds, "You know how to do that at least."

That's true, I do in a sort of way, but I'd far rather not. There are some other dancers on the floor already but as they become aware of us, they melt away and the floor is left entirely to us. Seeing me in my kilt, if they thought they were going to be treated to an expert dancing display, then they would have been severely disappointed. I thought my torture would never end but at last it does and to great applause and with my ears burning with shame, we return to the table. It's not easy being an ambassador sometimes.

"You're going to have to dance with some people," Iona says out of the side of her mouth.

"God, no! I'm not am I?"

There's no need for her to say anything else: the look says it all. We are the guests of honour after all and now I must dance for my supper. It's all right for her; she can just sit tight and hope no-one asks her, except she wouldn't hope that at all. She doesn't mind a bit of hoofing. In fact she was an excellent ballet dancer once upon a girlhood.

Whilst I am pondering who is going to be my first victim, Mary Mason sails up like a galleon in full sail and drops anchor.

"It was me who thought of asking the band if they could play any Scottish tunes," she announces proudly. If she were a dog she'd be wagging her tail, hoping for a bone as a reward. Fat chance! I have one to pick with her though. "So you're the person to blame," I want to say, but don't. The best I can muster is a weak smile.

"Do you have any bands in Scotland that play that kind of music?"

Good grief! Is the woman completely barking?

402

"Would you care to dance?" And it will serve her right if I stand on her toes, not that I would do so on purpose of course or out of revenge, but it's her own fault if I do.

Later on, Art leans nearer my shell-like and says into it, just loud enough to be heard over the band but by no-one else, "I'll buy you a beer, Dave, if you dance with Matt's wife."

I look closely at him to see if he's serious. He appears to be. "Make it two and I'll consider it."

"You've got a deal, Dave," and he offers me his hand below the table.

I grasp it and then set out on my mission. If I've got to dance with someone, I may as well make a bit on the side. It's only as I'm taking extra special care not to stand on *her* toes as well as endeavouring to keep my foot out of my mouth as we engage in small talk (which requires no small amount of ambidexterity on my part), that I realise this was a very polite and diplomatic thing to do. Sometimes I just can't put a foot wrong.

For the sake of appearances, to show I was not trying to "sook up" to Matt as we say in Scotland, I dance with some other ladies. I am fresh back from one of these dances of duty when Matt appears at my elbow with Patty, his wife. They are taking their leave although it is relatively early - which is when it occurs to me if there is anybody more on duty here than me, it is him. For him to come here to this den of iniquity where they sell alcohol must be akin to a Jainist being given a tour of the leather factory.

I try not to knock over our army of dead beer bottles as I stand up to shake his hand in farewell. I am the guest of honour after all. He has my permission to put this purgatory behind him.

"Really proud of you, Dave," he says, gripping my hand like a vice and swallowing hard. (I knew it was a good idea to dance with his wife.) Maybe he's more grateful than proud, for that's one dance it saved him from having to do with her. But probably it has more to do with people not attached to the school asking who the bloke in the skirt is and being told, "That's the exchange teacher from Scotland, in Matt Olsen's school."

People mingle and we are joined at our table by Ron Ackermann and his wife, Beth, who had substituted for Kathy Kuhn today. He's actually the psychologist for the special ed kids and at 11 pm precisely, I discover he is something much more exalted than that ⁓ the Exalted Ruler of the Elks, no less. I really can't help but be amused at the pretentiousness of the title.

A bell chimes eleven times and Ron goes to the dance floor to make a speech.

"Wherever Elks may roam, whatever their role in life may be, when this hour falls upon the dial of the night, the great heart of Elkdom swells and throbs. It is the golden hour of recollection, the homecoming of those who wander; the mystic roll call of those who wander; the mystic roll call of those who will come no more. Living or dead, an Elk is never forgotten, never forsaken. Morning and noon may pass them by, the light of day sink heedlessly into the west. But 'ere the shadows of midnight shall fall, the chimes of memory will be pealing forth the friendly message. [Pause. Raising his glass.] To our absent members."

"Great speech, Ron," I tell him when he gets back. Actually I thought it was a bit over-sentimental but not without a certain poetry, like *the dial of the night*. "Don't suppose I could have a copy of that could I?"

"No problem, Dave," he says, fishing it out of the breast pocket of his safari jacket. "It's not a state secret," he grins.

Actually I know its origins lie in freemasonry with all the ritual and secrecy that is steeped in. Wouldn't it be something if I could be an Elk for a year! That would be a real American experience. I'm sure you'd have to be nominated by someone and who more influential than the Exalted Ruler himself?

"It costs $50, Dave."

That is a bit of a disincentive I must admit. Maybe it's not such a good idea after all.

"And you've got to be an American citizen!" Ron adds laughing. It's as if he knew of my impecuniousness and had been toying with me.

"Oh that's different! That's all right then!" and we both laugh heartily.

Still it would have been nice to have been an Elk - just as long as there were no embarrassing initiation ceremonies like the freemasons have. Now I'll never know.

Chapter Forty-four

In which the holiday spirit is upon us.

We're off to get a Christmas tree, Montana style. Help yourself. The United States Forest Service, in association with the Bureau of Land Management, sells permits for a dollar. The forests are your oyster. You can pick any tree you like as long as it is on USFS land and not in a wilderness or recreational area and, for some reason, not within 150 feet of water. And so, armed with a trusty saw and with George cocooned like a mummy in his snow suit and Hélène wrapped up in her coat, we drive into Lolo forest in search of the perfect tree.

It's not as easy as you'd think. For a start, as far as we are concerned, it mustn't be too far from the track, mustn't be too tall and mustn't be too short. It mustn't be scrawny and must have a good shape, symmetrical, with an equal distribution of branches, not too bushy at the bottom and not too thin at the top. And preferably it will look as good from the front as it does from the back. The tops of more mature trees fit the bill but it is not allowed to top a tree however shapely it may be though I can see someone has done precisely that.

George can hardly walk in his snowsuit through, what is for him, waist-high snow, and has to be carried. He's as snug as a bug in a rug but not so Hélène who soon starts complaining about the bitter cold and has to be carried too and she's no lightweight I can assure you. And still the ideal tree refuses to reveal itself.

"You're just going to have to pick one," Iona says in exasperation after a while. "I've had enough of this."

And so have I, if the truth be told. What I had intended to be a happy family outing to harvest our Christmas tree has turned out to be a misery for everyone. I settle upon the sacrificial victim and begin to saw amidst the falling snow. I must not leave a stump higher than five inches, so down on my knees I must go among the deep, untrodden snow and before I am done, my legs are soaked through and the hand that gripped the saw is as cold as an executioner's heart.

Down in Mrs Bates' basement, I find a stand and the lights and by late afternoon the tree is installed in all its lovely scrawniness. What else can you expect for a dollar? But at least we are beginning to look a bit Christmassy.

And Christmas has broken out at school too. It's the start of Kris Kringle week and in my pigeonhole this morning, a poem and a twig of spruce. My present to Lesley Ibbotson was a bar of Lifebuoy soap. Don't ask me why. I thought it was a good idea at the time: a clean sort of joke and practical too but now I'm thinking it maybe wasn't such a good idea after all. What if she sees it as a barbed comment on her personal hygiene? But of course I have a get-out-of-jail card in that I can always refrain from revealing my identity on the last day if I so choose.

"Say, Dave, you got a minute?"

It's Matt summoning me into the holy of holies again. I enter without fear or trepidation of having done anything wrong: more a case of having done everything right and I am in for another dose of head-swelling sycophancy. It's an ominous sign that he doesn't ask me to close the door behind me.

Matt clears his throat, a sure sign that he's going to croak something he finds deeply embarrassing.

"Er, ahrrum, you know at the Elks on Friday, I just wanted you to know how well you did. [How did he know how many bottles of beer I drank?] I was really proud of you. You're a real credit to your country and the school."

I have the good grace to look at my shoes. If only he knew I only danced with his wife as a bet - which I've still to collect. I won't forget. And even now I am reaping a different sort of reward for my misdeed. "I was wondering, er, ahrrum, is there anyone back in Scotland who I could write to saying what a good job you are doing over here? So it could go in your file."

I stand and stare while my jaw hangs slack. That's three things I am capable of all at once which is pretty impressive for a male who is not supposed to be able to multi-task at all.

"Well, er, erm, my headmaster I suppose."

Matt nods. He's got all the necessary details. "Anybody else, Dave?" he adds expectantly, pen poised to take the details.

"Well, no, I don't think so really." I am sorry to let Matt down in this way especially as he apparently seems to think it might further my career if he trumpets my ambassadorial skills back home. Alas he doesn't understand the Scottish psyche, and why should he?

The truth is we Scots, and Aberdonians in particular, do not rush to praise (though we do to judgement) and, in fact, treat all unsolicited efforts in that respect with the gravest of suspicion. I can just imagine my headmaster reading it with passing interest and filing it in the wastebasket. And when, on my return, if he were to put his arm around me and call me by my Christian name and tell me he was really proud of me for what I'd achieved in Missoula, I would have run a mile in four minutes. I really would. Especially since he is a bachelor.

Meanwhile, in the classroom, the students are infected with holiday mood. Hard enough to get them to do any work in the first place, but this week, with a week to go before Christmas, they have already downed pencils. All right then, let it be a week of talks - see how they like that.

I've had trouble with this in the past, both at home and abroad. Kids who can yak, yak, yak to their hearts' content in an informal situation find it extraordinarily difficult to talk to as few as seventeen of their peers in a formal situation. I've overcome that difficulty to a certain extent since they no longer refuse to participate and although I wouldn't expect any of them to have the confidence to present a programme on TV any time soon, it is at least a step in the right direction. And then there was Jackencoke.

I'm not kidding, that's his real name, not something I dreamed up to protect the innocent and Jackencoke is very far from that. And before him came Leonard Kane and never was there a boy less able according to any criteria you'd care to go by. A new recruit to my homeroom, he'd been in trouble in the dining room for swearing and spitting food at people.

There is a notice in the kitchen saying "Positively no Expectorating" - not a word with which I am on very familiar terms and what's more, I would bet my pension that my students aren't either, so it seems an odd choice of word to use if you want to get a message across with absolute clarity. But since the kitchen is out of bounds to the students, the message must be intended for the consumption of the cooks, which is rather worrying, in that they feel there is a need to remind them to refrain from such a habit.

Notice, or no notice, in words which even Kane could understand, he should have known that spitting food at people is wrong. In the classroom however he'd been perfectly behaved - or at least no worse than any of the others.

But Jackencoke is not so biddable.

"Nuh! I'm doin' somethin' private," says the bold boy when it's his turn to go out and give his talk.

I have no idea what this "private" activity is and I dread to think but I publically wipe the floor with him and to my relief the now not-so-bold boy makes his way to the dais.

"Go, Tony, baby, go!" shouts out Kane who is seated at the front of the class, all the better for me to keep an eye on him lest he started expectorating or doing something else unsanitary.

For some reason a red mist descends in front of Jackencoke's eyes. In an instant he strides to the nearest chair, picks it up and has already begun to raise it over Kane's cranium before I manage to grab a hold of it.

"What do you think you are doing! Get down to Mr Olsen's office this instant and tell him what you just did!" I yell at him, at the same time opening the door in order to assist his passage.

A while later, back he comes, not at all in a timid or chastened way.

"What happened? What did Mr Olsen say?"

"Nuthin'."

Obviously I'll have to get the full story from Matt. But in fact, it turns out Jackencoke spoke not much short of the truth. No punishment, no warning, no deterrent, nothing.

Matt listens to what happened gravely. "I talked to

him, Dave," he says when I have finished. "If you've any more problems with him, just let me know." He swallows hard and sticks his jaw out. The interview is at an end. His face is red; I hope with shame at his failure to take any action. I can already feel my golden-boy image beginning to shine less brightly, bringing troubles to his door like this.

None of us has long to wait for the next incident - the very next day in fact. I have asked the class to write a set of instructions telling someone how to set about doing a task. I was thinking of things like how to mend a bicycle puncture or bake a cake, nothing that would be too taxing from a literary point of view, requiring no imagination and for once, brevity would be desirable, a change from my habitual plea for more words. Well, it is nearly holiday time after all. Time to take the foot off the pedal, a little.

Jackencoke, however, has come up with something different. He has written a list of tips on "How to steal something". Follow these tips and you won't get caught is the drift. I wouldn't be surprised if this has been inspired by Taylor and another, who at lunchtime yesterday, had been caught stealing from The Bon, a nearby department store. No doubt this is their alternative version of doing a spot of Christmas shopping. Taylor was another thorn in the side who had refused to give a talk to the class.

I take Jackencoke's handy hints without comment and without my face betraying anything. As soon as I can, I take it down to Matt.

"I'll call in the grandparents," he says, "but it won't be until New Year now."

I might have known. What's wrong with now? What's wrong with a phone call to alert them of his behaviour and at least set up a date? So that is the end of that and in the interim I bet Matt hopes the problem with Jackencoke will go away and when New Year comes Matt will point out it's a new beginning and a time to give him a fresh start. Meanwhile the brat himself thinks he's got off scot-free and it looks as if he has, which does not go down well with this particular Scot one little bit.

Grandparents eh? That's interesting. Probably Jackencoke's parents are divorced and for one reason or another, neither of them can look after their hellish spawning. But just imagine the poor grandparents - no sooner have you got rid of your kids into the big wide world and are looking forward to being Derby and Joan when you get one of the grandkids to look after for the rest of your natural. I've no idea how old the grandparents are but looking after Jackencoke is going to give them white hairs if they haven't got them already, poor sods.

* * *

Across the Atlantic, the Christmas spirit is abroad too. Art lets me see a letter from Marnie. She writes that she has been making Christmas decorations with the kids and some "cheeky" person had asked her what that had to do with English. That sounds like a very pertinent question to me indeed and I wouldn't mind betting that it was the head of the art department. I would expect that would feature in *their* lesson plans at the moment and he wouldn't be best pleased at having his department's thunder stolen like that.

And there's a more serious point, something that Marnie has not realised: she is contravening the guidelines laid down by the General Teaching Council. In a drive towards a more professional teaching force, it is forbidden to teach any subject you do not hold a qualification in - like English teachers making Christmas decorations. And there's another even more serious point that's worrying me. Since it takes a week for a letter to arrive from Scotland, this means that Marnie must have been engaged in this Mickey Mouse sort of stuff for at least a week.

Compare that with what I'm doing here. I'm still giving them homework (such as it is) and only three of Blake's homeroom had done it. "The holidays don't start until Friday," I tell them. "As far as I am concerned, we work right up until the last day. If you're running a race you don't go slow on the last lap do you? And neither are we going to." Mr Strict has spoken.

And there's another telling thing Marnie has written. She says she's going to have to see the headmaster about the writing on the wall of her (my) classroom. Hmm. I must say I'm not altogether surprised to learn she has discipline problems. Some of them can be a right handful and I had seen how her own two sons didn't listen to a word she said if it didn't suit them. I shudder to think of the sort of behaviour she is letting my pupils away with. Something they are going to have to unlearn when I get back and take up the reins again.

She finishes by saying that she's going to London for New Year. Now *that* is an incredible thing! Everybody knows that no-one celebrates Hogmanay, or New Year's Eve, better than the Scots. The BBC televises the countdown from Scotland and Edinburgh's Princes Street hosts a massive street party with live bands and fireworks. And Marnie, with all that on her doorstep, is going all the way to London where they hardly celebrate it at all! Madness!

If most of that is bad news, I have kept the best till last.

I also get a letter bearing glad tidings of great joy. It's from the bank to say that $1,500 has been deposited in my bank account from the Central Bureau. I'm rich! I'm rich! Rich beyond my wildest dreams! It's even more than I expected. This is going to be the merriest Christmas ever!

I'm not the only person to get a windfall. Blake has also received a bounteous cheque from his father in California and he's going to equip the whole family (he has two sons) with cross-country skis.

"We'll need to get you goin' on a set of these, Dave," he says.

It's lunchtime and we have come to the Army and Navy store for him to do some pricing.

"Actually, I wouldn't mind giving it a bash," I tell him. "I'll try just about anything once."

But of course he knows that already.

Monday was the start of Kris Kringle week and in my pigeonhole today, a keyring with a little penknife attached and "Missoula" written on it. Earlier, following on from the poem with spruce twig attached, my haul is a little sock with a candy cane sticking out the top and designed to be hung on the Christmas tree, and a little notebook. The gifts I gave were a packet of fags (60 cents from the Grizzly Grocery) and which might mitigate against any offence caused by the soap, and some paper napkins with Santas on them. Today's was a battery with a little note saying "To give you energy for the holidays". It may not work as I found it lying around the house.

Tomorrow is the final day. I'll find out what my three dollar gift is and perhaps who my mysterious Kris Kringle is. I can hardly wait.

After school Steve and I go to the Depot for a beer or two to celebrate the impending festive season and the break from the kids for a whole two weeks. It's very self-sacrificial of him considering his experience before his nuptials. Somehow the conversation turns to his college days at the Western University of Montana in Dillon in the mid Sixties, of which he seems to have an unlimited fund of stories.

"It was closin' time in this bar but this guy had just put a dime in the jukebox an' refused to leave. The barman told him he'd have to go or he'd throw him out. 'Oh, yeah?' says the guy. 'I'll go when my music is finished an' not a minute afore.' 'You're leavin' right this minute, buster or I'm gonna call the cops.'

At this point, Steve says, the customer lost his rag and reaching over the bar, went for the barman's throat. The barman shook off the attack and producing a gun from beneath the bar, shot him three times in the chest.

"Oh, my God! What happened?

"He died."

"No, I mean what happened to the barman?"

"He got a suspended sentence. It was self-defence, see?"

I stare at Steve to see if he's winding me up but his face is perfectly impassive. It's not as if Blake were here and they are doing their double act. Dead! And all because he wanted to hear a song on the jukebox! Life doesn't come much cheaper than a dime and it was probably some dire Country and Western ballad into the bargain.

But it's the barman getting off scot-free that really gets me. I'm sure in Scotland that would be considered excess use of force and he would have got I don't know how many years behind different sort of bars for manslaughter. Except of course in Scotland the worst that would have happened was a punch-up, since as far as I know, barmen are not in the habit of stowing loaded guns beneath the bar, not even in Glasgow which has a reputation of having some pretty mean streets and some pretty shady parts which respectable citizens would be advised to keep clear of at night if they value their health.

"That's not the only shootin' there was in that place," Steve goes on after a pull at his beer.

"Really?"

"Yeah, a man was shot in the head."

"Good God! Why?"

"Adultery, supposedly." Steve shrugs. He doesn't know any more details. That's just the way life is in the West.

My God! Two killings in the same bar! And Dillon is just a two-horse town out to the south east somewhere, a former gold-mining town.

"How big is Dillon? I mean how big was it when you were there?

"Same as now. 'bout four thousan'."

Imagine that! I would call what the barman did nothing short of "murder" so that makes two just in that bar alone. How many more were there elsewhere in the town, in other bars, not to mention the happy home?

"The fights there used to be in that place!" Steve reminisces, taking another pull at his beer and in what if I'm not mistaken, a nostalgic tone. He gives a chuckle. "I remember seein' this old-timer sittin' at a table by himself, mindin' his own business, just drinkin' his beer. Then he'd get up, punch somebody an' then sit down an' go back to his beer as if nothin' had happened."

I suppose that *is* quite a funny thing to happen as long as you are not the person at the receiving end. It's like he was suffering from some sort of nervous tic and he couldn't help himself. As for me, I would have been far too nervous to have enjoyed a peaceful pint there knowing the next moment I might get a punch in the throat. It doesn't surprise me that he drinks alone but it does surprise me no-one punched him back or even shot him stone dead in self-defence.

"You were saying something about fights," I prompt as Steve seems to have dried up for the moment.

"God yeah, there were fights there every day o' the week. The whole bar would be at it sometimes. The place would be rockin'. There was somethin' about that place... I've even stopped fights there between my friends - and I've been in them too," he admits.

"Maybe it's something they put in the beer."

"I remember once I was there with two pals," Steve continues with another chuckle and without apparently having heard me. "We heard the police sirens but the only way we could get one of them to leave was to knock him unconscious an' carry him out!"

Was that by hitting him over the head with a bottle, like I've seen in the movies I would like to ask, but forbear from asking. I'm also too surprised at this revelation to ask if they managed to make their escape. It can't have been easy carrying an unconscious body between them but since he says nothing more, I take it that is the end of the tale and they did succeed.

Talk about the wild and woolly west! And we're only talking about fifteen years ago! Well, Steve certainly seems to have led a very adventurous life compared to me, especially when you take into account the tales from the cathouse with which he regaled me on the backpacking trip to Idaho.

Hmm. Wonder if his wife knows about those. She will now, if ever she reads this book. Sorry, Steve, but the stories were just too good to miss out.

Chapter Forty-five

In which I go on the Great Kris Kringle Hunt, go over some old ground and a mistake comes to light.

Whoever my Kris Kringle is, he or she has a sense of humour. In my pigeonhole this morning, I find a roll of Scotch tape. Well actually I had been expecting that as one of the joke presents and it is a bit of a disappointment to find that that's the real one, the one that we can spend as much as $3 on. If that's it, I'm not surprised that he or she has not identified themselves.

Later, Sarah from my homeroom, who is extracted for remedial lessons, materialises in front of my desk bearing a message.

"You've got to find your Kris Kringle present," she blurts out, squirming with embarrassment.

Eh? What on earth is the girl blethering about? I've already got it. Has the girl gone completely loopy? It wouldn't take much. She frequently comes out with remarks that stun the class and which seem to be light years from what we are dealing with. She has a singular perspective on the planet. Sometimes I think she is on another one altogether.

"Where?"

"Dunno."

"Who sent you?"

"I've not to say."

"Thanks, Sarah," and off she goes, plainly relieved to have fulfilled her mission and be released.

So what happens now? Where do I start to look?

Any teaching today is impossible such is the fever pitch of excitement among the kids. Apart from stopping early at 2 pm there is the entertainment to look forward to. The middle floor is going to entertain us and of course there is the *pièce de resistance,* the staff song which we have been practicing assiduously under the baton of the itinerant music teacher, Karen Campbell.

Messrs Jackencoke, Kane and Taylor are absent today. They have probably sussed out that they will not be missing much in terms of ways to hone their reading and writing skills and have decided instead to improve the shining hour and their shop-lifting skills by taking the day off and doing a bit of last-minute shopping under the tutelage of the master. This absence of the terrible triumvirate means I feel it is perfectly safe to leave the rest of the class to their own devices so I go down to photocopy an article I had seen in the *National Geographic* about a literary tour of Scotland that I think may be of interest to Marnie.

"Have you a minute, Dave?"

It's Matt summoning me from behind his desk. For a moment I think he's going to ask me what I'm doing down here when I have a class upstairs. I've got my answer ready: "Well you see, I spotted this article in the National Geographic and I wanted to tell the students about these famous writers and where they came from. Just a two or three copies for them to share. Won't take a minute."

But subterfuge and deceit are not necessary.

"Ahrrum! Dave, here is a copy of what I wrote to your principal."

I scan it quickly. It's all about how professional I am, what a credit to the school etc etc. Modesty prevents me from quoting it. Besides it hardly seems a very professional thing to do, to abandon your class, even if it is the last day of term.

"Well, Matt, that is very kind of you indeed. I appreciate it very much."

Matt smiles and colours.

"Merry Christmas, Matt," I say as I hand back the valueless document. Actually I wish he hadn't done it as it makes me feel as if I am in his debt, that I must keep on being good and keep bringing kudos to the school.

"Happy Holidays!"

Oops! Have I already blown it? Are you not even allowed to use the C word in school?

It's as I head towards the photocopier that I spot an envelope in my pigeonhole. Inside is a single sheet of paper on which is written: "Go to the teachers' room". Prominently, lying on a shelf, I find another envelope and in that another note: "Go to the bulletin board". And so the Great Kris Kringle Hunt begins and ends three places later in the library, next to my room.

My present is a Santa Claus and his wife astride broomsticks, which makes a change to a boring old sledge I suppose and if you decide not to hang them on the tree, you could always use them as a hearthside brush. And just who is my Kris Kringle? With the Santas is a note: "Happy Holidays from Stephanie Monk!" Well that's a surprise! Who would have thought it!

I go straight down to her lair and give hearty thanks for the present and for the fun of the chase which she receives graciously. She's not all bad after all. It is the season for bygones to be bygones, even if she did grass me up to Matt. And have I not redeemed myself since then by bringing kudos to the school in spades and does not Matt think I am a shining and guiding light to not only the school but the teaching profession as a whole?

As for me, I decide not to reveal my identity to Lesley Ibbotson, as is my prerogative. I am still worried about the soap. I also choose not to reveal what my proper present to her was. That is another prerogative and another mystery.

And here's another. I happened to notice that my colleagues on the top floor have all received a little bag with a drawstring, all exactly the same. Now why is that? It's strange that I should see them in the first place since I am invariably the last of the faculty to arrive but the mystery deepens when I saw they were still there when I went down to do the photocopying for Marnie. And most puzzling of all — what a strange coincidence that they should all have landed up with the same Kris Kringle! I suppose the numbers may not pan out exactly but it's very odd that the poor unfortunate who got landed with three should all happen to come from the top floor. And another thing: why has not a single one been removed from the pigeonholes? Something very strange is going on. But what?

Because of the Great Kris Kringle Hunt and other routine matters, the opportunity does not present itself to ask those who could provide the solution to these mysteries before it is time for us to troop down to that multi-purpose room that I choose to call the dining room.

Iona is there, with the kids, to witness the entertainment on this last day of school. Sam's class is *the* class act: they sign *I'm Dreaming of a White Christmas*. It was utterly beautiful. While I am heartened by the thought that Kathy is teaching signing to Sam's class, at the same time I am depressed by the thought that George, profoundly deaf, will have to live in a hearing world and whatever he may become in life, so many job opportunities will never be open to him.

And then it is our turn. Since Blake is refusing to have anything to do with the staff choir, I hand him my camera to put on photographic record the phenomenon of me "singing" and jostle for a place as far at the back of the pack as possible.

At last we are ready to warble but we close our collective mouths again as an enormous amount of hissing and booing erupts from the audience. It's directed at Blake who is seated in splendid isolation on the bleachers. As he continues to sit there, the sound rises in intensity and shows no sign of diminishing. There is only going to be one winner here. Shamefacedly and burning bright red, Blake hands my camera to one of the students, and as he makes his way to join us, the jeers turn into a thunderous mixture of cheers and whistles and handclaps.

When we are finished, the applause is only half as loud as that and I dare say we don't even deserve that - unless they were clapping because they were glad it was over. In fact I would say that the standard of entertainment as a whole was not very high, apart from Sam's class. It seems utterly strange to celebrate Christmas without singing a single carol.

After the whole thing is over and we are free for the holidays, Sam, Art, Kathy and Molly and I repair to the Stockman's. It was my choice. I had been introduced to it by Al when we first arrived and he had given me a tour of the bars. I've never been back since. I like their slogan: "Liquor up front, poker in the rear". That's because the bar, a long mahogany affair, is at the front while at the back you can play poker. (Other card games are available.)

It's a bit of a dive to tell the truth, a working man's bar really with peanut shells littering the bare wooden floor.

Much in the manner you scatter feed to hens, the barman scatters the nuts along the bar to the customers who are sitting propped up in front of it on high stools. They drop the shells on the floor, just where they sit, as if they were not in the least domesticated. And maybe they aren't.

We sit at a wooden table, neither to the front or the rear, on hard wooden chairs. Maybe it wasn't such a good idea to come here. It's hardly the last word in comfort. Doesn't even have a happy hour, not that that matters as it's far too early for anywhere else to have one either.

"God, but wasn't Blake a prick?" says Sam.

We all agree that he was a bit of a spoilsport which is a bit odd really as there is no bigger joker than him.

"Yeah an' he didn't even do the Kris Kringle thing, either," Art remarks.

"What was that little bag in his pigeonhole?" I chip in. "Steve and Nat had the same thing and they just left them there. What is that all about?"

"It's a little lump of coal," Art explains. "It's like being blackballed."

Ah, I see now! Mystery solved.

"What's up with those guys?" Art goes on, shaking his head.

Nobody can come up with an explanation unless, being on the top floor, they think they are above such childish pursuits. I can see how Nat wouldn't be interested in it - he's pretty straight, but Steve isn't. He's a member of the Lion's Club International and he'd shown me a pair of three-legged underpants that he'd bought at a sale they'd held in aid of charity. That's right. Three legs. The middle one was a lot shorter than the other two. And you would have thought that Blake would have relished the opportunity to have put outrageous things like that in people's pigeonholes and remain anonymous. Except if they know him at all, his fingerprints would have been all over it, so to speak.

I decide in the present company it's probably not a good idea to reveal that my Kris Kringle was Ms Monk and I had found her very affable. Molly, especially, would find that laughable, in a risible sort of way.

When I return some hours later I find myself locked out of the house. Not to worry, I know where I can go where I'll be made welcome and where, if I am not given a drink, it'll be for the first time.

It turns out to be the first time I have had this particular drink. It's eggnog, a non-alcoholic drink which tastes like custard and very tasty it is too. Al is at work but Terri adds a mighty slug of brandy and it tastes even better. Custard with a kick. I suppose that makes it a type of advocaat.

She tells me that Iona is out doing the last of the Christmas shopping. She'd better get back before too long as I have offered to take Sam and Margaret to the airport. They are going to Minneapolis as that's where Margaret's folks come from. The airport's another place I have not been to since we arrived and when I deposit them there a while later, I find it's undergone something of a facelift. It's seething with people but that's only to be expected on this, the last Friday before Christmas.

It's snowing quite hard as I drive back. There was never any doubt in my mind that it would be a white Christmas.

* * *

Saturday morning and I do a bit of Christmas shopping myself with my newfound wealth. In fact, I am even richer than I thought as I found $18 in a pair of jeans that I hadn't worn for a while.

First stop is the liquor store where I buy a bottle of Dewar's, another thing I haven't seen since we first arrived and before I knew of Al's fondness for whisky and this brand in particular. It didn't last long what with the amount he drank himself and those he made drink it as it was so good, according to him. I doubt I'll see much of this either but I'm going to keep it under wraps until Hogmanay when it will come out to usher in the New Year. In the meantime, as a Christmas present, I buy him a selection of miniatures and the same for dear old Grandpa too.

I also buy a bottle of Black and White, a gallon of Bacardi and some Californian brandy to go in the eggnog. It sounds a lot and it is for me where I would have been hard pressed to have scraped up the money to buy even one bottle of booze back home. But it only costs a fraction of the price over here and it is the season to be merry after all and I may as well be merry while I can, for times of austerity lie ahead. It's a sobering thought that I am already halfway through the school year, although we will have two months of travelling after that, before we fly home.

After that it's on to Mr Wood to pay off my debts.

"Is it workin' all right for you, Dave?"

"Yes, not too bad. Would be better if I didn't have any kids though."

"How come, Dave?"

"Well I was listening to the football results. There was a bit of static but I could just about hear them OK when my daughter started crying. My wife went to find out what was wrong with her and she had vomited about a pint. She switched on the fluorescent light and that was it! Nothing but static. I never did hear my team's results," I finish ruefully.

"Can't do nuthin' about sick kids, Dave," Mr Wood laughs sympathetically.

Next it is on to Buttery's for the eggnog. It's my lucky day again. They are having a promotion and I buy two pints and finally it's on to the Chausée for Iona's Christmas present, a cute set of earrings shaped like daisies. I had been alerted to them by Mo Mokomo.

Iona, on the other hand, is not having such a good day. While I was out, she made a batch of mince pies only for them to turn out so crumbly they disintegrated as soon as you touched them. She made a second batch of two dozen and they turned out perfectly, only for George to reach up and pull them to the floor where they ended up in the same state as the first. If at first you don't succeed... She's making the third batch now.

I am looking forward to a nice, warming eggnog when the phone goes. Sure enough, Al's radar has detected the return of the Big Blue Mean Machine.

"You gotta come over an' have a Christmas drink, Dave." It's not often that he gets to issue that invitation, so how can I refuse him? With a bit of luck it might even be my new favourite tipple. It must be so good for you: egg yolks and brandy. A double whammy health drink.

But alas it is not on offer. Al always decides what you are going to drink and this afternoon it's whiskey. I suppose when you are abroad you should drink the wine of the country, but oh, to be in Scotland with a dram of real whisky now that Christmastime is near ‹ as the poet didn't quite put it. No, of course I didn't really think that at all. What I did think of was my little store of Christmas cheer just along the street and the bare cupboard there would have been back home.

"What you doin' Christmas Day?"

"We're going to Steve Knight's." After he'd heard that we weren't going to Canada any more, Steve had been the first to invite us. Actually we are going to his in-laws, the Petersens.

Al doesn't say anything but I am pretty sure his moustache bristled in disappointment. It's hard to see his eyes behind his dark glasses and it's impossible to be sure but I think they register the same emotion.

"What ya doin' this evenin'?"

"We're going to the Paxmans'. You know, the Math teacher at the school?"

The moustache quivers, the hand reaches for the bourbon and tops up my half-empty glass.

* * *

Picking up the babysitter is a piece of cake this time. It's the delectable Kelly on Crestview. I know precisely where I am going and ring the bell at the palatial-looking residence.

"I'm here to collect Kelly. For the babysitting." It must be her mom I am addressing.

"On my way!" shouts a disembodied voice from upstairs and a few seconds later the body appears and a very delectable body it is too - only it doesn't belong to Kelly but the girl I saw in the car who had directed me to the house!

"Er. Em. I was expecting Kelly," I blurt out, lost for words, a bit like the stupid miller in *Rumplestiltskin* who rather than suffer a few seconds' awkward silence has to say something. I suppose I could have said something anodyne like, "Hello," or something more personal like, "Nice to see you again," after our brief encounter on the road but I said what I said and there is no taking it back.

"I *am* Kelly!"

"So... er... who was that who babysat the other night?"

"That was my sister, Stephanie."

Stephanie! But Iona had said the babysitter was Kelly! How could she have got that so wrong? In fact, she had got nothing right that night at all.

Did I address Stephanie, whom I thought was Kelly, by name I wonder? Surely if I had she would have corrected me or perhaps she just let it go, too embarrassed to correct me. Feverishly I rack my memory, but embarrassment fogs the brain and I can't remember. But one thing I do remember is the culture shock I gave Stephanie, something that Kelly will not have the misfortune to be exposed to, since as we are only going for drinks at Nat's, there is no need for me to dress up.

When we get back it is to be greeted by the news that in the interim, Hélène has been sick again. Somewhat reluctantly, Iona says she will go to the party but tells Kelly that if it happens again she's to phone and we will come straight back home.

Chapter Forty-six

In which I receive a present, the kids are enchanted, and I do something I have not done for years.

"There's been a phone call from Kelly," says Mae the moment we step over the threshold.

A moment later Iona comes off the phone with the news that Hélène has been sick again and as we said we would, we are going back to relieve her of her duties. I knew it wasn't worth me taking my coat off, so I didn't. She can't help it, but following on from her spoiling of the football results, Hélène has now spoiled the party too.

"You can always come back yourself, Dave," says Blake.

Well that's true, so I could, wife permitting, but surely it is up to our hosts to suggest that rather than him?

I drop Kelly off back home with a couple of dollars for her trouble and then return to the company, having agreed this with Iona on the way. It's almost as if they had been waiting for this moment, for no sooner have I been admitted to the basement, as all the best-regulated American homes have, when Blake hands me a parcel.

"This is an early Christmas present, Dave," and it suddenly becomes clear why he had wanted me, at least, to come back.

"Oh, no! You shouldn't have done that! No-one told me there were going to be presents. I haven't got anything for any of you." I add lamely, all covered in confusion and embarrassment.

"No, no! It's all right, laddie," says Steve. "This is just a wee gift from all of us to you an' your lovely bride. Just a way of sayin' we're really glad you're here from Scotland an' thanks for bein' such a good sport."

How ironic is that in the light of Blake's lack of sportsmanship yesterday and the triumvirate's lack of participation in the Kris Kringle thing!

"We would have given it to you on Christmas Day," Steve goes on, "but then they wouldn't have gotten to see your reaction. We've got presents for the kids too," he adds, "but they'll get them on Christmas Day."

"Oh no, you shouldn't have! That's just far too kind and generous of you. But thanks very much indeed!" I had absolutely no inkling that anything like this was going to happen. I feel quite touched and feel moved to say a few words. "I would just like to say that you're the greatest bunch of colleagues anyone could ever have hoped for. I'm really, really lucky to have landed up with you guys."

"Just cut the crap, Dave," says Blake good-humouredly, "an' open the parcel." After all, they have been waiting an eternity for this moment, like children who can't wait to open their presents on Christmas Day.

My joke-alert antennae are out on stalks by now. This has all the hallmarks of one of Blake's jokes and this is confirmed a moment later by the sight of Mae kneeling down at the other side of the room armed with a camera. I immediately think of Steve and his three-legged underpants with a note pinned to the middle leg saying "Will shrink to fit" but this mysterious parcel is far too big for that. It's soft and square and light but those are the only clues. What can it be?

It's a habit ingrained from childhood, having been born in a period of postwar austerity, but I never rip the paper off a parcel in a frenzy to get at the contents. Instead I fastidiously and carefully open it so the paper can be used again if at all possible. This tactic serves me in good stead now as I begin to unwrap it as carefully as if I were defusing an unexploded bomb. This painstaking process not only must be driving my benefactors up the wall but it also gives me valuable thinking time as I try to work out what it could possibly be and what the appropriate response should be. For if there is one thing that is worrying me more that what the present is, it is that I spoil their fun by not being suitably shocked or whatever response they are expecting, and thus ruin my reputation as a good sport.

At last the contents have been laid bare and I can see right away that it's a couple of T-shirts, one for me, one for Iona. That's harmless enough isn't it? As it happens, Iona's is on the top, a beautiful turquoise colour. The front depicts the outline of the state of Montana with the peaks of the Rockies featured at the western end. Well that is very appropriate indeed, especially for a lady's T-shirt, and the back is even more so, for it says, "Missoula, Montana". Very nice indeed and a very nice souvenir which I am sure she will wear with pride. It is very easy indeed to enthuse about such an appropriate present and I am sure I must be smiling broadly when the flash goes as I am unfolding it and once more as I hold it up to display it to the camera.

But it's back to the nerves as I turn to my T-shirt. It's not nearly such a nice colour, a sort of bilious mustard. The back is uppermost. I can see the word "Schlitz" and then, when I open it out, a cartoon figure of a man wheeling his beer belly in a wheelbarrow. There is a slogan below which

435

reads, "Beer builds better bodies". I can't help but laugh. Flash! Yes, I really like it, so no acting is necessary and I also like Schlitz, my favourite beer. In a land where "beer" means one insipid lager after another with not a real ale to be found anywhere, I have found Schlitz to be the best of the bunch and had written in glowing terms to the brewers, praising their product and adding I was a teacher on exchange from Scotland. It would be nice if they sent me a case as a little token of their appreciation. I can but live in hope.

But it's the front of the shirt that they've really been waiting for me to see and what I'm worried about responding to in the appropriate manner. In velvet letters, in a semi-circle, is written, "The Home of the Scottish Whopper". It's the slogan of a burger chain but what has that got to do with me? Absolutely nothing. It's the arrow, lower down, near the bottom, pointing to something even lower down where the connection with me lies and I am sure I am looking suitably amused as Mae takes the long-awaited for photo. I have to pose for the camera again as I stand with it held up against me. And once again it's easy to look amused and pleased and it's a great pity Iona is not here to join in the fun, though perhaps on second thoughts, perhaps not. She might have been embarrassed to see one of her favourite things being made so much fun of in public like this.

"You know, in Scotland, when we use the word "whopper" it means something very big."

"Exactly, Dave!" says Blake. "You got it!"

"We got the idea from the porno shop near the school," Steve adds.

Right enough, there is one. Very discreet with nothing in the window except a drawn blind so I don't know how exactly they had managed to see what had inspired the idea, but they had seen me in the shower on at least two occasions.

Steve has brought some Schlitz, appropriately enough, and I took along some mince pies as well as the Californian brandy and a carton of eggnog, all of which I think would go very well together, but unfortunately no-one wants to try the concoction or the mince pies either for that matter. They are not big drinkers of course, this lot, but I feel sorry for Iona after all her hard work, though of course they did not know all the trouble she had gone to. It's just as well she's not here, right enough.

There is not a meal, as we knew, but there are lashings of Ben and Jerry's ice cream. Nat and Mae leave us to it and go upstairs to make coffee when, just for fun, as you do, Blake flicked some ice cream from his spoon across the room at Steve as I imagined those two naughty monkeys Jack and Jock might have done. After this initial shock and after wiping the ice cream from his face, Steve responds in like manner and the next minute, it's full-blown ice cream wars.

Splat! That was the sound of the ice cream hitting the wall behind Steve who, showing no consideration at all for the décor ducked out of the way of the incoming missile.

"Ooops!" says Blake, "better scrape that off the wall before straight Nat sees it!"

And that's what he's caught in the act of doing when Mae comes down the stairs bearing a tray.

"I was just giving your wall a bit of a dust," Blake says as calm and unflustered as you like.

Up above, Mae must have heard our hilarity if nothing else and Blake's remark sets us all off again. I don't know what she made of it, but she gives the wall a good look in the passing but there is nothing there to see now. Fortunately it's wood paneling so there isn't a stain but that was the last thing Blake and Steve were thinking of when they began the fight and I imagine the last thing Mae would have suspected as being the cause of the merriment was two grown-up men flinging ice cream at each other. When Nat comes down a moment later with some snacks we are all sitting as sober as judges like well-behaved grown-up people.

The evening passes with jovial banter if not with quite the same hilarity as before and at last Steve and Jackie get up to go, only for Jackie to return a moment later to ask Blake to move his truck as they are blocked in.

"Do you want the cheque for the $4 now or will I give it to Diane tomorrow?" she adds.

"Tomorrow will do, Jerkface," Blake responds, making a ball of a paper napkin and throwing it in her direction.

"Oooh! Sorry!" Jackie says, embarrassed at her faux pas.

It takes me a little longer to realise what this is about - their share of the cost of the presents and now she has let the cat out of the bag. A little mental arithmetic tells me what the total cost is and it also confirms that Blake had been the prime mover behind the presents, just as I suspected.

I take Steve's three cans of Schlitz back inside with me as well as the brandy and eggnog in their containers, just as I had brought them, but I categorically refuse to take back the mince pies. That is just taking generosity a bit too far. In fact, I'm not so sure it's not an insult.

* * *

Christmas Eve and I'm not feeling too good. Hélène had not been sick again yesterday evening and has not been sick today but today it's my turn. However, by the afternoon I feel well enough to do some path-clearing and later Steve drops by with a map he has drawn showing the way to his in-laws. They live out in the country somewhere on a smallholding near Stevensville about thirty miles towards Hamilton.

I take him down to Mrs Bates' basement room to show him the set of skis I'd seen down there as well as some boots which fit me. Last night we had talked about going cross-country skiing at some time, just as Blake had said. He'll be desperate to try out his Christmas present.

"The skis would do but the trouble is the boots don't fit the skis. You're outta luck, my boy."

"No problem, I'll just have to hire some."

"Yeah! Boy am I lookin' forward to seein' you on the boards!"

"Oh really? Why?"

But Steve just gives a chuckle and I'm guessing he reckons if my skiing ability is anything like the prowess I've shown in the other sports they've seen me try, then they are in for a treat. It also seems he does not rate my sense of direction too highly either for he goes over the directions once more.

"You got it?"

"Yep, sure."

"Sure? An' remember they are tee-total, so absolutely no alcohol, right?"

"Right. Got you! Don't worry!"

Imagine Christmas Day without even a glass of wine with which to wash down the turkey! Oh well, I said I'd try anything once and I may as well give this a go too.

"Oh, you should take a drive past Martha's Court," Steve says from the window of his truck, having just evidently remembered it. "The kids'll love it! See ya tomorrow! Oh, an' bring the sledge, we'll take the kids sledging." He must have spotted it in Mrs Bates' bedroom.

And so to Martha's Court we duly go, just as it's beginning to get dark and which happens to be the very best time because it is light enough to take photos but dark enough for the attractions to be lit up.

I've never seen anything like it in my life and never expect to ever again - for it is Santa Land complete with elves and coloured lights beyond number. Santa himself with sledge and reindeer is on the roof, all lit up with Rudolf sporting a big red bulb at the end of his nose, while at the other end of the roof is a six-foot high penguin. So now we know it's a myth that Santa lives in the North Pole. Nothing could be further from the truth in fact.

Other figures and animals are dotted about what will be the lawn once the snow has gone. But arguably even more remarkable than that is a "skating rink" with half a dozen figures and a workshop where elves are busy at work while Christmas songs (not carols) blast forth to keep them entertained. It is a wonderland of fairy lights and I can't help but wonder what the owner's electricity bill is going to be. There is a wishing well in which you are invited to put donations - not to help defray the bill, but for charity.

Hélène and George stare at it entranced, particularly George. Hélène can hardly believe her eyes but for George this is something beyond that - real, not a fantasy world. To see the delight and wonderment on their faces makes it as much a joy for us as it is for them. They have not yet attained the age when memory begins so they will have no recollection of this when they are older, but in the here and now they are drawn into a world of enchantment. You've got to hand it to them, whether it be Hogmanay or Christmas, the Americans really go to town. I can hardly wait for Valentine's Day.

* * *

In the evening, at Iona's behest, we set off to visit a Methodist church near Emerson. I'm not looking forward to it at all. I don't suppose I've been in a church apart from weddings, funerals and christenings since I got married six years ago but I can put this down as another of those Montanan experiences which I'll try at least once.

And in fact, as so often happens when you don't look forward to something, it turns out to be much better than I had feared. They say you can't beat the Methodists when it comes to singing but I think this is proof that you can. The carols are sung by the smartly turned out *Chevaliers*, a mixed choir and soloists from Hellgate High - the boys in light blue suits with big, black, velvet bow ties and the girls in long dresses of the same pale-blue hue. They look good but they sound even better. I am really glad Iona persuaded me to go.

It's not all singing: there are some readings also, the same old stories which everyone knows by heart, practically. Of course George can't hear them, just as he couldn't the choir and after what must seem an eternity to him, at first he begins to fidget, then to wriggle and then to start girning. There's nothing else for it - I'm going to have to take him outside and if it means I have to miss the sermon, well that's just my tough luck.

As I loiter outside, a little later along comes another little dissident, a boy called Kevin. Despite neither of them having a single intelligible word between them, they get on like a house on fire. Who needs words when you are not even two yet and there is snow which you can put in a fountain and watch it melt?

As they enjoy their play, I fall into conversation with Kevin's father and reprise my Scotland ambassador thing again, something I never tire of doing and as long as he has a question, I am happy to provide an answer. Thus time seems to pass quickly despite the cold until we are joined by Iona.

"I had to come out as Hélène was fidgeting," she explains.

"Pity. It was a really good concert."

"It was the sermon. It seemed to be going on forever. No wonder she started to get restless."

"So you just got up and left when the minister was in full flow?" I ask, astonished.

"I had to or Hélène would have started crying."

Personally I think that's a bit rude. If one of my pupils suddenly stood up and walked out the room when I was holding forth, I'd go ballistic! But then they make you go to school don't they and you don't *have* to go to church, at least, not when you are a consenting adult.

It's another Montanan experience for me to tick off and put under my belt. But I'm a bit like June Whitfield's character in *Carry On Abroad*, who memorably said (of wine and smoking), "I tried it once and didn't like it". Although I freely admit I did quite like it, at least up until I had to leave, I am aware it was a special occasion and I see no need to try it again.

If I need any sermons, this Innocent abroad will carry on looking for them in stones instead.

Chapter Forty-seven

*In which the Big Blue Mean Machine misbehaves
badly again.*

It's Christmas Day and it begins at the crack of dawn with
the kids opening their presents on our bed. After that
excitement, whilst Iona gets the kids dressed, I go
downstairs to get a fire going, then after breakfast, it's time
for us to open our presents.

From the kids I get a Charles M. Russell painting of
Native Americans crossing a river. The "M" stands for
Marion, poor devil. That's just asking to be bullied in the
playground if the other boys get wind of it. Some parents just
don't stop and think when they are naming their kids.

Although not a native of Montana, he came as a
teenager and fell in love with it, a bit like me, only I am quite
a bit older and can't draw for toffee. He made it his home,
working on a ranch as a cowboy, hence the sobriquet "The
Cowboy Artist" which I imagine he liked a lot better than his
middle name. To look at his paintings is to see Western life in
all its wonderful diversity: cowboys engaged in work and play;
the everyday life of Native Americans; the depiction of
historical events such as the exploits of those pioneering
explorers Lewis and Clark; and not least, dramatic landscapes.
I am a great fan of them all but I like best the paintings of the
first settlers, by which I mean the indigenous peoples, not the
early pioneers.

From Iona I get a Western shirt, a fancy affair with
embroidery and pearl-stud buttons. With my battered cowboy

hat from Al and the belt with a Native American chief on the buckle that I got in Canada, all I need now to make me the compleat Montanan, or at least look like one, is a pair of cowboy boots which somehow Santa has failed to deliver. Perhaps I have not been a good enough boy even although I never flung as much as a single drop of ice cream.

From home, my mother-in-law has sent a Guernsey. It's like the more common Jersey, a garment from another Channel Island, but different in that it has a straight neck and a slit at each side at the bottom. Traditionally it was knitted by the wives of the fishermen with stitches so tight, it is said to be waterproof.

From my sister-in-law, a very unusual gift which might come in very handy indeed on January 25th, the birthday of our national poet which is traditionally celebrated by the eating of haggis. I would mention the drinking of whisky but that happens every day whereas the consuming of haggis is not nearly so frequent. It is a do-it-yourself haggis kit consisting of a haggis skin, a hessian bag of oatmeal and another containing ingredient X which I will not go into in case it makes you boak.

I am luxuriating in a hot bath, Christmas music on the radio, a book in hand and an eggnog fortified with brandy near the other, when the doorbell rings. My extra-perceptory senses tell me who it is, confirmed a moment later when Iona shouts up the stairs, "David, Al and Terri are here!"

My Guernsey is much admired. So much admired in fact that Al wonders if I would be able to procure one for him. I tell him if first he would be so kind as to give me his measurements, I'll see what my mother-in-law can do. But if he likes the Guernsey, when I show him my new T-shirt, he throws his head back and laughs uproariously. I knew he would appreciate it, the very reason I showed it off to him. He doesn't ask where he could get one of those, however. Maybe he doesn't like to boast or maybe his mummy told him it was wrong to tell lies. Reader, I cannot enlighten you. I have never seen Big Al in the shower.

We all have some of the famous fortified eggnog, apart from Iona, who, to Al's obvious disapproval, only has the non-alcoholic version. But just like the last time he was here, he makes a big fuss of George which I am sure must do something to promote him up Iona's approval ratings, even if her non-alcoholic habits means she ranks pretty low down in his.

But now it's time we must set out for Steve's relations. And that's when the trouble starts. The Big Blue Mean Machine fires first time but then, unaccountably, dies. I try Nat's trick with the accelerator but it's no use. In fact it's worse than that. The starter motor makes a horrible grinding noise that makes me shudder. It sounds as if there is something very seriously wrong with it.

"I think we'd better phone and tell them we are going to be late," I tell Iona.

The problem is I don't know their number and the only person who could possibly tell me is Steve who will have been there long ago. What's to be done? There's only one thing - look up the phone book and pray that it's there. Mercifully, there is only one Petersen living in Stevensville. That must be it. Thank you, God. I guess You noticed I was in Your house yesterday. I swear to You, make this turn out all right and I'll pay another visit before another six years have passed. I promise.

"Hello, this is the Petersen residence."

Help! That sounds posh!

"It's David Addison here. Steve's friend from Scotland."

"Oh, yes, Dave. How can I help you? Would you like to speak to Steve?" The voice sounds warm, welcoming.

"Yes, well, erm, I think er, maybe that would be best."

"Hold the line." There is a brief pause then I hear Steve's voice. "What's the problem, Whopper Boy?"

"Well, it's just to say that the car won't start. Maybe it's flooded or something. I'm giving it a rest at the moment and I'll see if it starts in a little while. Just to let you know that we might be a bit late."

"Boy! That machine of yours is a whole pack of troubles, ain't it?"

"You bet! Well, we'll see you just as soon as we can."

"OK, Dave. Good luck! See ya!"

Why didn't I tell him about the starter motor? Hope maybe, that when I went back to it, miracles might happen and it will start first time - and keep going. But there was something else I hadn't told him and I know the reason why not. I was too scared. The thing is, I have somehow mislaid the map he gave me and because I knew that I could rely on Iona to read me the directions, I hadn't really bothered to look at it except in the most cursory of ways. Why should I clutter my brain up with a whole lot of unnecessary information when I am married to Iona the Navigator?

It seems to me a good idea to go on the Great Map Hunt whilst the BBMM is resting but to no avail. How could it possibly have got lost in such a short space of time? There can only be one possible answer - Mrs Bates has come out of her basement and hidden it with malicious intent.

And then I have another good idea. How about if I take some Schlitz? Maybe Steve and I could have a sly slug when we take the kids sledging? And it would be a quid pro quo for those I drank at Mae and Nat's. But as I lift the four-pack out of the fridge, I accidentally knock over a glass bottle of concentrated orange juice which lands on the hard, unforgiving floor and does not bounce. Smash! Splinters of glass everywhere and a thick, glutinous mass begins to spread its sticky tentacles across the black linoleum floor.

By the time I get the mess cleared up, by the time I transfer the Schlitz to the Big Brute of a Malfunctioning Machine, by the time we get the kids installed again, it has surely had time enough, like Noah, to recover from the flood ⸗ if that is what it was. Deep breath. A silent prayer. I put the key in the ignition and with the lightest of double taps on the accelerator, I turn the key.

Oh, my God! That is truly terrible! If there is a sound that could be said to have come direct from hell, like the sound of souls in torment, this is it. I immediately stop turning the key. I'm no mechanic, but as sure as there are eggs in eggnog, this starter will never start anything again.

Iona and the kids go back into the house while I go along to ask some help from our friendly neighbourhood cop, hoping he'll be able to get me out of this mess.

"I'll give you a tow an' you can jump start it."

"But you can't do that with an automatic, can you?" I've done it before with a manual but I didn't think it was possible to do so with an automatic.

"Sure you can," says Al, shrugging aside my objection. "I'll take you up Higgins. Keep it in neutral an' once we get up to about 30 or 35, put it into second gear, OK?"

I understand and it fills me with horror. It's the main street downtown and as well as any pedestrians who might be wandering about, has traffic lights which means we may not get too far before we have to stop again.

"Er, erm, why Higgins? Isn't there a quieter street we could go on?"

Al shakes his head. "It's got to be long an' straight," he explains patiently. It's hard sometimes being surrounded by idiots, not to mention dames who don't drink.

He tows me back out onto Lincoln and then removes the chains and puts them at the front. It's when we have to stop at the end of the street to turn onto South Higgins that I realise that although the speedometer works, the power-assisted brakes do not. I have to stand hard on the pedals as Al stops at the junction and the back of BIG AL looms terrifyingly large in the windscreen before I manage to bring the BBMM to a halt only a foot from it. Another thing that is worrying me is that to get to the Downtown area, we have to wait for a break in the stream of traffic. It's never the easiest of manoeuvres but fortunately, being Christmas Day, it is quieter than usual.

There is a jerk as the chain takes up the slack, we make the crossing safely and head towards N. Higgins and the bridge. That is when the second problem dawns on me - the power steering doesn't work either and it takes me all my strength to do what I can normally do with two fingers, if I have a mind to, namely to turn the wheel and point that big, blue bonnet in the direction I want to go. This is like trying to turn an elephant's head by pulling on its ear.

And then, as we gather speed, I realise just how alarmingly short that chain is and how hard I am going to have to stand on the brake pedal if I am not going to cannon into the back of BIG Al like a billiard ball. We're doing 35 as we cross the bridge and knowing traffic lights are only a few hundred yards away, I slip the gear into second, desperately hoping that that will do the trick, that the power will be restored and I'll have full control of the vehicle. Nothing happens. At least what I hope for does not happen. Instead there is a jolt, the chain tightens, but the engine remains as dead as the dodo. I release the gear and my foot hovers over the brake pedal as I see the lights are at red. And so are the beads of sweat on my brow if only I had the time to look in the mirror, or could spare one hand from wrestling with the steering wheel to wipe them off.

I leap out and rush round to speak to Al.

"It's not working and neither are the brakes or power steering!" Can he see the panic in my eyes and hear it in my voice?

"Try first," advises Al laconically.

I guess that means he can't see the hell he has taken me through. All too soon we're off into the second circle of those nether regions and to my alarm, the speedometer is saying 45 ´ and this in a built-up area which means we should be doing no more than 25 but when you're being towed, what can you do? Oh well, if we are stopped by the cops, I'll just let Al do the talking. Maybe he thinks we've been going too slowly and this combination of speed and in lower gear will do the trick. It doesn't. No matter how often I try engaging first, the result is just the same as before.

At last we have come to the end of the road, where a majestic and mighty old Northern Pacific steam locomotive has come to the end of the road too, spending its retirement near the railway depot, a reminder of how much the opening up of the Pacific Northwest was due to these mighty machines. I'm not sure what happened next but as BIG AL makes a U-turn to embark on the homeward leg, there is a rending of metal, a clang and a scraping noise. I have come to a dead stop and it didn't have much to do with the brakes either. It doesn't take long for Al to realise he has lost his tail. We both get out to inspect the damage.

The chain has snapped. That was the clang and the reason for it breaking is all too obvious to see; part of it is under my left wheel. As for the scraping of metal, that is because part of the bodywork beneath the bumper has come away from its moorings and is making contact with the road. Actually it was already hanging down slightly ever since Steve had tried to tow me out of the snowdrift.

All that is bad but there is still worse. Of all the places for this to happen! The Plymouth has come to a halt straddling the railway tracks. I suppose I am in no immediate danger myself. Long before I heard the mournful sound of an approaching train (almost certainly it would be a freight train and hardly travelling at the speed of light), I would have been out of the car and watching in awful fascination at the inevitable collision and its aftermath, the screeching of tortured metal as the locomotive ploughed remorselessly into it and crushed it into something only vaguely resembling what used to be my pride and despair. At least it would solve my dilemma about whether to cut my losses and get rid of it or not.

"Goddammit!" says Al and it's to his everlasting credit that that is all he says and does not blame me for running over the chain, let alone turning it to good use by hanging me from the nearest lamppost. Without any sense of urgency, without any fear that it might soon be reduced to something the size of a tin can, singlehandedly, Al pushes the BBMM back to free the chain, ties a knot in it, finds a piece of rag and ties the hanging down bit of metal onto the bumper and we are off again - not back to Lincoln though, but to Grandpa's where we are going to try and start it with jump leads. Now if only he had thought of that first, I wouldn't have sweated a pint of blood and my hair would still have been black.

But at Grandpa's, the leads fail to raise a flicker of life and for the first time Al hears the awful tortured sound of metal grinding against metal.

"Starter's broke," he pronounces.

If only I had let him hear it right at the start! But wasn't that what we were trying to do, bypass it so it would start? And now, belatedly, I realise that if it had started, how would I have got it started again at the Petersen's? It seems the starter wasn't the only thing that had a bypass.

The chain comes apart twice on the way back to Lincoln (nothing to do with me), and mercifully at a more sedate pace. An hour after we had set out on this nightmarish and fruitless journey, the BBMM is abandoned outside the house from *Psycho*. I feel drained, mentally and physically. Did I hear you laughing down there in your basement, Mrs Bates?

It's Terri to the rescue now as she offers us her beloved VW Bug, the one that I swore I would never drive again because of its "characteristics" as Terri called them, the brakes that were exceedingly spongy, the lack of a rear-view mirror and the lack of lights. I am glad to see that this fault, at least, has been attended to since I drove it last, away back at the beginning when we were carless and Terri had let us use it until such time as we got a wreck of our own. It was extraordinarily kind of her, especially as we had no insurance, something we might well have been in need of considering the "characteristics" and the very likely possibility, in this litigious land, of being sued in the event of an accident.

No point in taking the Schlitz now. It'll be the best part of an hour before we get to our destination as Terri has told us that we will need to stop for gas. And now there is the added problem of getting to the Petersen's in the dark, without a map and with only vaguely remembered directions...

Chapter Forty-eight

In which we experience a Christmas Day we will never forget.

I t's no good. We're never going to find it at this rate, going round in circles like this. I pull in at the Mini Mart and phone the Petersens.

Steve answers. He must have guessed it was me phoning at this time on Christmas Day. I briefly explain why we are so late and tell him, because of the dark, we can't follow the directions. Which is true. I didn't say "on his map".

"Where are you?" and then, "stay there. I'll come an' get ya."

It doesn't take long. I follow him, looking for landmarks so I can find my way back but all is black.

We apologise profusely as we are introduced to the family. It's not just Steve's mother and father-in-law, but Jackie's sister, husband and baby, and her brother Anchor. It sounds like he might be the mainstay of the family. Lastly there is Steve's mom.

They've all eaten, but before we do, it's time for the kids to receive their presents: a beautiful big doll almost as big as Hélène herself and a push-and-let-go fire engine truck for George. Both are delighted and Hélène sits on the hearth and holds her new baby as to the mother born. And then more embarrassment as Steve gives me a presentation pack of the year's US stamp issues (he knows about my habit) while Iona gets a very nice little necklace. It's just too embarrassing for words since we have nothing in return for them and even if we had, how embarrassing to give Steve and Jackie something and not the others!

Iona's mince pies seem a very meagre contribution to the feast, especially since they were hardly given a ringing endorsement the evening before. We have taken the precaution of taking a posh box of chocolates along as well, however. Normally I would have taken a bottle of wine, two even, but what can you do when you are expressly forbidden to bring any alcohol? It's a real problem. It's not as if their leader was against wine, was He, so why should our hosts be? I suppose I could have taken a bunch of grapes, wine in pill form, and hoped for a miracle ⁄ only I didn't think of it till now.

And so to table. But before we can tuck in, Howard, as I can now call Mr P, takes our hand in each of his and says grace. I find it a trifle embarrassing, firstly because of my lack of religiosity but mainly because of my lack of romanticism. It's the first time I have held my wife's hand in a long time and now, to my shame, I have to do it in public! Boys from the boondocks of Banffshire don't have any truck with handholding and other soppy sort of stuff ⁄ and neither do any other Scotsmen I know of for that matter. Like Terri's VW, it's one of our "characteristics". You will frequently see a Frenchman holding hands with his wife and if you travel a bit further south, you are more likely to see an Italian with his hand on his wife's bottom or more likely someone else's wife's bottom on the evening *passeggiata*. It comes with the blood: ours is cold from a cold climate; theirs is altogether much hotter. It's just the way we are and *Vive la différence*!

Just like Thanksgiving, the fare is as before: tasty turkey, potatoes, mashed and sweet, cranberry sauce, stuffing as before and gravy ⁄ only in place of the broccoli there is squash, and bizarrely, shredded carrots and pineapple in lemon "Jello" (jelly) and biscuits, which by our name of "scone" would taste just as sweet.

Alas, all this delightful spread is washed down, like the potluck at the church, with Kool-Aid instead of a cheeky little Chardonnay or sophisticated Chablis. Like then, it's really a bit of a crime against fine food, as despite this odd mixture (to our taste) of sweet and savoury, the latter in particular is very good indeed, and although I don't need any more, I have seconds as a sort of compliment to the cook, whom I presume, is Mrs Petersen. Besides, it means I have a good excuse for not partaking much of the sweet, or "dessert" as they call it, which consists of a fruit salad mixed with marshmallows and something bright pink and frothy which I really, really regrettably do not have any room for.

Iona is a sweet person, as you know, but unfortunately fruit salad is far too healthy a sweet for her taste despite the marshmallows, and so it is the frothy pink concoction for her and which she pronounces delicious, which it may or may not be, but she is a well-brought up "quine" as we say in the north-east of Scotland. As for the kids, they don't eat a morsel - they are far too interested in their new toys, much more, I must say, than those their fond parents had lavishly expended on them.

And now, fed and watered (no miracle happened to the Kool-Aid) we are able to join the party.

Howard, it seems, was in Helensburgh (near Glasgow) during the war so that is a useful ice-breaker, not that I have ever been there or know much about the place, nor that there is any ice to break amongst such a friendly family.

"Anchor" I also learn, is a Danish name. I think he might go far, the lad, with a name like that. I remember one of my teachers going through our names and on that basis alone, elevating us to fame and fortune or condemning us to obscurity and relative poverty - just like the souls, in paintings by Hieronymus Bosch and others, are either cast with impunity to hell and ever-lasting damnation, or uplifted to heaven and eternal happiness in paradise. It didn't take him more than a couple of seconds to make up his mind, rolling our names around in his mouth as if tasting a fine wine.

"David Addison? No."

Thus I am dismissed. I remember feeling deeply disappointed. And no whimsical judgement this either. I am already in my fourth decade towards hell, and no fame, and certainly no fortune, has come my way, so the seer's foresight was not in vain. Nevertheless, I live in the hope that I may be a late developer and may yet prove him wrong, though he, poor sod, will be long under it by now and will never see the error of his forecast. Having said that, methinks if Anchor had been in my class, I think that same prophet would have foretold a great future for him in the ships' chandlers business.

It's one of my beliefs, and there's nothing mystical about it, but I think you can tell a lot about people's characters simply by looking at the contents of their bookcases. In this instance, I don't even have to even look at the bookcase, for resting on top of the television there is an open bible, open at Luke, only I didn't like to look too closely to see if any particular verses had been marked for the improvement of our minds, lest Howard or someone else, misread that for interest or took it as an opportunity to do a bit of proselytising. Ever since a bunch of Christians in Dundee ganged up on me and tried to convert me, I have a morbid fear of those who try to save my immortal soul. I just don't know how to say politely I'd far rather be down below at the bar with my hell-raising friends than up in heaven, drinking tea to the tune of a harp played by some people dressed in white nighties.

A cursory glance at the titles in the bookcase reveals various books of a religious nature as well as a concordance on that worldwide bestseller, the same one that rests on top of the TV. Nearly every home the length and breadth of the land has one, but hardly anyone has read it from cover to cover and many never open it at all.

Conversation reveals that Ruth, Jackie's mother, is a quarter Native American through her grandmother, a Kootenai from St Mary's Mission which was founded in 1841 by the Jesuit Father de Smet. The Mission, in present-day Stevensville, proudly boasts, with some justification, that this is "where Montana began" - the first white settlement in what was to become Montana Territory, later the State, and one of the first places we visited when we got the Big Blue Mean Machine. Ruth's grandfather was a fur trapper from Canada. Now *that* is what I call romantic. How proudly I would have boasted having ancestors like them!

Ruth is on the tribal roll and so is Jackie's sister, Tony [sic] but not Jackie herself. Uncle Sam's benevolence does not extend quite that far, but they both receive $2000 a year, simply on account of the Native American blood that flows through their veins. The more Native American you are, the more you get. I suppose you could call it blood money: some attempt at reparations by a guilty government to the descendants of those whose lands they appropriated a century ago. It's a highly controversial policy. Many object to having to pay today for the policies of the past. What happened may be regrettable but it's as old as history itself - war and conquest with the spoils going to the victors.

While it may be commendable of Uncle Sam to attempt to atone for the sins of the forebears, actually it seems to me that it's counter-productive and breeds a great deal of resentment amongst the taxpayers who complain about Native Americans drunk on the white man's firewater without having to lift as much as a finger to earn the money. I was with Al once as he picked up one such individual and a rough handling he had of it.

"Would you like to see the turkeys, young man?" asks Steve, squatting down beside George.

Tough luck on the turkeys. Having survived the dangers of Thanksgiving and Christmas, little do they know that it is third time unlucky for them and they will not live to see in the New Year but provide, once again, the mainstay of the feast. It makes me think of those poor devils in the First World War who made it through four years of hellish torment only to be cut down on November 11th before 11 am. It is estimated there were nearly 11,000 of them. There is a certain symmetry to that, unfortunately.

Thanks to my signing class with Kathy, we have been learning words connected with Christmas. I squat down beside him and sign it as well as repeating Steve's question so he can read my lips. In response, George makes a fist of his tiny hand and bends it at the wrist a couple of times to imitate the nodding of a head. It's a wonderful thing, this total communication. Without it, how could I have got through to him?

"Come on, then, let's get you into your snowsuit."

Since Hélène expresses no desire to see, like the gladiators in a Roman amphitheatre, those about to die, it's just Steve, George and me who make the expedition into the snow. He's holding my hand and walking along quite happily despite the bulkiness of the suit making it difficult, when all of a sudden he stops, looks at me, gives an apologetic little smile ⁄ and ejects vomit like a figure spouting water on an ornamental fountain.

For a moment Steve and I are too dumfounded to move, while George, for his part, seems just as surprised but shows no signs of distress. And it really is surprising since he hasn't eaten a thing, so it can't be anything to do with the food but this nasty bug that is going around.

I get the worst off his suit with snow then carry him (at arm's length) into the house. Iona gets him out of it and despite her protestations that it's too much trouble, Ruth puts it straight into the washing machine. What a nuisance we are to be sure! Time for more abject apologies but, like The Carpenters put it, "We've only just begun".

The suit is tumbling merrily in the dryer when it happens again. This time projectile vomit over Hélène's beautiful long pink "princess" dress which she believes transforms her into one of that status. Iona made it herself and embroidered it with a double row of forget-me-nots on the front. As I said before, Hélène has not yet reached the age of memory, so in a few days she will forget the awful experience of being drenched in vomit by her little brother, but in the meantime, she sets up the most awful scream of surprise and horror, followed by real tears.

Macbeth wondered how the murdered King Duncan's body could contain so much blood; I wonder how George's little body could contain so much sick. Fortunately for us, if not for her, the dress and "Baby" as Hélène has chosen to name her new doll, get the bulk of the drenching and only a small amount lands on the shag-pile carpet. So, it's off with the dress and into the washing machine with that too while

Baby has to make do with a wipe-over as no-one thinks she will survive the christening by total immersion in the machine.

I don't know if this latest performance by George had anything to do with it or not, but at this point, Steve's mom decides it is time to go home and since Steve had brought her, he takes her back to Hamilton. I don't blame her for wanting to leave but it may be already too late - she, as well as everyone else, may have already inhaled some of the spores which George has liberally sprayed about the room.

In the unlikely event that he vomited again, Ruth had got some towels ready. But to our incredulous horror, George does it again - all over the carpet. Unbelievable that out of that tiny stomach he could be so sick again, if we didn't have the evidence of our very own eyes. All that is bad enough, but to our mounting alarm, his face is blue and turning a deeper shade of purple by the second. Is he holding his breath, like he did before? The doctor had told us that although it looks very alarming, the worst that would happen is he'd pass out and then the body's natural responses would take over and he'd start breathing again.

But as we watch and the agonising seconds pass and there is still no sign of him reviving, the terrible though comes to me, as it must have to everyone else - could he be choking to death on his vomit? By now his face is an angry, purple bruise.

Iona and I are paralysed with fear. Jackie, the nurse, who, up to this moment had been sitting on a stool reading Christmas cards, flings them aside and the next minute she and Ruth have swooped upon him and are holding him upside down by the ankles. I think one or the other may have slapped him on the back, I can't be sure - time stands still as I stand rooted to the spot, frozen with fear. The next minute, Jackie is holding him with his back towards her and is squeezing his diaphragm. I know what she is doing ⁄ the Heimlich manoeuvre. Like I did, she has come to the conclusion he must have some vomit lodged in his windpipe. In a moment it'll come shooting out and he'll start breathing again ⁄ and so can all of us.

But nothing shoots out and still he shows no sign of breathing. We can only gaze in horror as we see Jackie lay him on the floor, bend over him and administer the kiss of life.

Oh, my God! It's our last hope, the last desperate measure, the last throw of the dice. It must surely mean he is already dead and she is trying to bring him back. I can't bear to watch, but must, hypnotised, powerless to act, as if trapped in some nightmare. Before my legs buckle, I would cling on to Iona for support, holding her hand far too inadequate a gesture at this time of crisis, but some Medusa has turned us both to stone and she makes no move to hold on to me either as we watch, stricken, as Jackie works to bring our son back from the dead.

At last Jackie removes her head from his little one and looks for the tell-tale sign of the chest rising and falling, for that dreadful blue colour to disappear, for the rosy colour of life to return. But the chest stays still and flat and the face is as blue as ever. Not the slightest sign of life. Not a flicker. Not a spark. Oh my God! That's it. He really has left us.

I stand looking helplessly on ⁄ beyond shock, beyond belief, beyond being able to utter even a syllable but I know, in another few seconds, this paralysis will wear off, the awful numbness will go and I'll give vent to an ululation of grief which I won't even recognise as my own voice as nothing so utterly awful as this has ever happened to me before, not even when my father suddenly dropped dead.

And if that is how I am feeling, you can multiply that by two, and more, as the awful reality sinks into Iona and she too is released from this paralysis of mind and body, as we both begin to assimilate the awful truth that on Christmas Day, of all days, we lost our son.

How can we ever bear to celebrate Christmas Day ever again?

Chapter Forty-nine

*In which Christmas Day comes to an end and I am
infected with a dose of Shakespeare.*

Jackie is still on her knees in front of the little corpse. We are still standing, motionless, looking on, not having fully taken in the horror of what we have just witnessed. I watch as Jackie gently and calmly prises open George's mouth then I see her insert her finger into it and do something. Immediately George takes a gulp of air and that terrible blue vanishes like magic and Jackie props him up into a sitting position. Oh my God, first the miracle, then the relief!

"He'd swallowed his tongue," says Jackie, matter-of-factly, as you do, when you have just performed the miracle of bringing someone back from the dead, like Jesus.

What do you say to someone who has just saved your son's life? "Thanks" seems such an inadequate word.

That awful spell broken at last, Iona, sobbing, swoops upon George, picks him up and holds him to her. What I can see, but she can't because his head is resting on her shoulder, is that he is fast asleep, probably with exhaustion. Holding your breath for that length of time really takes it out of you. I should know. I've been doing it all this time too. Iona collapses on the sofa with him in her arms.

"You'd better sit down, Dave." I don't know who said it but it seems to me that there was more than one voice who did so. I'm vaguely aware of Howard's strong arm taking mine and leading me to the seat on the sofa next to Iona. As soon as I sit down, I can't help but notice my hand is shaking uncontrollably. Ruth fetches me a glass of water. Isn't brandy what you're meant to give people in a situation like this? But of course in this house, even the medicine cabinet would not stock such a thing, nor in the kitchen, cooking sherry, I imagine.

"You're a worse colour than the wee fella," I hear Howard say.

I take a sip of water and glance down to where George lies, sleeping, in Iona's arms. He is a deathly white, his hair plastered to his head, but he *is* breathing, even if it is in a very shallow way. I am sure of that because I take a long, long look and I can see he is. He looks peaceful and perfectly healthy, apart from his deathly pallor. If I am a worse colour than him I must look quite ghostly, "a whiter shade of pale", as the song has it.

But now that this crisis has passed, now that the worst is over, another worrying thought comes buzzing into my head, like a nest of scorpions.

"He'll be all right won't he, Jackie?" My voice is hoarse because despite the water, my mouth and throat are as dry as a desert. "I mean... brain damage. He was deprived of oxygen for so long..." My voice tails off.

Jackie looks at him carefully before she speaks.

"He looks all right. Keep your eye on him when he wakens up. If you're at all worried tomorrow, call the doctor. But I think he'll be all right."

Maybe he had not been blue for as long as I had thought. Maybe it had just seemed so, time had been reduced to slow motion and perhaps the whole thing had been over in not more than a minute. But what if she's just saying that to reassure us? And yet, apart from that awful pallor, he does look perfectly normal. But maybe there's no way to tell until he wakens up from that sleep that mercifully, was not the Big Sleep.

After a while he gets too heavy for Iona and she lays him gently down on the floor. He stirs and still asleep, changes position, one cheek on the carpet, his arms behind him and his bottom in the air. How could anyone find that a comfortable way to sleep? His hearing aid has come adrift from behind his ear and is sticking out at right angles.

A little later Steve comes back from his mother-delivering mission. As he listens to our tale, his eyes grow large above the walrus moustache which quivers in disbelief. To think he missed out on all this drama!

"Boy, you're some turkey," he says to the sleeping George. "Bet you had your mom and dad half scared to death!"

"You can say that again!"

"I can see that, laddie! You're as white as a sheet!"

Am I? After all this time I've had to recover! And the thing is I could have missed the whole drama myself. It had been on the tip of my tongue to suggest to Steve that I came along for the ride, for a bit of company on the way back. I can never get enough of Steve's stories and who knows what tales he may have had to tell on the way back!

But just imagine I *had* gone with him and George had died in the interim! Imagine the welcoming committee that would have awaited me. How they would have been dreading breaking the news, only no words would have been necessary - Iona's sobbing and shaking shoulders and the little mound under that blanket on the floor would have told everything I didn't want to hear.

But mercifully, that was just a nightmare scenario. The reality is that once Hélène's princess dress comes out of the dryer, we wrap the living and still sleeping body of George in a blanket and carry him out to the car.

With heartfelt thanks to our hosts for their kindness and hospitality and more thanks than we can possibly ever give to Jackie - in fact, I'm not sure we even thanked her in the first place, caught up as we were with relief and disbelief at George's resurrection. This is a Christmas Day they will dine out on; the Christmas Day they entertained the guests from hell from across the Pond. They will tell how they arrived late; how their kid threw up all over the carpet (look, there's the stain still there after all these years); how they all got sickness and diarrhoea on Boxing Day that lasted thru New Year; that the baby nearly died of it and the stress of all that came free, a non-optional extra. So this is the thanks you get for your hospitality! It's enough to persuade you not to be a Christian any more!

But at least they won't need to offer up any prayers against extending the hand of fellowship this time next year as they know this was a one-off with the wide Atlantic between us, not to mention two thousand miles and more of continent. We will probably exchange Christmas cards and inside it will say, "Remembering your visit with us last Christmas!" And never in the field of Christmas messages will so few words remind us of how much we owe to those poor, unsuspecting Petersens and the generosity of their forgiveness.

What sighs of collective relief did they give as they saw the tail-lights of the VW Bug disappear from sight? And how long did they wait on the alert, listening for and dreading to hear the distinctive putter of the engine that told them another crisis had occurred and would they please phone for an ambulance, even if we all knew it was too late?

The ice-slick roads are the least we have to fear as we

drive the thirty-plus miles back to Missoula. On the way George retches a couple of times but thankfully has nothing left to give and goes straight back to sleep and thus we are spared having to clean up Terri's Bug before handing it back. Before Lincoln, I stop by the Grizzly Grocery to get some ginger ale as both Ruth and Jackie had said to give it to George when he wakens up. I don't know what medicinal properties it is supposed to have but it is a drink I am very familiar with as a mixer for whisky, and boy, do I need one now!

As we draw into Lincoln there do not appear to be any unfamiliar cars parked outside the Hertz household, only BIG AL and the Thunderbird. This sight fills me with gladness for I had expected the place to be heaving with people and ever since we left the Petersens, I have been hatching a plan.

Whilst Iona deals with Hélène, I carry the unconscious George into the house. He does not stir as I remove his hearing aid and his clothes and get him into his sleeping suit. It seems to me sleep, what Shakespeare called "Nature's soft nurse", is what he needs most after the trauma he has undergone, whilst I know my mind is too full of scorpions to get any myself until I get the evening's events off my chest by telling them to a sympathetic ear.

Iona says she's exhausted and is going straight to bed. I tell her about the scorpions and say I'll take the Bug back and let Al and Terri know what had happened.

"Don't be too long," she admonishes but the tone is more resigned and weary than hostile and forbidding. She has no fight left in her; what she needs most is the sleep that "knits up the raveled sleave of care". You can't beat Shakespeare when it comes to finding an apposite image and for once I suspect she will have no difficulty going straight to sleep, as pity, "like a new-born babe", takes mercy upon her and she will pass out the moment her head hits the pillow.

"I won't," I promise. "Just as long as it takes to get rid of the scorpions."

I know how near to complete collapse she is when she doesn't even bother to give me one of her looks. As for me, it's amazing how restored I feel at even the prospect of a pick-me-up.

All the same, carefully, so it makes no tell-tale clink, I take the Dewar's from its hiding place and a couple of cans of ginger ale and drive the Bug the hundred yards along the street to park behind BIG AL. Let this be a surprise Christmas present for Al because I have not yet heard the chimes of midnight and it is still Christmas Day. If he was pleased by the miniatures I had given him earlier, this is going to absolutely make his day - the little of what's left of it.

And maybe my words are more prophetic than I imagine. For once Al and Terri are in the room with the big hairy carpet with the roaring Yule log in the fireplace watching some show on TV. I would have thought this day would have been the occasion for a real Italian family celebration, the walls resounding to the sound of mirth and laughter, but strange to tell, there is no sign of such a thing having taken place at all, not unless the dishes had already been consigned to the dishwasher. Maybe Grandpa had been here and had left long ago, long past his bedtime, the younger kids are still out partying and the older ones who live in the area are spending Christmas with their own families.

Anyway, I am glad to see that if ever there had been guests, they have gone, for I want Terri and Al's undivided attention, although I can see the moment I walk in, Al's attention has already been drawn to the Dewar's. And if I had been right about that look of disappointment I thought I had seen been behind his shades when I told him what we were doing on Christmas Day, little does he know I am just about to tell him how lucky he was that we were otherwise engaged!

What if we *had* come here instead? Would George still be alive? I know that Iona and I would have been too panic-stricken to have done anything useful. Would Terri have leapt into the breach? Would Al, with his training, have known what to do? Would he have been sober enough, even if he did? Would his enormous forefinger have even fitted into George's little mouth, let alone get a hold of his tiny tongue to fish it out? Whatever the truth of that may be, there is no doubt that we could not have been better placed for George's life to have been saved than where we were. Sometimes life or death can depend on something as random and seemingly inconsequential as acting on the whim of a moment.

"Hiya, hon!" says Terri, somewhat surprised at my appearance at this late hour, though it is not late by Hertz terms. "Had a good day?"

"I've brought the Bug back," I say, handing her the keys. "Boy have I got a tale to tell you, but first I need a drink! Remember this, Al?" I say, bringing the bottle of Dewar's up to eye level.

"Yeah. That is a good Scotch. It's sooo smooth."

"It's my New Year bottle." I may as well try to make that clear from the start. "And I can't stay long as Iona is waiting for me." I may as well try to make that clear too but Al has ways of bulldozing you along the track he wants to take. "I thought I would introduce you to a bit of Scottish culture," I say holding up the ginger ale.

Al doesn't look so impressed with that but we troop

through to the kitchen where I break the seal on the Dewar's and spring the can open.

"Instead of adding water, we often add some of this," I tell him. "Try it, see what you think. I like to take it fifty-fifty, but it's a matter of taste, really."

That's the measure I pour for my friends and await their verdict with as keen an anticipation as Al had done when he had asked me to give my verdict on a whisky he had bought and of which I had never heard of before. To tell the truth, it's Al's opinion I am the more interested in because I know Terri will be polite whatever she privately thinks of it.

Al takes a deep draught and smacks his lips.

"That is very good, Dave. Makes a good mix." His draught has been so deep he'll be needing another any minute. I have a feeling I may have made a convert. Isn't that an incredible thing, a mere beginner in alcohol teaching the master a new drink!

"So what's the story, hun?" asks Terri.

And so, seated round the bar, to the accompaniment of canned laughter from the TV in the room next door, which is singularly inappropriate, I regale them with the heart-stopping tale.

"No shit!" Al says, blinking behind his glasses. I know he is very fond of George. He's not all tough cop. Terri is suitably impressed too, more conventionally uttering various words of shock, horror and sympathy.

"I'll hope he'll be OK," she adds. Al is too tough to say anything more, but his glass is empty so, like me, he has evidently felt the need for something to steady his nerves.

"I know. We'll just have to see how he is in the morning. Listen, I'd better be going. I don't want to leave Iona alone for too long in case the little turkey does it again.

Here's one for the road, Al," and I pour him a good slug. "Terri?" She shakes her head. "OK, I'll see you tomorrow, let you know how he is."

Well, that's taken good care of the better part of half a bottle of the Hogmanay bottle. If it had been a bad day for us, at least it ended well for Al, who for once, does not press me to stay.

On my way back I can't fail to see the Big Blue Mean Machine. In all the excitement, I had totally forgotten about it, not even when I took the Bug back. I'm going to have to get a new starter for it. That may not be too easy with things running down to the New Year and slow to get into gear again after it. And how much is it going to cost? And will Iona say enough is enough - that's it, the Plymouth has to go? If so, where will I get another, at a price I can afford and will it be any more reliable?

But those worries are as nothing compared to the ones about George. Will he be as right as rain in the morning or will he show some alarming signs of brain damage? And will he do it again?

Reader, I can tell you that the very next day, for it is now the early hours of Boxing Day, on Wednesday 27th of December, 1978, he *did* do it again - only this time I was alone with him in the house from *Psycho* - unless of course, you count Mrs Bates.

David M. Addison

will return in

Less Innocent Abroad

Forthcoming from
Extremis Publishing Ltd.

About the Author

A native of Banff, Scotland, David M. Addison is a graduate of Aberdeen University. In addition to essays in various publications, he has written eight books, mainly about his travels.

As well as a short spell teaching English as a foreign language in Poland when the Solidarity movement at its height, he spent a year (1978-79) as an exchange teacher in Montana.

He regards his decision to apply for the exchange as one of the best things he ever did, for not only did it give him the chance to travel extensively in the US and Canada but during the course of the year he made a number of enduring friendships. The third instalment in his *Innocent Abroad* series, entitled *Less Innocent Abroad*, is forthcoming from Extremis Publishing.

Since taking early retirement (he is not as old as he looks), he has more time but less money to indulge his unquenchable thirst for travel (and his wife would say for Cabernet Sauvignon and malt whisky). He is doing his best to spend the children's inheritance by travelling as far and wide and as often as he can.

Also Available from Extremis Publishing

An Innocent Abroad
The Misadventures of an Exchange Teacher in Montana: Award-Winner's Edition

By David M. Addison

An Award-Winning Book in the 2015 Bookbzz Prize Writer Competition for Biography and Memoir

When, in 1978, taking a bold step into the unknown, the author, accompanied by his wife and young family, swapped his boring existence in Grangemouth in central Scotland for life in Missoula, Montana, in the western United States, he could never have foreseen just how much of a life-changing experience it would turn out to be.

As an exchange teacher, he was prepared for a less formal atmosphere in the classroom, while, for their part, his students had been warned that he would be "Mr Strict". It was not long before this clash of cultures reared its ugly head and the author found life far more "exciting" than he had bargained for. Within a matter of days of taking up his post, he found himself harangued in public by an irate parent, while another reported him to the principal for "corrupting" young minds.

Outwith the classroom, he found daily life just as shocking. Lulled by a common language into a false sense of a "lack of foreignness", he was totally unprepared for the series of culture shocks that awaited him from the moment he stepped into his home for the year – the house from *Psycho*.

There were times when he wished he had stayed at home in his boring but safe existence in Scotland, but mainly this is a heart-warming and humorous tale of how this Innocent abroad, reeling from one surprising event to the next, gradually begins to adapt to his new life. And thanks to a whole array of colourful personalities and kind people (hostile parents not withstanding), he finally comes to realise that this exchange was the best thing he had ever done.

This award-winning book, the opening volume of the *Innocent Abroad* series, charts the first months of the author's adventures and misadventures in a land which he finds surprisingly different.

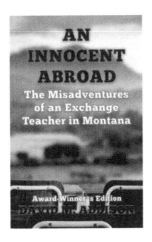

www.extremispublishing.com

For details of new and forthcoming books
from Extremis Publishing,
please visit our official website at:

www.extremispublishing.com

or follow us on social media at:

www.facebook.com/extremispublishing

www.linkedin.com/company/extremis-publishing-ltd-/

Lightning Source UK Ltd.
Milton Keynes UK
UKOW06f0127130416

272139UK00001B/4/P